VCs

OF THE FIRST WORLD WAR

THE AIR VCs

idea

Library Learning Information

To renew this item call:

0115 929 3388

or visit

www.ideastore.co.uk

TOWER HAMLETS

Created and managed by Tower Hamlets Council

VCs

OF THE FIRST WORLD WAR

THE AIR VCs

PETER G.COOKSLEY AND
PETER F.BATCHELOR

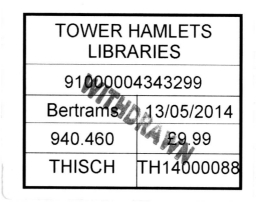
First published 1996
This new edition first published 2014

The History Press
The Mill, Brimscombe Port
Stroud, Gloucestershire, GL5 2QG
www.thehistorypress.co.uk

British Library Cataloguing in Publication Data.
A catalogue record for this book is available from the British Library.

ISBN 978 0 7524 8731 1

Typesetting and origination by The History Press
Printed in Great Britain

CONTENTS

ACKNOWLEDGEMENTS

When this work was originally published the late Peter Cooksley expressed his gratitude for the help given him by the following: Katherine Spackman and Joan Taylor, Bruce Robertson, John Smallwood, Derek Mottershead, G. Stuart Leslie (custodian of the GSL/JMB photographic collection), Stephen Snelling, Norman Gillam (medal and awards expert), John Garwood (Air Historical Society, New Zealand), Keith Keohane (The Australian Society of World War 1 Aero Historians), Alan Rowe and Alan Fraser (The Australian Society for Aero-historical Preservation) Mike Eddison (Chester Record Office).

Other sources of information have included notes from past conversations with, and letters from, the late Air Vice-Marshal Arthur Gould Lee, Major Wilfred Harvey and Charles Andrews, Cross & Cockade Society International – The Society of World War One Aviation Historians, museums in Britain and Canada, St Catherine's House, London and innumerable public libraries

Peter G. Cooksley, 1996

In addition to those mentioned above by Peter Cooksley I would like to thank the staff of the following institutions for their assistance in preparing this revised edition: Commonwealth War Graves Commission, Fleet Air Arm Museum, The National Archives and Royal Air Force Museum.

Individuals whose assistance has been invaluable include: Gerald Gliddon, who conceived this series, has given me much support and advice. Fellow Friends of the Great War Peter Harris and Steve Snelling have been generous with their time and help on numerous queries. I am indebted to David Cohen and Tony Freall for sending me the archive on Major Mannock as compiled by the late Tony Spagnoly. Others who provided material or assistance who are not mentioned here are acknowledged in the Sources section. As usual, my wife, Gill, has been of great support during the research and writing of this book.

Peter F. Batchelor, 2014

ABBREVIATIONS

A/A	Anti-Aircraft
AAP	Aircraft Acceptance Park
ADC	Aide-de-camp
AEG	*Allgemeine Elektrizitäts Gesellschaft* (German)
ANZAC	Australia and New Zealand Army Corps
AOC	Air Officer Commanding
AW	Armstrong Whitworth
B.	German two-seat aircraft category, regardless of engine power
BA	Bachelor of Arts
BE	Blériot Experimental
BEF	British Expeditionary Force
BSc	Bachelor of Science
C.	German armed two-seat biplanes of more than 150hp
CB	Commander of the Bath
CFS	Central Flying School (Upavon)
CMR	Canadian Mounted Rifles
CO	Commanding Officer
D.	Doppledekker (biplane) scout
DFC	Distinguished Flying Cross
DH	de Havilland
DSC	Distinguished Service Cross
DSO	Distinguished Service Order
E.	*Eindekker* (monoplane)
EA	Enemy Aircraft
FB	Fighter (reconnaissance) biplane
FE	Farman Experimental
FK	Frederick Koolhoven (designer)
GHQ	General Headquarters
HE	High Explosive
HLI	Highland Light Infantry

LVG	*Luft-Verkehrs Gesellschaft* (German)
MiD	Mention in Despatches
NCO	Non-Commissioned Officer
OBE	Order of the British Empire
OC	Officer Commanding
OTC	Officers' Training Corps
RAMC	Royal Army Medical Corps
RCAF	Royal Canadian Air Force
RE	Reconnaissance Experimental
RMC	Royal Military College (Canada)
RNAS	Royal Naval Air Service
RAF	Royal Air Force
RFC	Royal Flying Corps
RSM	Regimental Sergeant Major
RTO	Rail Transport Officer
SE	Scouting Experimental
SPAD	*Société Pour Aviation et ses Derives*
UPS	University and Public Schools' Brigade
VC	Victoria Cross
WFA	Western Front Association

Preface to the 2014 Edition

This book, first written by the late Peter G. Cooksley, was originally published in 1996 as one of the volumes in the thirteen-book series *VCs of the First World War* and The History Press are now reissuing these titles in a new format. I have been asked by the company to revise and update this work, and with their permission I have revised this particular book to bring it into line with the design of other titles in the series.

Interest in the First World War has increased dramatically in the past years as is evident by the numbers of books being issued together with the great number of magazine and newspaper articles being published as well as the amount of new programmes broadcast on radio and television. During this period access to primary sources including those of servicemen has become more readily available and the advent of Internet websites which provide facsimile copies of actual documents has been a boon to researchers, writers and family historians alike. However as with all secondary sources, other information available online should be verified where possible.

In 2012 the British Government laid out plans to commemorate the centenary of the First World War and as part of these commemorations it published a scheme in which every winner of the Victoria Cross would have a paving stone erected in his memory in his town of birth. It was quickly pointed out that this would exclude many VC holders who had been born overseas. The policy was then adapted to include the place or town in Great Britain with which the VC recipient was most associated. Even if this idea wasn't suitable the Government would hope that the country of birth would provide, if not a paving stone at least some form of remembrance.

After an open competition the winning design of the VC paving stone by Charlie MacKeith was unveiled on 4 November 2013 and it is both simple and effective. The stone also incorporates an electronic reader which can be scanned by a suitable device which would provide the user with further information on the life of the VC winner. Despite this idea being commendable it has run into problems with rival towns staking a claim when on some occasions they had no right to. Sadly of the nineteen aviators who I have written about in this book only ten of them were definitely born in the United Kingdom:

W.B. Rhodes-Moorhouse – Knightsbridge, London
L.G. Hawker – Longparish, Hampshire
J.A. Liddell – Newcastle-upon-Tyne, Tyne and Wear
R. Bell-Davies – Kensington,London
L.W.B. Rees – Caernarfon, Wales
T. Mottershead – Widnes, Cheshire
A. Ball – Nottinghamshire
J.T.B. McCudden – Brompton, Kent
A. Jerrard – Lewisham, London
F.M.F. West – Bayswater, London

The remaining nine men were born in the following countries and after each is the area(s) within the UK (if any) which is currently being considered by the British Government for a commemorative stone:

R.A.J. Warneford – Darjeeling, India – Stratford on Avon/Exmouth
G.S.M. Insall – Paris, France
W.L. Robinson – near Marcara, Southern India – Harrow Weald
F.H. McNamara – Rushworth, Victoria, Australia
W.A. Bishop – Owen Sound, Ontario, Canada
A.A. McLeod – Stonewall, Winnipeg, Manitoba, Canada
A.F.W. Beauchamp Proctor – Mossel Bay, Cape Province, South Africa
W.G. Barker – Dauphin, Manitoba, Canada
E.C. Mannock – Either Brighton, Sussex or Cork, Ireland – Brighton/ Cork

So although all nineteen of these early aviators fought, and in some cases died, whilst in the service of Great Britain, only the stories of just over half could be available via the commemorative paving stones. These stones will be unveiled commencing in 2014, in the years corresponding to when the VC was awarded during the First World War, 1914–18.

Peter F. Batchelor
Bury St Edmunds, Suffolk
February 2014

INTRODUCTION

During the First World War, 628 awards of the Victoria Cross were made and of these nineteen went to men of the Flying Services. The aim of this book, one of the thirteen volumes of the *VCs of the First World War* series, is to give a short biography of each of these servicemen.

When war was declared against Germany and her allies on 4 August 1914 the Royal Flying Corps (RFC) was only just 2 years old, its Royal Warrant having been granted in April 1912. By 15 August the four squadrons of the RFC, a little over sixty aircraft, were assembled at Amiens, France, under the command of Brigadier-General Sir David Henderson. The aircraft of the Royal Naval Air Service (RNAS) initially remained in England for home defence. These first RFC squadrons were composed of a variety of machines that were often extremely fragile in their design and not really suitable for military purposes.

The RFC suffered its first fatal air casualties in action when two airmen died after their machine was hit by ground fire on 22 August. It was also on this day that an RFC aircraft spotted and reported that the German First Army was advancing to threaten the flank of the BEF. This invaluable information enabled the British ground forces to be repositioned and avoid being cut-off. Field Marshal Sir John French, Commander of the BEF, in his first war despatch, dated 7 September, praised the RFC for their 'admirable work and accurate information'.

The initial war of movement became a more static, trench-bound conflict as both sides entrenched on the River Aisne before attempting to out-manoeuvre each other in the race to gain control of the Channel ports. This culminated in what was later to be named the First Battle of Ypres, which opened in mid October. By the close of operations a little over a month later the German advance had been finally halted.

The RFC, who had mirrored the movements of the BEF since August, established their HQ at St Omer and were actively involved in an important artillery co-operation role using wireless telegraphy in addition to their more usual reconnaissance duties. In the months that followed the aircraft also became involved in photography and rudimentary bombing raids.

It was on one such bombing raid that the first VC was awarded to a member of the RFC. On 26 April 1915, Second Lieutenant William Rhodes-Moorhouse was seriously wounded in an attack on Courtrai railway station but managed to return to base and submit his report before succumbing to his injuries shortly after.

Five further VC awards followed during 1915, each for differing acts of valour: Second Lieutenant Reginald Warneford was honoured for being the first airman to destroy an enemy airship; Captain Lanoe Hawker was the first to receive the award for aerial combat; Captain Aidan Liddell, although badly wounded, landed his damaged aircraft and saved the life of his observer; Second Lieutenant Gilbert Insall's aircraft was hit after destroying an enemy aircraft but he managed to land and save his aircraft; and the last VC award of the year went to Squadron Commander Richard Bell-Davies for his courageous rescue of a fellow pilot near the Turkish–Bulgarian border. This was the first VC to be awarded to a member of the RNAS and consequently had the blue naval ribbon.

The bodies of Rhodes-Moorhouse, Warneford and Liddell were all brought home for burial, contrary to the edict which was in force from April 1915.

In August, Brigadier General Sir Hugh Trenchard had been appointed GOC of the RFC. He adopted an aggressive offensive policy in support of the BEF, and always strived to take the fight to the enemy despite the fact that the German Flying Services were often one step ahead. The RFC machines were involved in the major conflicts of this year, and by the time of the Allied offensive at Loos in September over 160 aircraft in twelve squadrons were deployed on the Western Front.

Various experiments were employed in the pursuit of arming aircraft, the most successful of which being the synchronisation gear (enabling a machine gun to fire forward through the propeller arc) fitted to the German Fokker Eindekker machines. These took a heavy toll of the slow British reconnaissance aircraft during the winter of 1915–16 and it was not until fighter aircraft, such as the DH2, were organised into squadrons that the tide began to turn in favour of the British.

The most ambitious allied offensive of the war to date, later to be named the Battle of the Somme, commenced on 1 July 1916, and by then the strength of the RFC had been increased to over 420 aircraft in twenty-seven squadrons. It was on an early morning patrol north of the battle area, near Loos, that Captain Lionel Rees won his VC when he single-handedly attacked and scattered a formation of enemy aircraft.

It would be two months before the only other air VC of 1916 was awarded. Second Lieutenant William Robinson became a household name overnight after he shot down an enemy airship over Hertfordshire on the night of 2–3 September. This was the first such feat over home soil and his VC investiture took place a week later, no doubt the War Office, for propaganda purposes, wishing to take advantage of such good news.

Only one of the air VCs was awarded to to an NCO, Sergeant Thomas Mottershead, whose aircraft was hit when he was flying over Ploegsteert Wood, Belgium, on 7 January 1917. The machine caught fire but the pilot managed to land, thus saving the life of his observer. Tragically Mottershead did not survive his injuries and died less than a week later.

As the need for aircrew increased, more men from Commonwealth countries joined the RFC, one of whom was Lieutenant Frank McNamara, the only Australian airman to be awarded the VC during the First World War. On a bombing raid near Gaza, Palestine in March 1917 he was badly injured by a premature explosion of one of his own bombs but despite his injuries landed, rescued another pilot and flew them both to safety.

The tide swung against the Allies once more when the Germans grouped their single-seater machines into large hunting formations, *Jagdstaffeln* (*Jasta*), culminating in the air fighting during the Battle of Arras, known as 'Bloody April', in which the RFC suffered its worst casualties of the war to date, losing almost 250 aircraft with over 300 aircrew killed, injured or made prisoner of war. It was during this battle that one of the younger recipients of the VC, Captain Albert Ball, not yet 21, received his award, and unusually the medal citation particularly specified actions spanning the period 25 April to 6 May. Ball was killed on this latter date after achieving forty-four accredited victories over enemy aircraft, the highest number to date by a member of the RFC. The final award of 1917 was made to a highly decorated Canadian, Major William Bishop, following a solo attack on a German airfield early on 2 June. This was the only VC to be awarded based solely on the pilot's own combat report and without corroborating evidence. Bishop's total of accredited victories numbered seventy-two – a figure which is disputed to this day.

The final year of the war saw seven further VCs awarded to airmen. The first of these was made for actions over a period of time. The medal citation for Major James McCudden specifically noted his skill as a patrol leader, in addition to the destruction of enemy aircraft between 23 December 1917 and 2 February 1918. His final total of victories was to be fifty-seven.

The last major German offensives of the war commenced on 21 March with an attack south of Arras, and less than ten days later the youngest air VC winner, 18-year-old Alan McLeod from Canada, showed tremendous courage in rescuing his wounded observer after his bomber caught fire and he was forced to land in no-man's-land. During this enemy offensive the RFC lost over 1,000 aircraft in four weeks – over 200 more than during the 1916 Battle of the Somme, which had spanned over four months.

Italy had entered the conflict on the side of the Allies, but due to the heavy defeat of its army in 1917 by Austro-Hungarian forces support was transferred to that theatre late in 1917 including five RFC squadrons. One of the pilots was to receive the VC for service in Italy, Lieutenant Alan Jerrard. On 30 March 1918 he and two other pilots were involved in an attack on superior numbers of enemy in which, it was claimed, they were victorious over six aircraft, including three victories for Jerrard.

The RFC and RNAS amalgamated on 1 April 1918 to form the RAF, and four pilots from the newly designated force were to receive the highest military award. Captain Ferdinand West was the first airman of the RAF to win the VC on 8 August. He was very seriously wounded in his leg in an engagement with enemy aircraft but despite this injury flew back to base and submitted his important reconnaissance report. A South African, Captain Andrew Beauchamp Proctor received his VC in part for being the champion 'balloon buster' in the RAF as, over a two-month period from 8 August 1918, he had accounted for fourteen aircraft and twelve balloons, bringing his total of victories to fifty-four. On 30 October 1918 Major William Barker was attacked by superior numbers of enemy aircraft and in the ensuing melee he shot down four of these machines despite being seriously wounded. Barker was the third Canadian airman to be awarded the VC and the victories credited to him on this day brought his total to fifty.

The final member of the RAF to receive the award was Major Edward Mannock whose posthumous VC was gazetted on 18 July 1919 after much lobbying by his friends and supporters. The oldest airman to be so honoured, Mannock was 31, it is perhaps surprising that it took so long for the VC to be gazetted bearing in mind his achievements – probably sixty-one victories – and the great respect in which he was held within the RAF.

In the post-war years the general public were given the impression, through populist literature, of the heroic deeds performed by the aviators of the First World War, but it was not until many years after that serious aviation historians began to tell the real story. It is true that many RFC pilots came from privileged backgrounds and that those who began life in more humble surroundings had difficulty in being accepted. McCudden and Mannock both fall into this latter category but overcame these problems to become highly respected commanders who greatly influenced the men of the RAF who would later be fighting in the Battle of Britain.

Of the nineteen airmen who received the Victoria Cross only nine survived 1918 and all were initially employed in the Armed Forces in one form or another. Two of these, Beauchamp Proctor (1921) and Barker (1930) were to die in flying accidents but the remainder lived longer, and in some cases very influential, lives. The last air VC, Freddie West survived to the grand old age of 92, dying in 1988.

The motto of the RFC was *Per ardua ad astra* (Through adversity to the stars) and for the young men featured the words 'For valour' are also appropriate.

W.B. RHODES-MOORHOUSE

Courtrai, Belgium, 26 April 1915

On 22 April 1915, the Germans took the unprecedented step of releasing poison gas on a sector of the allied lines, north-east of Ypres, Belgium, with the result that, following the retreat of two divisions of French troops in the face of this new weapon, a breach in the lines 4 miles wide had been created. An airman who witnessed the release of gas was Captain L.A. Strange of No. 6 Squadron RFC who 'saw a sudden bank of yellow-green cloud spring up above the German trenches and move towards the line held by the French 45th Division. On the ground the French troops viewed it first with more curiosity than alarm, but soon the gas enveloped them and passed on, leaving blue-faced dead on an open road to Ypres.'

There followed some of the most critical days which the Allies had then seen following this German breakthrough at St Julien, near Ypres. Considerable efforts were made in the air in order to maintain reconnaissance patrols and keep commanders constantly informed of enemy strategy. In combination with these patrols, bombing operations were carried out by the Royal Flying Corps. Four days after the enemy gas attack several simultaneous operations were ordered against concentrations of enemy reserve troops in the vicinity of Ghent in an attempt to prevent them being moved to the front.

Among the three designated targets for No. 2 Squadron, based at Merville, near Hazebrouck, was the railway at Courtrai and Menin Junction. The pilot of BE2b 687 ordered to fly against this target was Second Lieutenant William Barnard Rhodes-Moorhouse, a 28-year-old married officer with a small son. His colleagues were ordered to attack Roubaix and Tourcoing, each with single two-seat aircraft, flown solo in order to take a bomb-load without reducing the machines' performance. Take-off was made by the aircraft at 3.05 p.m., each carrying a 100lb high explosive bomb under the fuselage centre-section. Normally an observer would have been carried, the allocated officer to aircraft 687 being Second Lieutenant William Sholto Douglas. Of concern to Rhodes-Moorhouse was that he would be flying an aircraft which was not his usual No. 492 which was under repair after it had been damaged the day before during a photographic reconnaissance flight with Second Lieutenant Douglas.

It was about thirty-five minutes flying time from Merville to the Courtrai railhead, and on arrival, Rhodes-Moorhouse took care to make sure he had reached the correct target before descending to 300ft to accurately drop his bomb. This was a common practice at the time when bomb sights, if indeed used, were primitive and of little accuracy, and none were carried on this occasion.

However, this very visible approach provided ground troops with a very easy target bearing in mind that the aircraft speed was less than 70mph. Also the BE was approaching in a shallow dive, despite its pilot having been strongly advised by his flight commander, before setting out, not to venture too low but to release the bomb at just below cloud level. It was added that he was free to use his own discretion on this. A hail of rifle and small-arms fire greeted the attacker and was augmented by a machine gun, which was almost level with the aircraft since it was firing from the belfry of Courtrai church. The damage done to the aircraft was considerable. Nevertheless Rhodes-Moorhouse unflinchingly held his course to drop the bomb on the line to the west of the station. He had then to run the gauntlet once more to retrace his course for home in an aircraft already riddled by splinters from the bomb he had dropped.

One burst of fire had entered the cockpit of the machine, hitting the pilot's thigh, and another hit his stomach. A bullet had also wounded him in the hand, and a continued loss of blood made him steadily weaker. Rhode-Moorhouse's flight commander Maurice Blake and several others were sitting on the bank of the Lys Canal, which bordered the south of the airfield, listening to the gramophone when the stricken aircraft came into sight at 4.12 p.m. It was flying very low, just clearing a hedge, but made a good landing with the engine turned off. Blake, Webb-Bowen and three others – the pilot's fitter, rigger and another fitter, 1175 Second Class Air Mechanic Percy E. Butcher, lifted the pilot from the blood-splattered cockpit and laid him on the ground. Before Rhodes-Moorhouse was taken to No. 6 Casualty Clearing Station, he was assisted to a nearby office for debriefing. Meanwhile his personal fitter counted ninety-five holes in the aircraft, some of them made by metal shards from the attacker's own bomb. Sholto Douglas also inspected the aircraft and noted that the observer's seat had been holed by half a dozen bullets. This would have been his observer's seat but Rhodes-Moorhouse had refused his request to fly, as his weight, in addition to that of the bomb, would have slowed the aircraft even more.

Although medical care was lavished on Rhodes-Moorhouse, it was soon clear that his wounds were too grave for the surgical skills available at the time to save his life. The task of informing the pilot that he was not going to survive was made by Padre Christopher Chavasse, twin brother of Noël, who was later to win the Victoria Cross *and* Bar. However the dying man, who had only been with No. 2 Squadron since March, had already realised his condition was hopeless. Earlier he had expressed a wish that his body be taken home to England for burial, his only recorded reply to the minister being, 'If I must die, give me a drink'. At about 2.30 p.m. he finally passed away having received Holy Communion as he requested, the faithful Blake still at his bedside since being called at 9.45 a.m.. In his good hand he clutched a photograph of his young son.

Less than four weeks later, Rhodes-Moorhouse was awarded a posthumous VC and the official citation published in the supplement to the *London Gazette* No. 29170 dated 22 May was as follows:

SECOND LIEUTENANT WILLIAM BARNARD RHODES-MOORHOUSE, SPECIAL RESERVE, ROYAL FLYING CORPS

For most conspicuous bravery on 26th April 1915, in flying to Courtrai and dropping bombs on the railway line near that station. On starting the return journey he was mortally wounded, but succeeded in flying for 35 miles to his destination, at a very low altitude, and reported the successful accomplishment of his object. He has since died of his wounds.

Perhaps the King's decision had been influenced by the hopes expressed in a letter of condolence to Rhode-Moorhouse's wife, Linda, from Douglas on 28 April: 'I do hope such courage will be recognised with a DSO although we all think a VC would be none too great an award for such pluck and endurance.' Maurice Blake, in a letter of 1 May to the dead airman's mother, revealed that he had written a long account of the raid 'to my father who sent my letter to my brother-in-law in the Scots Guards; it was shown to the King and my father has just written me that a VC is to be gazetted to your son for heroism'.

❖ ❖ ❖

William Moorhouse was born to Edward and Mary Ann Moorhouse, the second of their four children, at 15 Princes Gate, overlooking Hyde Park, on 26 September 1887. He had Maori blood in his veins, since his grandmother had reputedly been a princess of that noble race. William had been tutored at Harrow, after initial education in Hertfordshire, and later went to Trinity College, Cambridge, which he left in 1909. He was a vigorous young man with reddish-fair hair and brilliant green eyes. His background was sufficiently wealthy that he could devote himself to motorcycles and racing cars, the interests that always fascinated him.

He was the owner of several racing cars and attended motor rallies, trials and races, including events at Brooklands, where in 1908 he drove a 58hp Fiat named *Linda*, after his future fiancée, Linda Beatrice Morritt. However, he did not prove to be especially outstanding in this sport, so he turned his interests to flying.

Against a family background of inherited wealth (his maternal grandfather, William Barnard Rhodes, had amassed a large fortune in New Zealand, a considerable amount of which William's mother – who had been adopted by Mr Rhodes – inherited after contesting the will), Moorhouse found no difficulty in personally meeting the expenses of pilot tuition. On 17 October 1911 he gained aviator's certificate no. 147 in a Blériot monoplane similar to that in which the English Channel had first been crossed only two years previously.

The year had been a momentous one for young Moorhouse. He had, with his friend James Radley, designed a special version of this aircraft with a new Anzani motor – the Radley-Moorhouse monoplane, of which a silver model is still in the possession of the family. A photograph of this plane about to take part in the first Aerial Derby at Hendon on 8 June 1912 and bearing the racing number '8' on the side clearly show it with a 50hp Gnome engine. Unlike the majority of versions of the Blériot XI, the rear fuselage was covered, as were the wheel discs to reduce drag, measures which were seemingly successful as it was placed third.

The year before had seen Moorhouse entertaining friends and enthusiasts with demonstration flights. Much of this activity took place at the 360-acre Portholme Aerodrome, Huntingdon, established by James Radley in 1910. He also travelled to the United States with Radley where, flying a Blériot monoplane, he successfully competed in a wide variety of meetings and air races. One report later stated that he satisfied his adventurous spirit by becoming the first man to fly beneath the span of San Francisco's Golden Gate Bridge but as the bridge was not completed until 1937 it was probably the actual Golden Gate Channel down which he flew.

Before this, his name had been added to the American Hall of Fame by winning the coveted Harbor Prize, worth the equivalent of about £1,000, towards the end of a triumphant tour during which he collected a substantial total sum in prize monies. Having sold the Blériot to Earle Remington in Los Angeles, he returned to England in February 1911 on the SS *Lusitania*. In 1912 he still flew whenever the chance presented itself and made preparations for his marriage. William and Linda were married on 25 June at St Paul's, Knightsbridge and the event was later marked in its own way by him making the first aerial crossing of the English Channel with a pair of passengers – these consisting of his wife and journalist J.H. Lebedoer. The aircraft used was a French Breguet U2, two of which were entered for the British military aircraft trials at Larkhill to which delivery had to be made by 31 July. However, the weather was unfavourable and it was not until Sunday 4 August that it was possible to attempt the journey from Douai. It came as no surprise that, despite the Channel crossing being safely completed, it was carried out in the face of storms as the weather again deteriorated so that an early landing became essential. This was made at Bethersden, near Ashford, Kent, after a journey of 130 miles. Fortunately no one was injured except the clumsy-looking biplane with its narrow-track undercarriage, metal-skinned fuselage and two-bay wings. It had been blown against trees and damaged severely enough that there was no hope of entering No. 9, as it was known, in the trials as there was not sufficient time to repair it before the start of the competition.

In her wisdom Linda Moorhouse had realised the importance of aviation to her new husband. This was emphasised by her agreeing to the novel celebration of their honeymoon, but the experience it afforded also underlined the dangers of aviation. Therefore, although thrilled by her husband's success, she begged him to give up flying for the foreseeable future. Although he agreed, it was probably with reluctance, and it was not until 6 November 1914 that he flew an aircraft again.

But if the two previous years had been full of adventure, his motoring experiences had not been without serious incident. At a Gloucester court appearance in late January 1913 he was found guilty of criminal negligence after a man had been fatally run over by his own cart, his horses frightened by William's 'powerful racing motor-car'. This was his twentieth motoring conviction in Great Britain. Earlier in that month he had been involved in a serious motor car accident, when in foggy conditions, his car was in a head-on collision with another. Moorhouse 'sustained a severe scalp wound and concussion' and was detained in Northampton General Hospital. Ironically he was being driven to Northampton Police Court where his driver was summoned to appear on a charge of reckless driving the previous week. Six years earlier, in 1907, while practising for a motorcycle race on a beach at Wellington, New Zealand, he was in a fatal collision with a young boy. An acquittal on a charge of manslaughter was the verdict in court.

He stood to receive a considerable fortune bequeathed by his maternal grandfather, but in order to do this it became legally necessary to take the additional name of Rhodes, the confirmation of which duly appeared in the *London Gazette* dated 21 January 1913, so that his and Linda's only child, born on 4 March 1914, was therefore christened William Henry Rhodes-Moorhouse. Later in the year the couple bought Parnham House, a fine sixteenth-century manor at Beaminster, Dorset, where he planned to build a cottage on a prominent knoll in the estate for his family.

However this dream was never realised, as the international situation was leading inevitably to a European war and his plans were put on hold as on 4 August the First World War began and Great Britain declared war on Germany. Rhodes-Moorhouse bade farewell to his wife and child on 24 August 1914, just twenty days after the outbreak of hostilities between Britain and Germany, and joined the Royal Flying Corps as a second lieutenant. He soon made his first flight on 6 November and of twenty-five-minute duration over Brooklands, where he landed at 7.00 a.m. before leaving for South Farnborough, where he was to command the Aircraft Park.

His superiors' choice of occupation for him seemed to many strange since Rhodes-Moorhouse had been the first pilot to perform a tail-slide in the United Kingdom and was generally a very experienced flyer. However the decision was made on medical grounds, as he was physically not fit for flying. Instead he had to be temporarily content with testing Renault engines for BE aircraft, but it was only a matter of months before his frequent appeals to higher authority, coupled with a growing shortage of experienced pilots over the Western Front, brought a posting to Major T.I. Webb-Bowen's No. 2 Squadron at Merville with effect from 20 March 1915.

The Channel crossing from Folkestone to St Omer in BE2c 1657 was completed in one hour forty-five minutes. After a period spent familiarising himself with the surrounding countryside and in testing aircraft, trying out BE2b No. 492 on 26 March, Rhodes-Moorhouse was to find himself, with the rest of the squadron, involved in the air activity associated with the renewed struggle for Ypres. He flew the same machine on the following day when, at 7,500ft above Lille, he was 'introduced to Archibald', anti-aircraft fire. He was to describe this to

Linda as being, 'first a whistle, then a noise like a terrific cough', while the 'top centre-section of [No. 492] was hit by a shell' two days later when he found 'Archie in topping form'. These were the preliminaries to a struggle which was to take on a new and even uglier turn than previous battles with the introduction of poison gas.

❖ ❖ ❖

At the time of Rhode-Moorhouse's death on 27 April 1915 it was not government policy for the dead to be brought home, but as he had especially requested a wish to be buried in his homeland, he was indeed brought home for burial. This was on the orders of the general officer commanding the Royal Flying Corps, Hugh Trenchard, and with the support of Sir John French, commander of the BEF. The dead airman was also awarded a posthumous promotion to first lieutenant, backdated to 24 April. These gestures would have been of slight comfort to his wife and family, who received his coffin and had it conveyed to Parnham. There he was given a military funeral with full honours, before being borne to the crest of the hillock once selected as the site of his new home.

The funeral procession consisted of twenty men, six assisting with the wooden hand-bier on which lay the coffin wrapped in the Union Flag. A seventh, an officer, supported the grieving widow at the rear as the little procession climbed the Dorset knoll. With the committal, the crash of the firing party's three rounds blank and the sad, triumphant notes of the Last Post.

Twenty-two years later William and Linda's son, William Henry Rhodes-Moorhouse married Amalia, only daughter of Sir Stephen Demetriadi KBE, on 15 September 1936. William was a skier of Olympic standard and had been selected for the British team for the Winter Olympics of 1936, but an accident on the ski jump prevented him from competing. He had qualified as a pilot at the age of 17 while still at Eton, a little over two months before his mother qualified on 25 June 1931, at the age of 45, flying a DH Moth. In October 1933, William inherited his grandfather's estate of a quarter of a million pounds.

William was commissioned as a pilot officer (90140) in No. 601 'County of London' Fighter Squadron ('The Millionaires' Squadron'),Royal Auxiliary Air Force on 28 July 1937. This squadron was so named as its first commander, Lord Edward Grosvenor, reputedly only recruited members of White's Club.

The following year he purchased Mortham Tower, Rokeby, North Yorkshire and started restoration before the war interrupted the work. His mother, who later continued with the restoration, was to live here until her death in 1973 and had a plaque to her son erected above the mower room.

In May 1940 he was serving at Merville, as had his father, and after the retreat from Dunkirk in May 1940 took part in the Battle of Britain with several victories to his credit. On 6 September 1940 Flight Lieutenant William Henry Rhodes-Moorhouse DFC was killed in combat while flying a Hawker Hurricane near Tunbridge Wells. The crashed plane was buried so deep in a railway viaduct that the RAF left it there, but his father-in-law organised an excavation and William's remains were found some days later. These were cremated and his ashes were interred in a corner of his father's resting place on the hill which became Parnham Private Cemetery.

On his death, young William was 28 years of age and left recorded memorabilia housed in private collections which includes his father's flying logbook. Inside, a paper insert records his flight at Brooklands on 6 November 1914 with the remark 'Testing new machine, Very nice, Good climber'. The pencil claimed to be that used for entries in the logbook also survives. It is stamped 'Made in Bavaria' with a slide-on steel cap. Other items are a portrait of him, in its original card mount, in the cockpit of a Breguet biplane, possibly an L2 and probably taken at Douai, as well as the slightly rusted pin from a bomb together with an envelope on which is written by hand in ink: 'This is the safety pin removed from the 100lb bomb just before your father started off for Courtrai, just as he was going to leave. It was in his pocket when he came back, M.B.B.' – written by Maurice Blake, Rhodes-Moorhouse's flight commander.

Also there survives a letter from the father he never knew expressing, above all, his deep affection and admiration for the young wife he had left behind in England, and with whom, he stressed, he never had 'a quarrel or misunderstanding'. He urged his son always to seek the advice of Linda and expressed hope that the lad would eventually become an engineer with 'a useful knowledge of machinery in all forms'. Finally he encouraged the boy to 'keep up your position as a landowner and a gentleman'.

Early on the afternoon of Rhodes-Moorhouse senior's last sortie he had handed this letter to Blake after adding a prophetic postscript, 'I am off on a trip from which I don't expect to return but which will I hope shorten the War a bit. I shall probably be blown up by my own bomb or if not, killed by rifle fire.'

William Barnard Rhodes-Moorhouse is commemorated on the Lamport war memorial in Northamptonshire and a number of memorials exist in his name. In February 1948, the RAF Benevolent

Fund built twenty-six houses at Morden, Surrey. One group was called Trenchard Court, the other Rhodes-Moorhouse Court.

A parade was held at Beaminster on 3 July 1965 in honour of the first air VC, with a graveside ceremony at Parnham House. In 1982 the RAF Museum issued an aero-philatelic cover commemorating the VC bombing raid, which was flown on the anniversary in Jaguar T Mark 2 XX843, from RAF Laarbruch, over the route that was used. His name is also included on the roll of honour at St Clement Danes Church, on the Strand, London.

In September 1991, the medals awarded to William Barnard Rhodes-Moorhouse were sold by Sotheby's at the RAF Museum, Hendon, and the proceeds used to set up The W.B. Rhodes-Moorhouse VC Trust which provides scholarships through the Air League and charitable donations. The selling price of £126,500 was then a record for a Victoria Cross. The medals awarded to William Barnard Rhodes-Moorhouse (VC, 1914–15 Star, BWM, Victory Medal) are now displayed in the Lord Ashcroft Gallery, Imperial War Museum, London.

In 1966 No. 10 Squadron RAF was re-formed and equipped with VC 10 CMK.1K aircraft, and almost thirty years later, in March 1995, it was announced that the squadron's fourteen aircraft would carry the names of selected Flying Services recipients of the VC from both the First and Second World Wars. The name of William Rhodes-Moorhouse VC was inscribed on VC 10 serial No. XV108. later the scroll bearing his name was transferred to VC 10 serial No. ZA148. This aircraft was taken out of service in 2013, and it is planned that it will be put on display at the Aeropark, East Midlands Airport. During the normal decommissioning process at Brize Norton the name-bearing scrolls have been removed from each aircraft and it is planned for these scrolls to be put on display at Brooklands Museum.

R.A. WARNEFORD
Ghent, Belgium, 7 June 1915

Reginald Alexander John Warneford was one of five children of Reginald William Henry Warneford and his wife Alexandra and he was born in Darjeeling, India, on 15 October 1891. His father was an engineer organising the construction of the Cooch Behar railway in West Bengal. Alexandra was unhappy with the life at Cooch Behar and increasingly 'homesick for the gaieties of Darjeeling'. Consequently she spent more and more time visiting her parents and sister at Darjeeling, taking her four daughters with her. The young Reginald, often known as Rex, had an adventurous childhood spending the days with his father and his 'education' comprised riding the footplates of the engines, learning how they worked. He also spent time on climbing expeditions, river journeys by raft, elephant riding and even being present at a tiger shoot. This 'education' was much disapproved of by his mother and her family and, late in 1899, when Reginald was away working, she had her belongings packed and with her four daughters caught the train to Darjeeling. At the time, Rex could not be found so she left without him and he was waiting when his father arrived back that evening.

There was silence from Darjeeling but a few days later Alexandra's father and brother arrived and took a very unhappy Rex away with them. His father did not get over the loss of his family and descended into bouts of depression and heavy drinking. He died in a Bombay hospital in 1900.

Not more than twelve months after her husband's death Rex's mother married again, to a Captain Corkery, but as her son was rebellious and did not get on with his stepfather, his mother's family decided that he should be sent to England. He travelled alone, and once in England, was placed in the care of his grandfather, the Rev. Thomas Lewis Warneford, in Satley, a few miles west of Durham. Rex enjoyed the village life during the winter of 1902 and, on learning that Rex 'had a true, clear voice', his grandfather sent him to study for a choral scholarship and he became a boarder at King Edward VI school at Stratford-upon-Avon. Here Rex particularly enjoyed subjects that required a practical application and quickly earned a reputation as 'a character', while the teaching staff described him as 'individualistic'. These happy days were sadly not to last and ended after the summer term of 1904 when his grandfather's health deteriorated so that he had to relinquish his work for the church. A lack of funds necessitated a move to Ealing where Reginald lived with his aunt Maude and became increasingly miserable living with his cousins.

On 11 January 1905, Reginald was entered for service with the P&O Steam Navigation Company's subsidiary, the British India Steam Navigation Company. He was 13 years old and began an apprenticeship with the company, serving on board the liner SS *Somali*, a relatively new ship, and would work his passage to Calcutta. One of his main duties was to attend to the needs of the first-class passengers. At the end of the year he received the news of his grandfather's death.

During his time with the shipping lines, when he served on no fewer than fourteen ships, Rex visited numerous countries and their ports and reportedly 'enjoyed every minute of it'. In the early summer of 1914, when he was on leave from his ship in London, he found out from his aunt that his mother now lived in Woolwich and visited her there. After eleven years' absence with only an occasional postcard from Rex, it was an awkward and brief meeting, with one of his sisters not recognising him, and he and his mother not knowing what to say to each other.

Rex heard the news of the outbreak of war when crossing the Atlantic as first officer on the oil tanker *Mina Brea*. The tanker made her way through the Panama Canal and up the coast to San Francisco where a cargo of oil was taken on before heading south, her destination Antofagasta, Chile, where the remainder of her cargo would be loaded. Due to the moving of a light used for navigational purposes the ship missed her correct course and ran aground in the early hours of 19 September, ripping holes in her hull and shipping aboard quantities of seawater. It was just possible for her to be re-floated at high tide and to make a slow progress across the bay to Antofagasta. After superhuman efforts by her crew and local workers it was possible to pump out much of the water and also offload 3,000 tons of oil so that on 23 October the *Mina Brea* was able to make a triumphant departure from the dockside. Cheering crowds and the local band saw her off on her 900-mile journey to the dry dock at Talcahuano which she reached on 28 October.

The damage, caused when running aground, was found to be more severe than thought, with one of the holes in the hull 44ft long and half as wide! As repairs would take some considerable time, the captain sent Warneford back to the owners, the London and Pacific Petroleum Co., with a sketch made by Rex showing the damages, photographs and a full report of the situation. Rex arrived in Liverpool in the middle of December and celebrated Christmas at Ealing with his aunt Maude and her family.

In common with many of his generation, Rex Warneford was keen to serve his country and his experience with the Merchant Navy seemed to make the sea most appropriate, but he was to be disappointed. As his attempt to enter the submarine service failed, he volunteered for the army. He attended the London recruiting offices of the Sportsman's Battalions, a part of the Royal Fusiliers, and was interviewed by a blustering self-important sergeant in the recruiting hut which had been erected in the forecourt of the Hotel Cecil, the RNAS headquarters during the First World War. Rex was accepted into the 2nd Battalion and sent to Grey Towers, Hornchurch, an unattractive mansion where a large hutted camp had been erected in the grounds.

Warneford summed up the situation at Hornchurch when he called the Sportsman's Battalions 'a sort of Boy Scouts Jamboree for old gentlemen'. Disenchanted, he subsequently applied for a transfer to the Royal Naval Air Service in the belief that it would combine the excitement he craved with proximity to the sea. The transfer was granted, and although Warneford's behaviour with the Sportsman's Battalion is not recorded by biographers, that he made his presence felt may be judged by a memo added to the transfer papers by the commanding officer stating that the RNAS would doubtless find their new recruit 'illuminating'.

Accepted as a probationary pilot by the navy on 10 February 1915, Warneford knew very little of flying. He was sent to Hendon for training, and gained his Royal Aero Club Certificate No. 1098 flying a Bristol biplane only fifteen days later. He was then posted to the Central Flying School at Upavon and whilst there he took the opportunity of driving his bright red sports car to Warneford Place near Sevenhampton, which had been the home of generations of Warnefords before being sold by Rex's cousin Francis in 1902. Rex saw some of the Warneford coats of arms in stained glass in the mansion and later visited the church of St Michael at nearby Highworth where the verger showed him the Warneford chapel and memorials. The eighteenth-century Warneford Place had been built on the site of a Tudor building and was sold again, in 1960, to the author Ian Fleming who had it pulled down and a new building, known for some years as Sevenhampton Place, built in its stead. Fleming died in 1965 and is buried in Sevenhampton Churchyard.

Possibly owing to his unconventional upbringing Warneford still had a habit of juvenile behaviour, which at times could be extremely annoying to those around him. The dramatist Ben Travers for one, who knew the young man, described him as 'a brash character ... his cocksure and boastful nature annoyed us all'.

He was briefly posted to No. 2 Squadron RNAS at Eastchurch, where his behaviour did not improve. On one occasion, having paused in the doorway of the wooden hut which did duty as the officers' mess, he:

> strode into the middle of the room, pulled out his revolver, twirled it round in his hand, cowboy fashion and said 'Hi suckers! What about this?' before firing six shots into the roof. He then replaced his gun in its holster and left without another word. No sooner had he gone than the silence maintained while this exhibition was going on was broken as 'All hell broke loose'.

When in the air he appeared to fly recklessly, but was always in effect in complete control, his skill never questioned. This was just as well, as he had earlier earned official displeasure by landing a Bristol aircraft on top of another, wrecking both, so that at Eastchurch, in Ben Travers' words again, he was 'received with mixed feelings'.

Such events culminated in him being banished from the station with a recommendation that he be dismissed from the service. However, he did have one sympathiser at Eastchurch as the station commander, Lieutenant Colonel E.L. Gerrard, was impressed by the young man's flying ability. It can be assumed that it was Gerrard who was responsible for Warneford being posted to No. 1 Squadron RNAS at Dunkirk on 7 May 1915. Flying operations were carried out from the adjacent airfield of St Pol, commanded by Wing Commander Arthur M. Longmore, one of the early aviators.

Having watched one of the impeccable landings of which Warneford was capable, the wing commander summoned the newcomer to his office and declared that whatever 'unsavoury reputation' he had earned at home, he would now be judged entirely on what he did under his command. Unfortunately the opportunity to begin afresh was short-lived – that night, Warneford succeeded in driving one of the squadron's tenders into a ditch. On learning this, Longmore was better than his word, giving the younger man one more chance.

The following day saw Rex making his first operational sortie in a Voisin, with Sub-Lieutenant John H. D'Albiac as observer. When they failed to return after two and a half hours, it was assumed that the machine had run out of fuel and made a forced landing. This was not the case as the aircraft did get back, but with only a few pints of fuel remaining in the tank. Afterwards, a shaken D'Albiac demanded never to be sent up again with a pilot who decided to pursue an enemy machine back to its base, often at treetop height, taking potshots at it with a rifle!

One of the duties of No. 1 Squadron at the time was to implement measures to prevent Zeppelins from reaching England or returning to their home bases. On 17 May, the squadron was alerted at 3.15 a.m. by the sighting of an airship passing Dunkirk going slowly east. This was LZ39, commanded by Hauptmann Masius, returning from an aborted raid on England. Flight Sub-Lieutenant Warneford in a Nieuport two-seater, with Leading Mechanic G.E. Meddis as observer, took off at 3.20 a.m. When he found the airship off Ostend at 5,000ft, Meddis opened fire from below at a range of about 1,000ft. Warneford was unable to climb higher due to the load on board, including Lewis gun and ammunition, hand grenades and a 0.45 rifle and ammunition. Squadron Commander Spencer Grey, also flying a Nieuport, was the next pilot to attack and came abreast of the airship at a height of nearly 10,000ft. He fired his Lewis gun at the rear gondola at about 50 to 100ft distance while being subjected to heavy fire from the two machine guns in each gondola. Flight Commander A.W. Bigsworth, in an Avro 504, overtook the airship near Ostend and 'passed over her from stern to bow about 200 feet above her, and dropped his four 20-lb bombs in a line on her back'. When passing abreast in the opposite direction, '... he noticed very heavy black pungent smoke ... coming out of the airship about 100ft from her tail'. He was then forced to head out to sea due to 'heavy and accurate gunfire which opened on him from Ostend'. The airship was last seen about 5 a.m. at approximately 11,000ft heading towards Ghent. The LZ39 'reached Evere, where the body of an officer and some wounded men were removed, and was finally housed at Berchem'. The damage was severe, with the starboard aft propeller blown off and five gasbags damaged, and this airship did not reach England again.

Realising that Warneford was a swift learner, Longmore was about to give the new pilot a roving commission to fly as he pleased, an attempt to prolong his life as much as possible. Travers commented that this decision would have 'meant only a brief postponement of his farewell to arms'. Almost simultaneously, with a view to expediting anti-airship patrols, the squadron was equipped with a pair of French high-wing monoplanes, Morane-Saulnier Type 'L's known as Parasols. These were both capable of armament with unsynchronised machine guns and fitted with racks for 20lb bombs. One would be used by Warneford, with L3253; the second, being at first intended as a reserve, was in fact usually flown by a Flight Sub-Lieutenant Neville.

During the period immediately after this, Rex appeared to be more relaxed than he had been since his seafaring days, with the small difference that contemporary photographs show him wearing his uniform cap at the accepted angle. Hitherto he had taken to wearing his Royal Navy headgear on the back of his head, no doubt a gesture calculated to show a hint of humorous contempt for the service and its attendant discipline.

Two military airships, LZ37 and LZ39, had set off from their Belgian bases during the evening of 6 June 6 together with LZ38, which had to return almost immediately with engine trouble. Earlier in the afternoon, naval Zeppelin L9 had lifted off from Hage in Northern Germany on a course for London. Weather conditions, a freshening south-westerly wind and patchy fog, forced Kapitänleutnant Heinrich Mathy to amend his plan of attack and he now headed up the coast towards Hull. Finding the town not well defended against aerial attack, Mathy brought his craft down from his approach height of about 10,000ft and dropped bombs and incendiaries, a little before midnight, from a height of about 5,000ft. About forty houses and shops were destroyed, with civilian casualties totalling sixty-four, including twenty-four killed of whom seven were children. Such was the outrage in Hull that rioting broke out in the early hours of 7 June, with troops having to be called out to restore order. All shops belonging to Germans (or perceived to be) were sacked.

Meanwhile, radio messages from the two Zeppelins, LZ37 and LZ39, were intercepted by the Admiralty which contacted Longmore at his No. 1 Squadron RNAS headquarters advising that two airships were now heading back towards their Belgian bases. Evidently fog over the sea had prevented the German craft from finding their targets on the English coast. Longmore took immediate action, ordering Lieutenants Warneford and Rose, both in Morane 'L's, that they were to attempt an interception of the airships and if this could not be achieved they were to bomb the Zeppelin sheds at Berchem St Agathe. He also ordered two Henry Farmans, flown by Flight Lieutenant John Philip Wilson and Flight Sub-Lieutenant John Stanley Mills to bomb the airships' home sheds at Evere. The Farmans took off from St Pol, Wilson at 4 a.m. and Mills shortly after. Wilson arrived over Evere just after 2 a.m. after circling the area for a few minutes endeavouring to locate the airship shed, which he saw just as the sky became lighter. He released his three 65lb bombs from 2,000ft, the second of which caused a large explosion and '... clouds of black smoke'. Mills then arrived and was forced to climb up to 5,000ft by fire from the ground before dropping his bombs. The British pilots turned for home and 'the sky behind them was suddenly lit with the glare of intense fire, LZ38 had also been destroyed!'

At around the same time as the two Farmans left St Pol, the Moranes were being prepared at the Belgian airfield of Furnes from where Warneford and Rose were to depart. Loaded with six 20lb bombs apiece Warneford noted that it was 1 a.m. when he checked his instruments prior to taking off in Morane 3253. Warneford soon lost sight of his companion as he climbed through the layers of mist. In fact Rose had become lost as his instrument lights failed and he made a bad landing, in a field near Cassel. He was not hurt but had overturned the Morane. For an instant Warneford glimpsed a slim grey shape to the north which vanished almost immediately before reappearing as he changed direction. It was about 20 miles away on a south-easterly course so he steadily climbed behind and above the airship to achieve a good bombing position. When, after about three-quarters of an hour and a few miles south of Bruges, Warneford manoeuvred for a bombing attack, he was fired on by the airship's top gunners, forcing him to fly out of range. The Zeppelin changed course to port to give its gunners a better target and again when Rex came in for a bombing attack his plane was 'swept by a hail of bullets'. Warneford later recalled, 'After several attempts to get above again, I came to the conclusion that the best thing I could do was to try and make him think I had chucked the game and was going home.' The Morane headed west, well out of range.

A waiting game had now developed between LZ37's commander, Oberleutnant von der Haegen, and Warneford in 3253. Although he knew that his machine possessed superior speed, this was not matched by the aircraft's rapid climb so that the right moment would have to be carefully judged; closing in for a kill too early would only promote an order for the Zeppelin's crew to slip ballast and the vessel would rise like a lift and all would be lost. Already the element of surprise had been sacrificed so that everything now depended on how long a wait the aircraft's fuel reserve permitted.

The 'cat and mouse' game lasted until 2.15 a.m. and it was clear that the crew of LZ37 were preparing to land their craft at Gontrode as the huge ship was 'turning south and dipping her nose'. Warneford pulled hard on the stick of his machine, sending it clawing its way through the swirls of mist up to 11,000ft. He knew that to delay any longer would present his machine as a silhouette against the approaching dawn, an easy target for the airship's gunners.

Having gained height he made a silent dive at the huge airship, taking the precaution of switching off the engine. As the great green bulk filled his downward vision, he released the first of his bombs at 150ft above the Zeppelin. Believing it had no effect, 'I loosed another, but the third definitely did the trick ...' Rex pulled the toggle once more, dropping all the remaining missiles in quick succession. A savage eruption seemed almost about to split the LZ37 in two, the explosion being so great that Warneford's machine was overturned and tossed high into the air like a toy. Rex fought to maintain control of it, a battle which seemed to be everlasting until the monoplane responded to the pilot's attempts to right it and put it into a dive. Now as he plummeted down he was scarcely conscious of the smoke about him, through which pieces of burning debris shot upwards, so preoccupied was he with frantic adjustments of the air and fuel controls to his rotary engine. Rex later told one of his fellow airman, Flight Lieutenant Marsden, 'I looked down and watched it burning. I had the strangest feeling of detached curiosity, almost as though its death agonies had nothing to do with me.'

The airship plummeted down more than 6,000ft in six seconds, the twisted hulk, spewing flames, incandescent metal and burning fabric, fell on the Convent of St Elizabeth in the Ghent suburb of Mont St Amand. One crewman, Höhensteuermann Alfred Mühler, survived. He recalled men in the forward control car trying to protect themselves from the flames, some even flinging 'themselves into space'. This car broke away from the main structure and Mühler was seen by eyewitnesses falling from the burning gondola at a height of about 100ft. He fell through a skylight into an attic on to a bed which broke his fall, suffering burns, cuts and bruises. After hospitalisation in Ghent he later returned to the airship service.

The large convent of St Elizabeth, home of 700 souls, was a walled community made up of a number of houses and a church. The orphanage population had been swelled by the arrival of refugees and the bulk of the burning airship fell in the middle of their community. The ensuing fire caused the deaths of two nuns and a child despite the rescue attempts of two men, one of whom died and the other who fell some distance, breaking his legs. German sources record that nine crew died and one survived although some reports state that a number of engineers were also on the Zeppelin.

After rescuing children from their dormitory some of the sisters managed to enter by the rear entrance of a burning orphanage building and rescue most of the smaller children. A roll-call was made and as the sisters searched for those missing they could see the dead and hear the cries of dying airmen. German soldiers, who had quickly arrived, would not allow the nuns to help the injured men and even the convent chaplain was forbidden to give the last rites to those dying. It took the Germans two weeks to clear and cart away all the wrecked Zeppelin from the convent.

But the man who had wrought this destruction knew nothing of this, having no idea where the airship had fallen, and his priority was to restart the engine of his aircraft, without success. He was forced to find a place to land which would be in enemy-held territory. Extending the glide as far as possible, he put the machine down on what, despite the dank mist, appeared to be unobstructed land, and the Morane rumbled over the rough grass to a halt. Warneford climbed stiffly from the cockpit and began an examination of the machine, which appeared to be undamaged, and to check that there was sufficient petrol in the reserve tank, but the fuel feed was broken. He broke off part of a cigarette holder and forced this into the broken pipe.

A couple of experimental turns of the airscrew confirmed all was well, and culminated in a final turn with the ignition switched on. The motor roared into life and, the wheels being unchocked, the Morane began to move down the slope on which it stood after some determined pushing by Rex who now had to nimbly scramble aboard before it gathered speed, just as a party of German cavalry burst out from an adjacent wood.

After a rather tense time following a forced landing, due to lack of fuel, near the coast south of Calais when he was arrested by French soldiers before able to confirm his identity, his plane was refuelled and Rex 'fortified by their cognac' returned to his base. He was back at St Pol by 10.30 a.m. and after briefly reporting to Longmore he was driven to his sleeping quarters where he got eight hours' welcome sleep. He arrived back at the airfield to a hero's welcome which he found embarrassing. He tried to persuade his CO to allow him to escape the publicity he was receiving but Longmore had received instructions that he should '... keep Warneford on the ground for as long as his value as propaganda was fully exploited, and until he had returned from London'. He then passed Rex a telegram which had been sent by King George V offering his congratulations and conferring upon him the award of the Victoria Cross. This was the first VC to be conferred by telegram! Wing Commander Longmore then asked Rex to sit down and go through his report again and so it was that a clerk typed the following:

No. 1 Naval Aeroplane Squadron.
8th June, 1915.

Sir,

I have the honour to report as follows:

I left Furnes at 1.00 am on June the 7th on Morane No 3253 under orders to proceed to look for Zeppelins and attack the Berchem St Agathe Airship Shed with six 20lb bombs.

On arriving at Dixmude at 1.5 am, I observed a Zeppelin over Ostend and proceeded in chase of the same.

I arrived at close quarters a few miles past Bruges at 1.50 am and the Airship opened heavy maxim fire, so I retreated to gain height and the Airship turned and followed me.

At 2.25 am he seemed to stop firing and at 2.25 am I came behind, but well above the Zeppelin; height then 11,000 feet, and switched off my engine to descend on top of him.

When close above him (at 7,000 feet altitude) I dropped my bombs, and, whilst releasing the last, there was an explosion which lifted my machine and turned it over. The aeroplane was out of control for a short period, but went into a nose dive, and the control was regained.

I then saw that the Zeppelin was on the ground in flames and also that there were pieces of something burning in the air all the way down.

The joint on my petrol pipe and pump from the back tank was broken, and at about 2.40 am I was forced to land and repair my pump.

I landed at the back of a forest close to a farm house; the district is unknown on account of the fog and the continuous changing of course.

I made preparations to set the machine on fire, but apparently was not observed, so was able to affect a repair, and continued at 3.15 am in a South Westerly direction after considerable difficulty in starting my engine single handed.

I tried several times to find my whereabouts by descending through the clouds, but was unable to do so. So eventually I landed and found out that it was at Cape Griz Nez, and took in some petrol. When the weather cleared I was able to proceed and arrived at the Aerodrome about 10.30 am.

As far as could be seen the colour of the Airship was green on top and yellow below and there was no machine gun or platform on top.

I have the honour to be, Sir,

Your obedient servant

R A J Warneford

Flt Sub-Lieutenant.

The VC citation appeared in the *London Gazette* 29189 dated 11 June. Both Wilson and Mills were later awarded the Distinguished Flying Cross for their attack on the airship sheds at Evere. Warneford, when asked by Longmore to receive the congratulations of the crews, after quietly thanking them very modestly said it was only what any of them would have done. Rex was later told that before his London visit he was to be awarded the Cross of the Légion d'Honneur in Paris. He would then return to duty and fly a new aircraft back to the squadron at St Pol.

Rex was flown to Coublay airfield, 2 miles east of Versailles. He was met there by Flight Lieutenant Michael Marsden. The two men had known each other since Hendon days, where Marsden had helped in his training. At Longmore's request, Marsden was to 'keep an eye' on Warneford. Warneford was given a civic welcome on landing, followed by dinner. Warneford and Marsden finally arrived at their 'billet' late that night. Even here, at the Ritz Hotel, Paris, yet another reception awaited them and it was some time before they could get to their luxurious rooms. As Marsden recalled, 'The tables … were banked with flowers, surrounded by several bottles of champagne … we were too tired [for further celebration] and contented ourselves by riffling through the neat piles of telegrams, invitations and even envelopes containing photographs of beautiful mademoiselles who wished to make Rex's acquaintance.' Rex would appear to have been overwhelmed by all this attention as Marsden had to persuade him to stay, telling him how discourteous it would be if he did not attend the receptions.

On 12 June Rex was accompanied by Lieutenant Marsden to the Ministry of Marine, where he was awarded the Légion d'Honneur by M. Alexandre Millerand, Minister of War. He actually pinned his own medal on Warneford's tunic, telling him that he would be proud to wear the one destined for the young man instead.

A visit to the opera, dinners, receptions and presentations occupied their time, which Rex found 'quite good fun', but in the streets it was very difficult to get away from the hordes of well-wishers even with the assistance of gendarmes detailed to keep back the crowds. Amongst the numerous invitations they received was one offering to show the two officers Paris by motor car. This was from the beautiful Baroness Raymonde de Laroche, the first French woman pilot, having received her Aero Club of France *brevet*, No. 36, in March 1910. She put her chauffeur-driven motor car, a dark green Hispano-Suiza, at the disposal of Rex and she frequently accompanied him and Marsden during their time in Paris. Marsden recalled that 'people could not help noticing that they [Rex and Raymonde] had only eyes for each other'. and that Rex 'treated her … with more of a relaxed confidence than

I had ever seen before ... For the first time in his life, I should say, he was in love.'

'In an elegant restaurant in the suburbs of Paris', a newspaper reported, Warneford was entertained by 'friends and admirers' celebrating his two awards. This was Wednesday 26 June, planned to be Warneford's last evening in Paris before returning to St Pol. Rex received loud cheers when, in response to congratulation he had received by one of the distinguished guests, stood and cried, '*Vive La France! Vivent les Alliés! Et à bas le Boche!*' Later when nearly all the guests had gone and only Marsden, Warneford, Raymonde and another girl were left at their table, Marsden noticed that the cigarette girl, who was standing directly behind Rex, wanted to approach him. She had a bunch of red roses, which he stood and gratefully accepted. As he did, the petals, wilting from the heat of the room slowly fell over the cross of the Legion d'Honneur. The girl was very tearful and full of regrets as she tried to explain that she had brought them, 'to wish you happiness when you go back to England'. Rex took her hand and said, 'Mademoiselle, thank you for your flowers; but they will be for my grave, for I shall not reach England. I will not live to see England again.' Still later, at the Ritz, Warneford, smoking almost continuously, talked to Marsden about his life, India, his grandfather, his years at sea, a short comment about his 'beautiful' mother and lastly much about his father and how he had built the Cooch Behar Railway. Warneford considered his father's achievement as, 'something which really justifies one's existence'. Rex never thought that the bringing down of the Zeppelin was anything but 'routine' but he did admit, 'I wish I had never shot it down over a convent.' As Rex left the room to retire he said, 'I seem to have lost touch with reality these last few days'. Bearing in mind the constant adulation and attention he had recently been receiving it is not surprising he felt this way.

It has been suggested by some that his wild streak, possibly created by an inferiority complex, was replaced by a defensive arrogance. This was typified when, on entering a lift in the Ritz, he was approached by Robert Fitzgibbon (his name was legally changed to Robert Lee-Dillon in 1924), a lieutenant commander in the Royal Navy with the words 'You're Warneford, aren't you?' only to give the tart reply, 'I look like him don't I?' This perceived attitude may be compared to comments made by others like Lady Algernon Gordon-Lennox who, talking to Rex in Paris, found him 'so modest' as did Fitzgibbon's wife Georgette, who said of him, 'He described a good deal of his experiences in the most simple and natural and unaffected way.'

Marsden thought that Warneford's mood had changed for the better the next morning. Rex was due to give an acceptance test to a new

Farman F27 before returning for duty at St Pol in this plane. Henry Beach Needham, a prominent American journalist, had been given permission by the French military authorities for an interview with Warneford, and so the two met for lunch on 17 June. He returned to the Ritz after the lunch, where Fitzgibbon, to whom he had promised a flight, was waiting. Finding that Mrs Fitzgibbon would be left alone, he asked her to join them. They then went to the RNAS Headquarters and, collecting Needham, travelled in a RNAS car, with military driver, to Buc airfield. Mrs Fitzgibbon recalled that Rex was recognised, and saluted by, many officers on this drive.

Arriving at Buc, the men got out. Warneford and Fitzgibbon climbed into a new Farman F27, and after instructions for the passenger to tap him three times on the shoulder when he had had enough, Rex made a long, steady take-off run and the pair were away. The flight was uneventful, the lieutenant commander's initial fears of flying having vanished, and when it was over the proposal was made that his wife should next take to the skies. However, Fitzgibbon, who distrusted flying, began to object and since, as Warneford pointed out, time was slipping away, and the weather was not improving, it was agreed that Needham should go next. He handed his hat and notebook to Georgette Fitzgibbon, gave a pathetic smile, and climbed aboard. 'God,' he had exclaimed while her husband was aloft, 'I wish it was me coming down and that it was all over! I am scared blue, but I have to go up on account of the article for my paper. Oh well, I guess when all's said and done it is no worse than some of our express elevators!' Needham started to fix his safety strap, but he was told that they would not be airborne for long, so he need not bother.

As the plane began to taxi, 'a man appeared, running fast across the grass, shouting and waving his arms', but when he was not seen by Warneford the man 'shrugged his shoulders and turned away'. No one ever found out who this man was or what he had wanted! About then the green Hispano-Suiza belonging to Baroness de Laroche arrived at the airfield entrance and she alighted. Raymonde had wanted to be there before Rex took off, as she was a little concerned by his comments the previous evening, but had been delayed by heavy military traffic. Take-off with the two men 'went beautifully'; they rose to about 300ft and turned to port, then making a steep dive to about 50ft (there are conflicting accounts of the actual heights), straightened out before what seemed to be another dive commenced. This developed into a spin, and the Farman turned upside-down throwing out both Warneford and Needham to fall into a field of wheat. At once the wings crumpled and the machine began to disintegrate, finally crashing ¾ mile away from the horrified watchers, the majority of whom, including Fitzgibbon, joined a group of soldiers from an adjacent fort, all rushing to the field where the two flyers had fallen.

Needham was quickly found, and only a glance was enough to confirm that he would write no more reports. Warneford they took a little time in discovering; he was lying on his face and 'in a terrible state'. Fitzgibbon felt under the sub-lieutenant's tunic to confirm that his heart was still beating and noted that the French insignia he had so recently received had been driven through his jacket and deep into his flesh by the impact.

The RNAS Fiat in which the party had come to Buc could not be found, but the soldiers commandeered another vehicle into which Warneford was carefully placed before the driver was ordered to make all possible speed to the British military hospital (No. 4 General Hospital) at the Trianon Hotel, Versailles. The Baroness quickly instructed her chauffeur to follow, and on the 4-mile journey she and her car were seen by Marsden travelling in the opposite direction. He had been testing a Nieuport and, returning to the Ritz, heard the news of the crash. Marsden turned around and followed, to arrive at the hospital almost at the same time as Raymonde. They saw Rex taken into the hospital and Marsden later recalled:

> I do not know if he knew we were there ... he gave a little sigh and opened his eyes ... he looked straight at me, almost as if he was going to make a sign that he knew us. Then his head turned away, and before the orderlies had wheeled him out of our sight he died. I took Raymonde home and left her with her maid, whom I told to phone the doctor.

A post-mortem was to discover the extent of his injuries, which included a fractured skull, both arms broken and fractures to the right hip and leg.

Many theories for the cause of the crash were aired, and at the official inquiry it was suggested that Warneford might have pulled up the Farman too hard from a dive, causing the wing to break under the strain. The man seen running towards the aircraft just prior to take-off was not identified. A reporter from an English newspaper who had spoken briefly to Rex in the early afternoon had apparently made his way to the airfield as his sketch of the accident depicting the two men falling from the plane was adapted for use in the *Daily Express*.

Warneford's coffin was covered with a Union Jack surrounded by flowers, many picked by patients, nurses and doctors at the hospital. Numerous floral tributes arrived throughout Friday 18 June, including one in the shape of an aeroplane, on the right wing of which was a copy of the Cross of the Légion d'Honneur and on the left that of the Victoria Cross, made entirely of red and white roses with the propeller, of white roses, tied with a ribbon inscribed: 'Honoured by the King, admired by the Empire, but mourned by all.' Police were needed to control the numbers of those wishing to pay their respects. In the little wooden chapel beside Warneford was the coffin of Henry Beach Needham covered with his national flag. A simple funeral had been planned for Sunday 20 June with a service in the hospital chapel followed by an internment in the nearby military cemetery at St Gonards. (This cemetery already contained the remains of one RFC casualty who had been buried in May.) RNAS men were to attend, including Albert Hawkins, the fitter who serviced Warneford's aircraft at St Pol who had requested that he be a pallbearer. This plan was suddenly changed during the weekend and a decision was made to return Warneford's body to England for burial. This was contrary to the wishes of the newly formed Imperial War Graves Commission and the adjutant general who had decreed in April that all casualties should be buried near where they fell.

Warneford's body was returned to England on Monday 21 June after leaving the Versailles hospital early in the morning and having been conveyed by train to Dieppe. On the train journey, aviators from Buc travelled with the coffin in its funeral coach and a guard of honour made up of troops from Belgium, France and England was present at the quayside when the crated coffin was loaded aboard. All passengers were disembarked at Folkestone before the flag-draped coffin was loaded into a railway van of the specially provided train with many wreaths, including that of the massive aeroplane placed in another carriage.

Contrary to the scenes in France, where the departure had been carried out with some secrecy, streets surrounding Victoria Station, London, were crowded over an hour before the arrival of the train. The platform was closed to the public and only Admiralty representatives, two of Rex's sisters and Lieutenant Colonel Corkery, RAMC, his stepfather, met the train. The flag-covered coffin was placed on a gun carriage with the largest wreaths and pulled by twenty seamen of the Royal Naval Division up the crowded Victoria street and on to Brompton where it lay overnight in the mortuary chapel of Brompton Cemetery before the burial service the next afternoon at 4 o'clock. The coffin was taken to the graveside on a gun-carriage drawn by Blue Jackets with a firing party of fifty men to give a valedictory salute while the crowds were reported as numbering 50,000. Later, Alexandra Corkery was to receive the Victoria Cross awarded to her son from the Admiralty, and a year later a memorial stone was raised over his resting place, not far from that of Thomas Warneford, the grandfather he had adored. It was subscribed for by the *Daily Express* and was unveiled by Lord Derby on 11 July. It has been described by some as being in poor taste and extremely ugly, but does pay tribute to this 23-year-old.

In August, 1915 Rex's mother, then living in Exmouth, was called to the Admiralty where she was presented with a replica of the Légion d'Honneur. This cross, subscribed to by *all* those connected with the construction of the Morane-Saulnier aircraft, was manufactured with jewels replacing the enamels. 'The usual white ... by diamonds, the green part by emeralds, and the red portion by rubies. The Cross is set in platinum and the centre part in gold ... inscribed ... in a plush case.'

On 29 July 1919, in the town square of St Amandsberg, Gent, a plaque commemorating the event was erected on the wall near to where the Zeppelin had crashed. The number of the airship had to be corrected to LZ37 as it was originally inscribed LZ36. A nearby road has been named Reginald Warneford Straat. Engels oorlogspiloot 1891–1915.

The Morane aircraft used in the epic event, after an exhibition tour of Britain, was eventually broken up despite having survived at Crystal Palace as late as 1922. In the Warneford Chapel of Highworth Church, Wiltshire, is a memorial to members of the family dedicated by the Rev. H.L. Warneford on 21 August 1917. In the following year Hackney saw its Gotha and Victoria Streets renamed Warneford Street, there also being a thoroughfare of the same name in Harrow, while Watford had a Warneford Place. A blue plaque was also erected, by the Exmouth Society, at the Dolphin Hotel, 2 Morton Road, Exmouth, the address where his mother had resided.

Warneford's had been the first Royal Navy VC bestowed in the war, a fact marked by a display including his awards (VC, 1914–15 Star, BWM, Victory Medal, and Knight, Légion d'Honneur) in a special niche in the Fleet Air Arm Museum at Yeovilton where a restaurant also bears his name. Warneford's name appears on the roll of honour in St Clement Danes Church, the Strand, London along with all other VC winners of the RFC, RNAS and RAF.

Raymonde, Baroness de Laroche, carried on with her flying and in 1919 achieved a record height for a woman pilot of 4,800 metres. Sadly, the Baroness, who also held the Légion d'Honneur, was accidentally killed whilst training for an air race at Crotoy on 18 July 1919.

On the day of Warneford's death the *Paris Soir* wrote: 'He who defied the storm has been killed by a breeze.'

L.G. HAWKER

Belgium, 25 July 1915

In Northern France and Belgium, the year 1915 had seen the first major British offensives of the war at Neuve Chapelle, Aubers Ridge and Festubert, followed by the first use of poison gas by the Germans in their attack on the Ypres Salient in April. While these land-based battles continued, the fledgling Royal Flying Corps played its part in providing reconnaissance, bombing and artillery spotting while attempting to cope with an aggressive adversary.

On 25 July 1915, Temporary Captain Lanoe Hawker, at the controls of Bristol Scout C 1611 – a single seat rotary-engined biplane which was armed with a single Lewis gun mounted on the left side of the fuselage – took off for an early evening offensive patrol on the hunt for enemy aircraft. The first of these he spotted, at about 6 p.m., was a two-seater over Passchendaele about 5 miles north-east of Ypres, Belgium. The Bristol Scout attacked at the cost of a whole drum of Lewis gun ammunition, firing at about 400yd range, with the result of sending his opponent into a spin, and out of control.

A second enemy was encountered twenty minutes later over Houthulst Forest, 10 miles north of Ypres, a machine of *Flieger Abteilung* 3, with which Hawker immediately closed and opened fire, again at about 400yd range, causing it to dive away and make a forced landing behind enemy lines, a victory that was later confirmed by an anti-aircraft battery.

Hawker then gained altitude to 11,000ft, the time being about 7 p.m. when his attention was attracted by a heavy concentration of anti-aircraft fire over Hooge, about 2 miles east of Ypres. Closing in to a range of 100yd and making his approach out of the setting sun, Hawker noted as he opened fire that his target was an Albatros two-seater, probably a CI. The aircraft at once burst into flames and turned over so that the observer fell out to his death, the aircraft with its pilot plunging down to crash south-east of Zillebeke. A few days later in a letter Hawker admitted that he felt sorry for the German pilot as he crashed in flames.

The result of this action was an immediate recommendation for the Victoria Cross, and the citation was published in the *London Gazette* No. 29273 dated 24 August 1915:

CAPTAIN LANOE GEORGE HAWKER, D.S.O., ROYAL ENGINEERS AND ROYAL FLYING CORPS.

For most conspicuous bravery and very great ability on 25th July, 1915. When flying alone he attacked three German aeroplanes in succession. The first managed eventually to escape, the second was driven to ground damaged, and the third, which he attacked at a height of about 10,000 feet, was driven to earth in our lines, the pilot and observer being killed. The personal bravery shown by this officer was of the highest order, as the enemy's aircraft were armed with machine guns, and all carried a passenger as well as pilot.

This was the first of Britain's supreme awards to be made for aerial combat between aircraft and it was curious that it should be awarded to an officer of an army co-operation squadron.

Hawker was granted a brief leave followed by a further period in France, during which he 'sought out enemy aircraft at every opportunity'. Hawker was involved in aerial combats on a number of occasions and with confirmed 'victories' on 2 and 11 August (two) and a final shooting down of an enemy scout over Bixschoote on 7 September, his official total came to seven.

On 20 September, after almost daily carrying out operational flights, Hawker was posted home with a strong recommendation that he be promoted to major and given command of a squadron. While he was in Britain he attended the investiture at Buckingham Palace on 5 October 1915 where he was awarded by King George V both his DSO (see below) and VC so that he 'had to trot round twice' to receive them.

❖ ❖ ❖

Lieutenant Harry C. Hawker RN and his wife Julia Gordon Lanoe had six children. His son Lanoe George was born at 'Homecroft' in the village of Longparish, Hampshire, on 31 December 1890. This was only a very short distance from the Georgian Longparish House, traditional home of the Hawker family, whose traceable service to their country goes back to the time of Elizabeth I.

Lanoe learnt to read early and before long, having a very enquiring mind, developed an uncanny ability to dismantle mechanical toys and then accurately reassemble them. When his father left to fight in the Boer War both Lanoe and his younger brother Tyrrel were sent to be educated in Geneva for two years followed by attendance at Stubbington House School, on the River Solent, Hampshire, where they were prepared for entry into the Royal Navy.

Lanoe Hawker was nominated for naval service in March 1905 by Prince Louis of Battenberg, father of Lord Louis Mountbatten, and entered Dartmouth Naval College in July. This service was suddenly cut short when over-exertion strained his heart, causing him to leave the college. The family moved to Broxwood Court in Herefordshire, some 15 miles from Hereford.

Lanoe decided to enter the Royal Military Academy at Woolwich and embarked on a period of preparatory study, residing with his brother at the house of a tutor at Cricklewood for the purpose. It was at the local cinema that the pair first saw a film of a Wright biplane which so fired their imagination. Lanoe was successful in entering Woolwich in February 1910 and was rewarded with the present of a Triumph motorcycle.

During the summer of 1910 the two brothers attended the Bournemouth International Aviation Meeting on 13 July, where Charles Rolls had had a fatal crash the previous day. This visit was followed by trips to Hendon air shows, which inspired the construction of flying models and the study of books on the subject. Four months later the young Hawker brothers joined the Royal Aero Club. Included in the privileges of membership was free entry to Hendon, and during one of these trips Lanoe Hawker made his first flight in one of Horatio Barber's Valkyrie aircraft which were constructed there.

The experience he had of flying deeply impressed Hawker, and having borrowed the requisite instruction fee of £50, he joined the Barber school at Hendon using the Valkyrie machines of the same type as that in which he had first flown.

Meanwhile his studies at Woolwich had gone well with the result that he was made second lieutenant in the Royal Engineers in July 1911, being immediately posted to the School of Engineering at Chatham. His pilot training was temporarily suspended when Barber closed down his school and sold it to Handley Page. Hawker's aviation training was not resumed until the spring of the following year, still at Hendon, but this time with the Deperdussin school. He obtained his Royal Aero Club Certificate, No. 435, on 13 March 1913.

The death of his father – whose estate was later valued in excess of £127,000 – as the result of a horse riding accident, in effect left Lanoe as head of the family, which was now living in Dorset. Hawker was promoted to lieutenant in October 1913 and posted to 33rd Fortress Company, RE, at Cork Harbour, Ireland.

Hawker had made frequent requests to be accepted by the Central Flying School. His application was accepted and he was posted to Upavon, Wiltshire, on 1 August 1914 where he joined D Flight for his training, three days before the outbreak of war. On 3 October he qualified as a military pilot, and was immediately posted to No. 6 Squadron at Farnborough, Hampshire. This squadron, with its mixture of aircraft including BE2s of several sorts (fast machines mostly reserved for the CO and flight commanders), BE8s and Henry Farmans (one of which was flown by Hawker), successfully flew from Dover to Bruges, Belgium, on 7 October 1914. On the morning of the following day the squadron's first war sortie began at 7.10 a.m. with Hawker acting as observer to Captain A. Marsh, flying BE2a 492, for a reconnaissance flight over German troops who were advancing towards Bruges so rapidly that Ostend racecourse was to be the squadron's base for the next few days.

As a 'jack of all trades' unit, officially described as a corps reconnaissance squadron, No. 6 had a wide spectrum of duties connected with the army to perform, none more demanding than that of target spotting to assist the artillery. Perhaps it was the training and predilection that Hawker enjoyed as an engineer that caused him to carry out this duty in a very personal manner. This, a highly dangerous but effective way of distinguishing enemy guns concealed in camouflage, he described thus, 'First, fly low and draw their fire, then mark it [the position] down on the map'.

Enemy aircraft were seldom seen during the winter of 1914–15 although Hawker did manage to fire all the shots from his revolver at the first enemy aircraft he encountered, at the end of October. Few other chances came his way for such aggressive action although in addition to his revolver he usually carried a rifle.

On 22 April 1915, Hawker, in BE2c 1780 of No. 6 Squadron, now based at Bailleul in Northern France, was on a bombing attack, his target the Zeppelin airship sheds at Gontrode, near Ghent, Belgium. Arriving at 4,000ft, he dropped two of his three 20lb Hales bombs in order to 'test the defences', but then noticed a captive balloon moored nearby with its basket underneath containing a machine-gunner. To deal with this Lanoe flew past in a steep turn, coming in at close range to toss hand grenades in the direction of the basket and at about 200ft releasing the other bomb, his proximity to the balloon having protected him from some of the fire from the ground. Small wonder, therefore, that the return flight to base called for a high degree of piloting skill of the damaged aircraft which was later found to have sustained twenty-four hits. Hawker was not to know that the shed was empty, as Zeppelin LZ35, normally based there, had previously crashed.

For this action Hawker was rewarded with the award of the Distinguished Service Order and promotion to Captain, Flight Commander of A Flight. The DSO citation appeared in the supplement to the *London Gazette* dated 8 May 1915:

LIEUTENANT LANOE GEORGE HAWKER, ROYAL ENGINEERS AND ROYAL FLYING CORPS.

For conspicuous gallantry on 19th April, 1915, when he succeeded in dropping bombs on the German airship shed at Gontrode from a height of only 200 feet, under circumstances of the greatest risk.

Lieutenant Hawker displayed remarkable ingenuity in utilizing an occupied German captive balloon to shield him from fire whilst manoeuvring to drop the bombs.

His report on the material effect of the operation, however, reflected a note of disappointment since the third bomb fell 'six or ten ft short', although he added, 'I expect I did some damage'. The same touch of self-criticism attends his recollections of the grenade-throwing incident, these being 'impossible to aim going round at that speed'.

On another occasion, in April 1915, Hawker, on a reconnaissance patrol near St Julien, Belgium, was attempting to ascertain who held a particular large farm when he was hit near his left ankle by fire from that direction. As he later reported, after having 'placed the farm carefully on the map' he had 'solved the problem as to who held the farm!' Despite his injury Hawker insisted on flying – having to be lifted up to the cockpit – until the ground fighting eased. He successfully used a rifle on enemy aircraft in this and another patrol. He then took two weeks' sick leave and was then sent for training on single-seater aircraft before his return to the squadron in May.

On 3 June the first of a new aircraft, a single-seat Bristol Scout C, No. 1609, was received by the squadron, now based at Abeele on the French–Belgian border near Poperinge. Hawker, with the help of Air Mechanic Ernest Elton (later flight sergeant DCM MM), devised a mounting for a Lewis gun fitted on the left side of the cockpit. At that time no British aircraft was equipped with armament synchronised to fire through the propeller blade so with this improvised new mounting the gun would fire forward, outside of the arc of the propeller.

Hawker was delighted with this machine, which he described in a letter as 'a beauty and no mistake' and, after a flooded airfield had prevented further 'tests', on 8 June he wrote, 'I have badly frightened one or two Boches'. This was a reference to an encounter with an Aviatik the day before, and on 21 June in this machine, Hawker attacked a DFW – a two-seater German biplane used for reconnaissance duties – which was last seen trailing a plume of smoke, but as he did not see it fall, made no 'victory' claim.

The euphoria he enjoyed for the new machine was damaged on 22 June when, after three encounters with enemy aircraft, he ran out of petrol and during his forced landing overturned near a wire fence. Concerned that his commanding officer would take a very dim view of the damage to such a valuable aircraft Hawker was relieved, and pleased, when Bristol Scout C, No. 1611 was delivered from the 1st Air Park to No. 6 Squadron on 26 June. It is reasonable to assume that the replacement aircraft was quickly fitted with Hawker's individual Lewis gun mounting.

No. 24 Squadron had originally been formed at Hounslow Heath Aerodrome on 1 September 1915 and, at the end of that month, Major Hawker took up his appointment as commanding officer with the task of building a scout (fighter) squadron from scratch. Despite the rigours of having been on almost continuous active service for many months he immediately threw himself into this new challenge. The squadron's new aircraft, the de Havilland 2 (DH2) were delivered during January 1916 and this single-seat pusher quickly earned a reputation for spinning, which caused fatalities. Consequently Hawker, in full view of the squadron pilots, took one of these aircraft up and proceeded to put it into a series of spins, from each of which he safely recovered. After landing he described to the pilots, in detail, the correct techniques for getting out of a spin in the DH2. Such instructions were of great assistance to the squadron pilots whose confidence in this very manoeuvrable aeroplane grew rapidly. One of his pilots in training, after Hawker had explained the importance of accurately allowing for the range of the target, commented that, 'He was one of the first to realise that many a pilot can get close to his man, but few can shoot straight enough to shoot him down'.

The unit flew to St Omer on 7 February 1916 and was preceded by Hawker on 2 February, the day before his promotion to major became effective, and on 12 February the squadron flew to Bertangles, 3 miles north of Amiens. Here Hawker's engineering skills were tested due to various engine faults in his aircraft, but despite such work and leading his squadron he had also found time to invent the fleece-lined thigh-length boots ('fug boots') that were later to become standard issue, introduce a ring-sight (the 'Hawker fore-sight') for machine guns, allowing automatic deflection, and modify the standard 47-round ammunition drum of the Lewis gun which almost doubled its capacity. These aids were all aimed at improving the efficiency of his new unit and many of his ideas were taken up by the other RFC squadrons.

That his value was recognised by his superiors is illustrated by the fulsome terms adopted by the commander of the 4th Army, Lieutenant General Sir Henry Rawlinson, in his report for 23 May 1916 when he said, 'I cannot speak too highly of the work of these young pilots, most of whom have recently come out from England.' Hawker had commented during April that when Allied planes crossed the lines, a few Fokkers would come up and 'hang like minnows in a stream, but they would not fight', but as for personally flying over enemy territory, he was now, as squadron commander, forbidden to do so. He did, however, 'bend the rules' at times and it was not unknown for him, at the last minute, to take the place of pilots who were about to take home leave or just to omit his name from flying orders.

In May the squadron aircraft strength was increased from twelve to eighteen in readiness for the Battle of the Somme which began on 1 July 1916 and involved twenty-seven RFC squadrons with 421 aircraft on charge. No. 24 Squadron was thrown early into the fray (an instruction pinned to the squadron notice board by Hawker was to the point: 'Attack Everything!'), mounting patrols composed of six or seven machines each, while Lanoe had personally conducted two reconnaissances by the end of the day, one at midday and another in the evening. The earlier order that squadron commanders were forbidden to fly had been amended to a prohibition of crossing the lines, but Hawker now chose to ignore this second directive despite some overcast skies. These conditions, with only a few bright intervals, were not to change for a week when a partial improvement brought increased activity in the air from the other side of the lines. Although few sorties were mounted against Allied targets, and lacking any appreciable degree of other activity, Hawker ordered his pilots to attack German troops on the ground whenever encountered. He personally obtained a supply of tracer to use against observation balloons, realising the harm which accurate reports from these could do to troops on the ground. Unsurprisingly official records show that during the Battle of the Somme, No. 24 Squadron took part in more combats than any other unit.

The Battle of the Somme officially ended on 18 November 1916 and by this time the German air services were being equipped with aircraft such as Albatros DII and Halberstadt DIII which had superior performances to the RFC machines.

Reconnaissance flights were ordered in the region of Bapaume during a brief spell of fine weather, the photographic machines being escorted by DH2s of No. 24 Squadron, and one such operation on 23 November at about 1 p.m. hours found Lanoe Hawker in DH2 5964 participating with two others flown by Captain John Andrews and Lieutenant Robert Saundby. Fifty minutes later the three were at 11,000ft just crossing the lines towards Bapaume, when two German two-seaters were seen by Andrews, flying below at 6,000ft. Andrews later recorded that, 'I attacked two Hostile Aircraft (HA) just North East of Bapaume and drove them East when I observed two strong patrols of HA Scouts above me. I was about to abandon the pursuit when a DH2 Scout, Major Hawker dived past me and continued to pursue.' The enemy aircraft were *Jagdstaffel 2* flying Albatros DIIs.

Meanwhile Hawker cut the fuel to his engine to prevent it choking in the dive, but on switching on again the motor was obviously not functioning properly so that altitude was lost at each turn. An enemy was also now on his tail, Manfred von Richthofen, and the experienced pair were in a situation where neither could bring his gun to bear so that, now close, they waved to each other. Von Richthofen detailed what happened next:

> I discovered that I was not meeting a beginner. He had not the slightest intention of breaking off the fight ... When we were down to about 6,000 ft without achieving anything particular, my opponent should have discovered that it was time for him to take his leave ... The gallant fellow was full of pluck [and] at that time his first bullets were flying around me, so far neither of us had been able to do any shooting ... When we had come down to about 300 ft he tried to escape by flying a zig-zag course ... That was my most favourable moment [and] I followed him firing all the time. The Englishman could not help falling ...

A single bullet through his head had killed Lanoe Hawker.

Von Richthofen, in his autobiography, wrote, 'I was extremely proud when ... I was informed that the aviator I had brought down on 23rd November 1916, was the English Immelmann.' He arranged for Lanoe's Lewis gun to be retrieved from the wreckage and this trophy was hung above the door to his quarters. Hawker was von Richthofen's eleventh victim and after this victory he had his aircraft painted red.

The wreckage lay in the mud about 250yd east of the battered Luisenhof Farm, roughly 2 miles east of Bapaume, and the next day Lieutenant Bergmann, troubled by the fact that the body had lain in the open all night, reported this to Major von Schonberg and asked permission to bury Hawker. Permission was granted and Hawker was laid to rest beside the remains of his aircraft, some wreckage from which the major's batman, Grenadier Paul Fischer, used to make a cross on which he carved details of 'der Englische Major Hawker vom British

Royal Flying Corps' and the date, 23.11.16. Subsequent fighting over this area later in the war led to the actual burial site becoming lost.

In a letter dated 23 November 1916, one of the young pilots wrote: 'We have lost three people this last week one of whom was our major.' He then went on to describe Hawker's last action and later in this letter to his brother in No. 32 Squadron (who was ill in hospital) he wrote: 'I only hope we can survive till we get the new buses ... don't come out for ages. T'isn't worth it.'

Major Lanoe Hawker VC DSO was posted as missing and it was not until July of the following year that *Flight* recorded that he was officially reported as killed.

On 31 July 1932, Lord Trenchard, marshal of the Royal Air Force, unveiled the Arras Memorial to the Missing and the Flying Services Memorial, Fauborg d'Amiens, Arras. It was designed by Sir Edwin Lutyens. Commodore Richard Bell-Davies VC represented the Admiralty at the opening ceremony. The name of Major Lanoe Hawker is listed, together with those of 990 other airmen who have no known grave, including his fellow VC winners, Captain Albert Ball and Major Edward Mannock on the Flying Services Memorial. Twenty-three of these engraved names are 'aces', having been credited with ten or more aerial victories.

In St Nicholas Church, Longparish, a large stained-glass window was installed in 1967. Designed by Francis Skeat the window depicts St Michael flying over an airfield, biplanes on the ground and two airmen in the foreground. The window is dedicated to Major Lanoe George Hawker VC DSO RFC. A copy of this window is held at the Museum of Army Flying at Middle Wallop. Lanoe Hawker's name is also on the Longparish War Memorial. In St Clement Danes Church on the Strand, London, his name appears with those of the other VC winners of the RFC, RNAS and RAF.

Lanoe Hawker's original Victoria Cross was lost when family belongings of the Hawker family, left behind after the fall of France in 1940, were looted and stolen in their absence. A replacement is now displayed by the Royal Air Force Museum, Hendon, having been issued to Hawker's brother on 3 February 1960. His medal entitlement is VC, DSO, 1914 Star, BWM and Victory Medal. A VC 10 aircraft Serial Number XV101 was inscribed with the name Lanoe Hawker VC and later his name was transferred to Serial Number ZA150. This latter aircraft was withdrawn from service on 24 August 2013 and is now at Brooklands Museum. It is the intention of the Museum to refit ZA150 with the last three names it bore, including Hawkers, with the remainder of the fourteen names displayed inside the aircraft.

J.A. LIDDELL

Near Bruges, 31 July 1915

During May 1915, Captain John Aidan Liddell was provisionally seconded from the Argyll and Sutherland Highlanders to the Royal Flying Corps. Probably due to his previous aviation experience, he had obtained his RAC flying certificate in 1914, his service flying training was brief. At first he went to Shoreham, a War Office station which had been almost deserted until four months earlier when No. 3 Reserve Aeroplane Squadron had arrived, then to Dover St Margaret's where No. 15 Squadron, described as preparing for overseas service, was actually engaged in flying instruction. Finally Liddell was to be sent to Farnborough where on 20 July he was officially accepted as an RFC officer and posted to No. 7 Squadron. Three days later he joined its A Flight at St Omer, France.

The squadron had arrived in France on 8 April. Its duties were artillery observation, reconnaissance, bombing and photography. Its aircraft comprised seven of the clumsy-looking RE5 two-seaters which had only entered production during the previous year and a number of Vickers pushers.

Although this type of RE5 was used for bombing, reconnaissance missions were also flown. Six days after his arrival, Liddell was to make his first operational sortie when he flew RE5 No. 2458 for a long reconnaissance flight carrying himself and his observer, Second Lieutenant H.H. Watkins over Ostend, Bruges, Ghent, Audenarde and Heestert. At the time this sort of operation was in its infancy and, although enemy aircraft were encountered, the resultant combats were inconclusive. This was probably owing to their crews being unable properly to retaliate.

Liddell's next reconnaissance mission took place on 31 July, this time with him at the controls of 2457. His observer on this occasion was

Second Lieutenant Roland H. Peck, who is reputed to have attempted to augment the standard armament by also taking along a loaded 0.303 service rifle. In a machine capable of a maximum speed at sea level of only 78mph, the use of such a weapon would have been by no means impossible. However, as matters turned out, this sortie over enemy territory, Liddell's second, was to be his last.

Take-off from the Belgian base at Furnes was made late in the morning and a course was set for a routine reconnaissance over the vicinities of Ostend, Bruges and Ghent. The aircraft arrived over Ostend at an altitude of some 5,000ft. An enemy aircraft had been seen earlier above the trenches but it had made no attempt to attack, so it was probably another aircraft that suddenly did so from above as the RE5 flew over Bruges.

The machine left no more impression of itself than that of a two-seater with the gunner standing in the rear cockpit, crouching over his Parabellum machine gun and opening fire on the RE5. (In his report Peck described the 'Hostile Machine' as, '… similar to a Bristol Scout but at least twice as large … Armed with a machine gun.') To this Peck replied with his Lewis gun, using a full drum in doing so, and it was while replacing this that he suddenly became aware that in the swift, surprise attack, his pilot had obviously been hit, as the machine began lurching into a dive, nearly throwing out the unrestrained gunner. Peck managed to save his Lewis gun although all the ammunition fell out when the aircraft 'turned completely over'. The aircraft then fell for about 3,000ft with no hand on the controls since Liddell in the rear seat had lost consciousness. Small wonder that he had done so, since the enemy's fire had blasted away part of the starboard side of the cockpit. It had cut through his thigh so deeply that for a moment the white of the exposed bone could be seen through the gap in the flesh that had been torn out.

Perhaps it was the rush of air, perhaps the instinct for self-preservation, but Liddell somehow managed to arrest the machine's headlong plunge. No doubt pleased by this, Peck was then handed a scribbled note stating that he proposed to attempt to reach the Allied side of the lines. An immediate landing might well have brought him medical attention but would have meant both men becoming prisoners of war. However part of the controls had been destroyed, jamming the throttle. In addition the right side of the cockpit was shattered and part of the undercarriage badly damaged. Despite this Liddell managed to operate what was left of the aileron controls with his right hand and operate the rudder cables with the other. In this manner, he set out on the half-hour journey where landfall was made on la Panne airfield He then cut the engine at the last moment as a substitute for closing the throttle.

The first, reaction of the crowd of men that surrounded the stricken RE5 was to assist Liddell from the cockpit. But he would have nothing of this, indicating that he regarded it safer to remain in his seat until a doctor arrived. While he waited half an hour for one to do so, he took some pieces of wood and with them put together first a splint and then used the second as part of a tourniquet to stem the flow of blood. This done, he was lifted from the cockpit and placed on a stretcher, managing to smile and raise a feeble wave of the hand at the camera that one of the Belgians had the presence of mind to seize. This man was able to record several good photographs before Liddell was transported to hospital, the Belgian Red Cross Hospital at the Hôtel de l'Ocean at la Panne, where the senior physician was a skilled surgeon from Brussels, Dr Depage. Due to the shortage of available Belgian nurses the British Red Cross had sent VADs and nurses to la Panne, one of whom was probationer Mrs Elsie Fenwick who, on 31 July 1915, noted the arrival of Liddell in her diary. 'Just before lunch an English aviator called Captain Liddell was brought in with a bad smashed leg. I saw the observer with him, Mr Peck, such a bounder ... He [Liddell] is very bad but they hope he'll be all right.'

The Liddell family, at their home of Sherfield Manor, Hampshire, received the telegram advising of John Aidan's injuries on 3 August, the same day on which he wrote them a long letter which would seem to indicate an improvement in his condition. Peck was sent back to England for a few days' leave by his CO Major Hoare, so that he could give the family a first-hand account of the action. By now Liddell's fame was spreading and on 14 August the front page of the *Daily Mirror* was taken up with photographs of the injured Liddell sitting in his aircraft under the headline 'British Airman with fifty wounds in his leg, Unconscious when plane turned turtle'. However, on the previous day, Elsie Fenwick noted in her diary, 'I'm afraid Captain Liddell's leg is doing badly and will have to be cut off after all, but we still hope not', and on 16 August, 'Poor Captain Liddell is not doing well'.

A short telegram which read, 'Have been given Victoria Cross will be in gazette Saturday' was received at Sherfield Manor on 17 August (the VC citation was published in the *London Gazette* No. 29272 dated 23 August). Elsie Fenwick noted:

Poor Captain Liddell is much worse and they settled to have his leg off tomorrow morning. It's too sad, after a fortnight's pain for nothing. In the afternoon Prince Alexander [Prince Alexander of Teck from the British Military Mission] came up to say he'd been given a VC. It's splendid, but it was very sad going to congratulate him, knowing that his leg was doomed and he didn't know it. One felt such a humbug, but he was so happy.

A senior consultant serving with the BEF had also concurred with the decision to amputate, and the operation was duly carried out. Liddell's condition did not improve and on Saturday 21 August, the day when, the British Military Mission (Lieutenant Colonel Tom Bridges) wired his family and suggested that his mother should come over and that he would have a car waiting for her at Boulogne. Emily Liddell was at the la Panne hospital by Monday and reported home that although the operation had been successful she was concerned about the blood poisoning. She was, unfortunately, right to be fearful, for on 31 August John Aidan Liddell passed away, his mother at his bedside. This was the feast day of St Aidan, after whom he had been named.

As mentioned earlier, in the chapters on Rhodes-Moorhouse and Warneford, it was not army policy for the dead to be returned for England but once again, for an airman who had been awarded the VC, the rules were bent! In order to repatriate the body to England it was necessary for the family to make arrangements with army general lines of communication and it seems likely senior military figures smoothed the way for them. The coffin was accompanied on the journey to England by an officer from No. 7 Squadron, Lieutenant Benegough, and the British matron from the hospital. On 2 September a service had been held in the hospital chapel and was very well attended including by many senior officers from the RFC. The coffin lay overnight in the Church of the Immaculate Conception at Farm Street, Mayfair, and, after a Requiem Mass the next morning celebrated by the Rector of Stonyhurst, a motor hearse conveyed the body to Basingstoke. The funeral procession began at London Street and was led by five pipers from the Argyll and Sutherland Highlanders with the hearse flanked by an eight-man strong RFC bearer party. Amongst those following behind were two senior NCOs from the Argylls including Company Sergeant-Major Conroy. The streets of Basingstoke were crowded as the cortège slowly made its way to South View Cemetery where waited the clergy: the Bishop of Portsmouth, the Canon of Winchester, Canon Scoles, and the Rector of Stonyhurst. After the service volleys were fired by men of the RFA and the military pipers played laments. On 1 October 1915 most of Liddell's family attended a Solemn Requiem Mass at the Church of St Peter at Stonyhurst College. This was followed by the playing of the Last Post outside the church where the College OTC were formed up.

On 16 November John Liddell received his son's Victoria Cross from King George V at Buckingham Palace after being only given three days' notice of the ceremony. This was the fourth VC to be awarded to an aviator and the second of three to be gained by Old Stonyhurst (Stonyhurst old boys) in the First World War – the first by Maurice Dease at Mons in August 1914 and the third by Gabriel Coury on 8 August 1916 during the Battle of the Somme.

Sherfield Manor had been used as a military hospital which closed late in 1915 and the then commandant, Liddell's sister Dorothy, continued her nursing career at the Belgian Red Cross Hospital at la Panne which had cared for her brother. She was later honoured with an OBE.

The observer in Liddell's aircraft, Roland Peck, stayed in the RFC and, when serving with No. 30 Squadron, was killed in combat over Mesopotamia on 5 March 1916. He is commemorated on the Basra Memorial, Iraq.

❖ ❖ ❖

John Aiden Liddell was the first child of John Liddell and Emily Catherine and was born in Benwell Hall, Newcastle-upon-Tyne, on 3 August 1888. There were five more children to come, three daughters and two sons. The family moved to Prudhoe Hall in 1898. This hall was built as the seat of the Liddell family in 1870 and is about 11 miles west of Newcastle-upon-Tyne. Another move followed in 1904 to Sydmonton Court near Newbury where the family remained until their desired property, Sherfield Manor, was purchased and made ready for their occupation in 1908. This old established manor house stood in over 800 acres of parkland a few miles from Basingstoke, and was of considerable size. It was 'a most suitable home for an Edwardian gentleman and his household' and included the Lordship of the Manor. John and Emily Liddell were much involved in local life and were very generous to the village associations and clubs. They were devout Roman Catholics and worshipped at Basingstoke although a chapel at the manor was often used.

John Aidan developed a talent for mechanical matters and at school an interest in scientific subjects. His first education was at Mrs Ware's Academy, Frognall Hall, Hampstead, which he left in the summer of 1900. A fellow student at Frognall Hall, and distant relative through marriage, was Maurice Dease, a year younger than Liddell. On 20 September 1900 Liddell undertook the long rail journey from Prudhoe to Stonyhurst College where the fees were sixty guineas per term. He did well at Stonyhurst where the Catholic-influenced education by the mainly Jesuit staff suited him and he was awarded several prizes and medals. Sport, however, did not feature in his achievements and his chief fascination was in modern technology and science, resulting, in 1904, in passes for his lower certificates in chemistry and mechanics. His interests also included astronomy, naturalist pursuits and country sports and he also played the flute.

Prior to Liddell's arrival at Stonyhurst two old boys had been awarded the Victoria Cross, Lieutenant Edmund Costello on the north-west frontier in July 1897 and Captain Paul Kenna in the Sudan, gazetted on 15 November 1898. Both these heroes had visited the school where they enthralled the boys with their stories. The Boer War was in progress when John arrived and shortly after, in October 1900, the school cadet corps paraded for the first time. In 1904 the school records show that Cadet J.A. Liddell was classified as a 'Very Good' shot with a score of 128 out of 168 in the annual musketry competition. This he improved to 131 the following year, well above average. In 1901 the school celebrated the end of the Boer War and a request for donations elicited the large amount of £5 from John's father towards the costs of a Boer War memorial in memory of old boys who had not returned.

John's interest in astronomy was greatly helped by a science teacher, Fr Aloysius Cortie, who was an astronomer of national repute and the director of the solar section of the British Astronomical Society. John, with Fr Cortie, travelled to Spain to view and photograph a total eclipse of the sun in August 1905, and the successful photographs were published in the Stonyhurst magazine. He also obtained the School Certificate in that year with excellent marks in advanced mathematics.

His final two years at Stonyhurst were spent in preparation for college, during which time he was elected to be a member of the British Astronomical Association. In 1908 Liddell, although failing to win a scholarship, started the autumn term at Balliol College, Oxford, reading Natural Sciences. A photograph of the 'Balliol Freshmen 1908' shows Liddell, now over 6ft tall, towering above most of his fifty-three fellow students. Amongst his contemporaries at the college were Cyril Asquith (son of the prime minister) and Friedrich von Bethman Hollweg (son of the German chancellor), Ronald Knox, Billy Grenfell, Walter Moncton and Aldous Huxley.

Liddell did not shine academically during his time at Oxford, graduating with third-class honours in zoology, maintaining an interest in science and the natural world while still developing his interests in engines. He competed in a number of motorcycle events as a member of the Varsity Motor Cycle Club and his practical interest in the maintenance of such machines earned him the nickname of 'Oozy' Liddell, although many of his college friends knew him by his family nickname of Peter.

John Aidan was offered a travelling scholarship to investigate changes in fauna following the Krakatoa volcanic eruption of 1883, but decided to remain at Sherfield Manor. Much of the time during that summer of 1912 was spent helping his mother in laying out the extensive gardens.

Also that year, in keeping with 'not wishing to be a slacker', to use his own words, he joined the Special Reserve of Officers and in June was granted a commission with the 3rd Volunteer Battalion, Argyll and Sutherland Highlanders (A&SH). The commitment required by such a commission was not inconsiderable, with much time spent training with regular battalions, in Liddell's case, 2nd A&SH. In December he was stationed at Fort George, near Inverness on the Moray Forth and he wrote to his sisters at home describing the memorable activities at Christmas and New Year, 'where there were innumerable other drinks with all the sergeants … so that it will be days before I am myself again'.

Liddell was sent on a Maxim gun course at Hythe in September 1913 where he did well. He continued to be interested in all things mechanical and inevitably became interested in aviation. He enrolled with the Vickers Flying School at Brooklands, Surrey, on 19 April. Here, on 14 May 1914, he successfully gained his RAC pilot's certificate Later in the year he received promotion to the rank of lieutenant.

When war was announced Lieutenant Liddell was at Sherfield Manor, and like other special reservists received his mobilisation orders by telegram. His assembly point was Stirling Castle and a photograph taken on the morning of Wednesday 5 August portrays him in service dress at the manor before starting out from Basingstoke Station on the long journey to Scotland. The 3rd Battalion was to be stationed at Woolwich Arsenal, and, as the machine-gun officer was off sick it was Lieutenant Liddell who was delegated command of the two Maxim guns. After much effort, particularly by Liddell himself, the 3rd Battalion machine guns, with all ammunition, men and horses, were entrained, and left Stirling about midnight on Friday 7 August, arriving at Woolwich Station some twelve hours later. Camped on a marshy area not far from the River Thames the battalion's strength grew steadily and was about 1,300 men by the end of August, even though the first draft of nearly 100 had departed on 26 August to join the 2nd Battalion as reinforcements. On the same day this battalion, which had disembarked at Boulogne on 12 August, was involved in the Battle of le Cateau where it suffered very heavy casualties – 461 killed, wounded or missing – whilst valiantly supporting units of the 14th Brigade. During the subsequent retreat the 2nd A&SH reached the village of Néry, not far from Compiègne, at 7 a.m. on 1 September. The battalion war diary records, '7 am Halted in NERY. Village a shambles as QUEEN'S BAYS and L Battery RHA shelled in billets and suffered heavily …' It was in this action that three VCs were won by members of L Battery. The remains of the 2nd Battalion were joined by reinforcements en route and by Lieutenant Liddell with his draft of eighty-four other ranks at La Haute Maison, south of the River Marne, on 7 September. Liddell left Arsenal Station on the morning of 30 August and embarked on the SS *Lake Michigan*, along with nearly 3,000 other troops, before sailing from Southampton early in the morning of the next day. The troops disembarked at St Nazaire on 2 September where a muddy unfinished rest camp (a ploughed field!) was their home for two days before they embarked by rail. After a trying, and confusing, journey Liddell and his fellow reinforcements arrived to join their comrades of the 2nd A&SH, 19th Brigade at La Haute Maison.

On the following day, 19th Brigade was ordered to advance towards the Marne in an attempt to cut off the enemy retreating over the bridge at La-Ferté-sous-Jouarre. Lieutenant Liddell and his men started at 4.30 a.m. and spent a large part of the day under fire from enemy artillery on the far side of the river, which caused one fatal casualty. The following day the Marne was crossed by a pontoon bridge and while the weather deteriorated the battalion followed after the retreating enemy amid scenes which Liddell recorded in his diary: 'La Ferté badly sacked by Germans. Houses turned inside out, furniture broken, bedding in the streets ... Bridge absolutely destroyed. Marched to Vendrest ... whole road littered with bottles and dead horses. Stench appalling.' On 12 September, the battalion endured a punishing march from 5.30 a.m. to 5.45 p.m., during which the commander of the BEF, Sir John French, briefly stopped and delivered a short message of thanks to the 2nd A&SH 'for their work at Le Cateau'. This was followed by a much shorter four-hour march the next day, which brought them close to the River Aisne where the sounds of battle could be heard on the heights of the Chemin des Dames. In a letter home on this day Liddell wrote that he had 'got quite a good start of a beard' and 'in spite of all the sleeping out we've done, am keeping very fit and well'. His requests from home emphasised 'cigarettes, chocolates (Menier for preference) ... and any kind of sweets' reiterating this later in the same letter, 'something to eat during the march and something to smoke'.

The battalion spent several days in the vicinity of Venizel and nearby villages, often under heavy shellfire and torrential rain. Liddell was much involved in working parties, finding and burying the dead and the seemingly endless numbers of horses who had become casualties of the shelling. On 20 September the battalion marched to Septmonts as they were now in corps reserve, their spell as support troops over for the time being. Billets were found and on the next day Liddell had his first shave since St Nazaire! Three days later two machine guns, replacing those lost at le Cateau, were delivered and, due to his previous experience and expertise with these weapons, Liddell was made machine-gun officer. He had under his command two NCOs and twelve privates with others trained as replacements. An advantage for the officer in charge was that he was mounted and Liddell was also given some 'spare' riding breeks which had belonged to Major McLean, killed at le Cateau in a gallant attack whilst supporting the Suffolk Regiment.

During this period Liddell made several entries in his diary relating to aircraft, and on seeing an enemy aircraft at about 1,500ft when in Soissons he considered that his machine guns would 'have had a chance of knocking it down'. In his letter of Saturday 3 October Liddell was complaining that the requested supplies of cigarettes, chocolates and boiled sweets had yet to arrive, writing '[I] detailed my needs in my first letter'. He also noted that the casualty lists had named his friend from childhood, Maurice Dease. On the following Monday the battalion began a move north toward the railhead at Pont-St-Maxence, travelling at night and on 5 October his first mail parcel arrived containing the requested cigarettes and chocolate. Two days later Bethisy St Pierre was their stop for the night, the nearest village being Néry, where, a little over a month earlier, many of the 2nd A&SH had seen the carnage following L Battery's gallant stand.

Following a slow train journey via Amiens and Étaples the battalion arrived for a short stay at billets in St Omer and later found themselves marching between various towns and villages arriving, during the afternoon of 20 October, at Fromelles. Fourteen German infantry divisions had launched strong attacks from la Bassée to the coast and were opposed by only seven British divisions together with three smaller divisions of dismounted cavalry. This was the beginning of what would later be termed 'The First Battle of Ypres'. Shortly before dawn on 21 October Lieutenant Liddell set up his machine guns south-east of le Maisnil and within an hour was subjected to German artillery fire which he later described as, 'all kinds of guns, Black Marias and high explosive beasts with green, white, black and yellow smoke'. French cavalry who had been supporting the British troops began to withdraw and the enemy infantry mounted strong attacks all along the line. The A&SH machine guns were in action until ammunition ran short late in the afternoon. The section by then had only three men and Liddell left. When withdrawing with his guns Liddell found a badly hurt NCO, Sergeant Conroy, and stopped to help him get towards an aid station. Conroy was convinced that if it had not been for John Aidan he would have perished in the freezing conditions.

The battalion withdrew to la Boutillerie having suffered over 200 casualties, many of the wounded not being recovered in the darkness.

This had been Lieutenant John Aidan Liddell's first serious enemy encounter and he, with his section of two machine guns, had acquitted themselves very well.

The Germans kept up artillery bombardments and frequent attacks, many during the hours of darkness, over the next several weeks and it was not until 25 November that Liddell had his first bath since arriving at St Omer. He and his machine guns had seen action regularly during this period, at times with other units, and he had witnessed what was to become known as the 'Massacre of the Innocents' helping to bury some 200 young German soldiers whom he later described as, 'the 224th Reserve Bavarian regiment who ... were all lads from 17 to 20 ... they seemed to have primed them up with rum and sent them off to attack ... I only heard of one officer being buried.' This last comment refers to rumours circulating that some German officers only accompanied their young charges halfway to the British trenches and then returned to their own lines. The trench conditions during the last three months of 1914 were terrible, with many men reporting sick as well as the daily losses from artillery and snipers. The Argylls occupied trenches at La Boutillerie, Pont-De-Nieppe, Ploegsteert Wood, Houplines and Armentières where the battalion was housed in the lunatic asylum – an irony not lost on many. Lieutenant Liddell and his machine-gun teams were attached to other battalions for some time, rejoining his own battalion on 16 November in Ploegsteert Wood.

Christmas was spent in the trenches near Houplines and the battalion war diary accurately describes the day as very quiet, with unarmed Germans coming out of their trenches and asking leave to bury their dead. Liddell's diary was more descriptive: 'In the afternoon the Germans brought two barrels of beer over to the Welsh Fusiliers. Our men and theirs walked over to the halfway fence and had a chat ... Walked over, Kennedy, Thompson and all of us ... met man from Glasgow and gave him tobacco in exchange for cigars.'

The New Year brought more rain and waterlogged trenches with the troops thoroughly exhausted, so it was with great relief that Liddell's long-expected leave pass arrived and on 9 January he departed for the comforts of England. One wing of Sherfield Manor had been turned into a Convalescent Hospital and one of his sisters, Monica Mary, was nursing there. He spent three days of his leave salmon fishing in the River Eden at the home of an uncle who lived in Warwick Hall, Cumberland. Liddell returned to the battalion's flooded and muddy trenches near La Vessee late in the evening of 18 January 1915. An entry in his diary of that week noted that more officers were off sick and on Saturday 23 January he recorded, 'Felt pretty seedy'. By the Monday morning the war diary recorded that, 'Lt Liddell sent away sick', as the medical officer had him taken to the field ambulance at Erquinghem. The next morning he was transported by motor ambulance to CCS No. 2 at Bailleul from where he was moved by ambulance train to No. 7 Stationary Hospital at Boulogne, arriving on Wednesday evening. In a letter home he admitted that he had been feeling run down before his leave and had hoped this break would, 'put me right', but that now he was 'feeling very washed out'. By 28 January Liddell was in the Herbert Hospital, Woolwich, having arrived at Dover on the hospital ship *St Edward* where he was diagnosed as recovering from an attack of influenza, and by the end of the month a medical board awarded him three weeks' sick leave. He went home to Sherfield Manor for further convalescence and while he was there, over the next few weeks the family was cheered by some good news. Firstly the *London Gazette* (*LG*) of 7 February announced that Cuthbert, one of his younger brothers, had been Mentioned in Despatches (MiD) for his services with 15th Hussars (he was to receive another MiD on 22 June 1915), then, in the *London Gazette* dated 17 February, five officers and three OR of 2/A&SH were named as Mentioned in Despatches. Included was Liddell's name. The *London Gazette* of the next day also included five awards for officers and NCOs of the Argylls including the newly instituted Military Cross for both Lieutenant Liddell and Sergeant-Major Kerr. This award was probably for John Aidan's work atle Maisnil in October 1914.

A medical board on 24 February awarded him three further weeks' sick leave with a diagnosis of rheumatism – hardly surprising considering the conditions he had been living and fighting in since September 1914. At the end of this period of sick leave he was pronounced as fit to return to duty at Woolwich with the 3rd Battalion. Clearly a return to his duties as machine-gun officer would further affect his health. However, he could still serve his country by putting at its disposal another of his interests and skills, that of a qualified pilot. The *LG* of 29 March 1915 announces his promotion to captain dated 2 February. This was followed by his secondment to the RFC in May and his subsequent VC action which proved fatal.

After his son's death his father continued with local philanthropy by financing a new heating system at Basingstoke Cottage Hospital where a brass plaque bore his son's name. A fine portrait of Captain J.A. Liddell VC MC, in full dress uniform, by William Carter, RA, was commissioned and donated by the family, in 1918, to Stonyhurst where it hangs in the refectory beside portraits of six other VC winners. His name is to be found among those on the First World War memorial at

Balliol College in the Chapel Passage, West Wall. At the Scottish Naval and Military Residence seven beds for veterans were endowed by 3rd A&SH and above each is a brass plaque, one of which is in memory of Captain J. Aidan Liddell VC MC. His name appears on the war memorial cross at Sherfield-on-Loddon as well as on the war memorial at the end of the Upper Gallery at Stonyhurst. In 1934 a brass tablet was unveiled to Liddell by the Duke of Montrose in Stirling at Holy Rood Church, the last line of which reads, 'Greater love has no man than this, that a man lay down his life for a friend.' Liddell's name appears amongst those members of the RFC, RNAS and RAF who have been awarded the VC, on the roll of honour inside St Clement Danes Church, the Strand, London.

A memorial commemorating the British Air Services personnel who perished in the First World War was unveiled at St Omer by Air Chief Marshal Sir Brian Burridge, Commander-in-Chief Headquarters Strike Command, and Lieutenant-General Jean Patrick Gaviard of the French Air Force, on 11 September 2004. Present at this ceremony was Henry Allingham, who, at the age of 108, was returning to France for the first time since his service in the RNAS. The history panel at St Omer pictures and names two airmen, Captain Liddell and Major Mannock, both winners of the Victoria Cross.

Other connected items include the alleged tip of RE5 2457's propeller, whereon a silver plate is inscribed with the VC award citation. The aircraft, 2457, used in the historic action of 31 July 1915 was later repaired and sent to No. 12 Squadron on 26 November, and to the Aircraft Park on 12 December, before returning to England on 30 December. Here it was used for flying instruction by No. 7 Reserve Squadron at Netheravon before presumably being either wrecked or struck off charge and broken up.

The medals awarded to John Aidan Liddell were never worn by him; records show that his 1914 Star was requested by his mother in January 1919 but the clasp is not fitted on the medal ribbon. His family proudly displayed his medals (VC, MC, 1914 Star, BWM and Victory Medal with oak leaf) together with other memorabilia until in the 1980s these were sold privately to an overseas collector. In 1997 Spink sold the medals at auction for £85,000 to an anonymous buyer, while a set of miniatures was purchased separately by the family. The medals are now displayed in the Lord Ashcroft Gallery at the Imperial War Museum, Lambeth, London.

G.S.M. INSALL

Achiet, France, 7 November 1915

No. 11 Squadron RFC was based at Bertangles airfield situated about 6 miles north of Amiens, Somme, where they had moved in late October 1915. Flying Vickers FB5 aircraft, the most frequently encountered enemy type over that sector of the front were LVG BIIs, excellent enemy fighter aircraft. One of the pilots was Second Lieutenant Gilbert Insall, whose brother Jack was an observer/gunner in the same squadron. Gilbert had a reputation for frequently taking his aircraft in as close as 50yd range from the enemy aeroplane in order to give his gunner the best chance of a hit. Earlier, on 6 September, Gilbert, flying with Second Lieutenant Manley in the front seat, was on a photographic reconnaissance over Albert, Somme. When an enemy LVG was spotted 200ft above them, Insall immediately turned and attacked this aircraft, forcing it to dive towards the ground. A second German aircraft then arrived and Insall closed to very short range and drove this plane away to the east. Other similar encounters occurred in the ensuing weeks but, despite such bold tactics, as far as it is known, none of these attempts were successful in bringing an enemy down.

However all was to change when, on 7 November 1915, Insall took off from Bertangles, flying Vickers FB5, 5074. He was accompanied by 21-year-old First Class Air Mechanic Thomas Donald in the forward seat of the nacelle acting as gunner.

They were flying between 7,000 and 8,000ft when an enemy observation balloon was seen behind the German trench lines near Achiet-le-Grand, about 3 miles north-east of Bapaume. Insall flew down towards this balloon with the intention of dropping an incendiary bomb on the target, but was unable to achieve a good bombing position.

He abandoned the bombing attempt as a rocket battery (described by some pilots as firing 'flaming onions') situated near the balloon winch, fired at the British aircraft and commenced his climb to safety. Spotting an enemy two-seater, probably an Aviatik, about 2,000ft higher than the Vickers, flying along the trench lines, Insall changed direction and Donald was able to fire a few shots using the Lee Enfield rifle the aircraft carried. The German aeroplane turned east while Insall kept the FB5 in its climb, which persuaded his adversary that he was not continuing the attack. This deception was successful, enabling the Insall to manoeuvre into a position where Donald could open fire with the Lewis gun. The German aircraft immediately banked and dived away in the direction of the rocket battery Insall had previously encountered, which possibly was a deliberate ploy on the enemy's behalf. Insall put his aircraft into a steep dive and although under machine-gun fire from the enemy observer/gunner, followed the enemy craft until Donald was close enough to fire accurately a complete drum at the German aeroplane with the satisfaction of seeing its engine stop just as both aircraft entered cloud.

As the cloud layer was exited the German aircraft was seen 'coming heavily to earth in a ploughed field' and the two occupants were sighted getting out of the machine with one carrying a machine gun. Donald opened fire upon them, possibly injuring one, who lagged behind his comrade. Insall now made another low pass over the downed aircraft and Donald's aim with the incendiary bomb was good as the LGV could be seen 'enveloped in smoke'. The DB5 was under intense enemy fire from ground troops and batteries so Insall made all speed towards the British side of the lines, but a bullet pierced his petrol tank as they crossed no-man's-land. Insall narrowly avoided the trees of a small wood and landed the DB5 in a field, about 500yd behind the French front lines, close to the village of Agny, to the south-west of Arras.

The enemy artillery gunners who had watched much of the preceding action had seen where the Vickers had made landfall, and those within range at once began to shell the area. Insall and Donald quickly left their aircraft and sought cover and they watched as their aircraft survived the artillery attack, in excess of 100 shells. Insall then found a senior French officer and, being fluent in French, explained the situation to him so that in a short while Gilbert was able to telephone the airfield at Bertangles and speak with his CO, Major G. Dawes. There was a witness to this conversation in No. 11 Squadron's office: one of the pilots, Lieutenant Robert Hughes-Chamberlain, who at a later date recorded his memories of that time and explained that 'Dawes did not like Insall until he did this job ... then he was racing about ... to get Insall this VC'. Major Dawes had been berating Insall's non-arrival when the telephone call arrived and he quickly ordered Chief Flight Commander Lionel Rees, 'Take a tender, a new tank and all the appliances ... and everything else you want ... He's on the French Line, fifteen miles away.'

Rees and the mechanics arrived and under cover of darkness screens were erected to hide the work lights while essential repairs were made and the replacement fuel tank fitted and filled. By dawn the DB5 was ready for flight. An initial attempt to start the rotary engine failed and a pipe leak had to be found and repaired. This achieved and with weighted sandbags replacing the weight of Donald in the front seat, Insall took off across the shell-cratered field – although French soldiers had toiled in the night filling in the larger holes created by the earlier shelling. Insall managed the take-off and headed back to Bertangles airfield leaving the applauding French soldiers diving for cover as enemy machine-gun bullets cut through the trees. Gilbert later told his brother Jack, 'he took care to show himself to the enemy in their front-line trenches'!

Second Lieutenant Gilbert Stuart Martin Insall was awarded the Victoria Cross, the citation appearing in the fifth supplement of the *London Gazette* No. 29414 dated 23 December 1915. 3022 First Class Air Mechanic Thomas Hain Donald was awarded the Distinguished Conduct Medal, the citation gazetted on 22 January 1916.

On 14 December Insall and Donal carried out a routine patrol in the same Vickers pusher which had featured in their epic action. An enemy two-seater, later identified as being piloted by Hauptmann Martin Zander, was seen over Albert, flying from the direction of Bapaume, and Insall at once engaged with the enemy aircraft. Despite much twisting and turning by the Zander, Donald's fire disabled it very quickly, but at almost the same time bullets fired by the German observer put the DB5 engine out of action and wounded Donald in the leg. This time there was no hope of the British machine returning to base, as the fight had taken them west of Bapaume. Insall turned and attempted to set course in that direction, but quickly realised that a landing in enemy territory was as inevitable as their subsequent capture. The Vickers was in a shallow glide when an anti-aircraft shell exploded close by, the base of which wounded Insall in his left buttock. Despite briefly passing out he managed to land safely not far from Achiet-le-Grand and made attempts to destroy the aircraft with the tube bomb carried by these aircraft, but German ground troops arrived before this was accomplished.

Stretcher-bearers quickly arrived and by an amazing coincidence one of them was a German hockey player the Insall brothers had played against before the war when on a visit to Hanover, Germany. The wounded airmen were quickly transported to hospital and after an operation Insall was to spend several months being cared for at Cologne as a prisoner of war, an enforced period of inactivity which enabled Insall to devise in his head a number of escape plans that might prove workable when he was sent to a prison camp.

The first camp he was sent to was at Heidelberg, and from here he was successful in escaping to enjoy five days of liberty before being recaptured and later sent to Crefeld. From here he and a number of companions were able temporarily to regain their liberty after using a tunnel that had taken them months to complete. Once again he was recaptured and this resulted in his being sent to Strohen and from here, released from punitive solitary confinement, he was lucky to escape once more. This time, in August 1917, he was successful along with two others. Nine nights of travel in which 150 miles were covered took them to the Dutch border and eventually home, where Insall was to receive a Military Cross in recognition of his several bids for freedom. This was announced in the *London Gazette* dated 12 December 1919.

It is interesting to note the comments later recorded by Lieutenant Hughes-Chamberlain:

> It wasn't a VC job in my opinion, it was very ordinary, shooting down a machine and escaping over the trenches. I should have reversed it. What he did in escaping from Germany was a VC job in my opinion ... I always thought that was an extraordinary job, the other one was an MC job. He got them both but the wrong way round.

Back in England Insall, promoted to captain on 10 August 1917, was attached to the training staff at Gosport. In the same year, on 26 September, in the forecourt of Buckingham Palace, he was invested with the Victoria Cross by King George V who, it was reported, pinned the Cross beneath the pilot's wings on his left breast. Newspapers also commented on the wound stripe sewn on his left sleeve.

In 1918 he was posted as a flight commander to No. 51 (Home Defence) Squadron, Bekesbourne, Kent and by the Armistice was still stationed in Kent at Harrietsham, on the staff of No. 53 Wing, also designated to Home Defence.

❖ ❖ ❖

Gilbert Stuart Insall was born in Paris on 14 May 1894, the son of Gilbert Jenkins Insall and his wife, Mary Stuart (née Read). His father practised as a dental surgeon in the French capital and also held the post of honorary professor at the École Odontotechnique. Gilbert had two younger brothers, Algernon John (Jack) and Cecil Dudley and a sister, Marguerite Esmé.

Gilbert and Jack were first educated at L'École Anglo-Saxon before going on to study at the Sorbonne, Paris. France was virtually the centre of European aviation, and advances in the science of flight were frequently featured in the newspapers. Such early developments in aviation were of great interest to the brothers, who began to develop a passion for flying.

Seeing the way the international situation was developing, the boys' father closed his Paris practice and the family was on the *Maid of Kent*, crossing the English Channel, when it was announced that Great Britain had been at war with Germany since 11 p.m. the previous evening.

Both Gilbert and Jack enlisted as privates in the University and Public Schools' Brigade (the UPS) 18th Battalion Royal Fusiliers in September 1914, training in Surrey throughout the autumn and winter. When a War Office appeal for volunteers to join the Royal Flying Corps was read out on the parade ground early in 1915 the platoon commander approached the two brothers and encouraged their applications. Later that day they filled in the application forms under helpful military guidance and beside the heading of 'Previous Experience', was entered 'Close interest in progress of aviation while resident on the Continent (Paris). Passenger ascents at Buc (Versailles) with M. Maurice Farman.' They had spent time watching pioneer airmen at Buc and also at Issy-les-Moulineaux near their home at Auteuil. It was here, in 1909, that Blériot had prepared for his Channel crossing and they had often watched his very short, experimental attempts at powered flight.

Happily both applications were granted quickly, Jack's with effect from 12 March and his elder brother's two days later. They both went to Brooklands, Surrey, for flying training later in the same month at the same time that Captain Lionel Rees was an instructor. Gilbert was granted his Royal Flying Club Certificate No. 1110 some four weeks later, which enabled him to be accepted for training in military flying.

No. 11 Squadron Royal Flying Corps had been established on 14 February 1915 at Netheravon. This was the first RFC fighter squadron formed, the equipment for the new role being the pusher Vickers FB5s or 'Vickers Fighting Bi-planes'. It carried a gunner in the nose and taking its complement of eight of these machines, later augmented by a further three, No. 11 went to France on 25 July 1915. At first it went to St Omer and finally settled down at 'the clover-field at Vert-Galand, astride the Amiens–Doullens *route nationale*', numbering among its new officers Second Lieutenants G.S.M. and A.J. Insall who had been posted to it at Netheravon on 16 July. The squadron was to stay at this airfield for the following three months.

❖ ❖ ❖

Gilbert Insall remained in the RAF after the Armistice, posted first, with the rank of flight lieutenant, to Germany with the forces of occupation. In 1919 he was promoted to squadron leader on 1 November and the award of the Military Cross, for his activities whilst a prisoner of war, was gazetted on 16 December.

Group Captain Gilbert Insall was present at the garden party given for VC winners by King George V at Buckingham Palace on 26 June 1920, and was part of the VC guard of honour for the Unknown Warrior at Westminster Abbey on Armistice Day of the same year.

He was then posted via No. 6 Flying Training School to the RAF Depot at Uxbridge on 1 April 1922 and in December 1925 Insall, while flying over Wiltshire, took photographs of what was later to be called Woodhenge, near Stonehenge. This very important site had probably been constructed between 2400 and 2000 BC, about the same time as Stonehenge, with the concentric oval rings covering an area some 120yd in diameter.

Meanwhile his brother Jack, who had lost the sight of an eye, was working for the Air Ministry and was one of the co-founders of the Imperial War Museum, Lambeth. Jack was responsible for many of the aerial photographs used in 'then and now' publications relating to the war.

On 22 July 1926 Gilbert was married to Olwen Scott Yates at Berkhamsted Parish Church and they were to have two sons, Richard and David. Following his marriage he was known as Stuart in preference to Gilbert. The following year promotion to squadron leader saw him in command of No. 70 Squadron in Iraq. This posting enabled him further to pursue his interest in archaeology, one that he was to continue after returning to Great Britain in March 1929 to command No. 35 Squadron.

An illustration of this interest took place in the same year when, during summer flying near Norwich, Insall, now a wing commander, noted in Bridge Meadow, Old Lakenham two concentric circles of dark green grass which contrasted with the surrounding parched brown of the larger area. His interest was fired and an aerial photograph subsequently taken was to reveal round the centre nine postholes where long-vanished wooden poles had marked an ancient site, excavated in

1935, that was to be known subsequently as 'Norwich Woodhenge'. Commands at Upavon, Kenley and a further overseas tour in 1935 to command No. 4 Flying Training School were to follow before a return to Uxbridge in time for the Battle of Britain. Insall served in various capacities before eventually leaving the service at the end of July 1945.

Gilbert Insall was one of those present at the second reunion dinner of the Victoria Cross Association on Thursday 7 July 1960 at the Café Royal, London.

Group Captain Insall retired to live in Nottinghamshire, but on 7 October 1969 a break-in at his home precipitated a heart attack in the 72-year-old. Fortunately his medals and decorations – including his Victoria Cross – stolen in the burglary, were recovered and returned to him the following year. Group Captain Gilbert Stuart Martin Insall, VC, MC died of pneumonia in RAF Nocton Hospital, Lincolnshire, on 17 February 1972. He was given a funeral with full military honours and the procession proceeded through the streets of Bawtry before a funeral service at Bawtry Church. His son David, a captain in the Northern Frontier Regiment in Oman, returned from active service for the funeral. The coffin was carried by six serving station commanders from RAF Strike Command. He was cremated at Rose Hill Crematorium, Doncaster (Ref 15321) and his ashes were interred in Nocton Churchyard. Those of his wife, Olwen were laid to rest near her husband after her death on 16 August 1983. In August 2011 pupils from Nocton Community Primary School, Lincolnshire, were granted permission by the Nocton PCC to take over the maintenance of the memorial in Nocton churchyard to Group Captain Gilbert Insall VC MC, and that of his wife. Following schoolwork related to remembrance, a pupil had suggested that Year 6 pupils from the school might look after this neglected memorial.

His medals are displayed at the Royal Air Force Museum in Hendon, his full entitlement being: VC, MC, 1914–15 Star, BWM (1914–20), Victory Medal (1914–1919), General Service Medal (1918–62) and MiD, 1 clasp: 'Iraq', Defence Medal (1939–45), War Medal (1939–45), King George V Silver Jubilee Medal (1935), King George VI Coronation Medal (1937), Queen Elizabeth II Coronation Medal (1953). Group Captain Gilbert Stuart Insall VC, MC, is also commemorated in St Clement Dane's Church, the Strand, London.

R. BELL-DAVIES

Ferejik Junction, Bulgaria,
19 November 1915

Son of civil engineer William Bell-Davies (also known as Bell Davies) of Ricksmansworth and his wife, Mary Emma (née Beale), Richard Bell-Davies was born on 19 May 1886 at 3 Fopstone Road, Earl's Court, Kensington. He entered the Royal Navy at the age of 15 after receiving basic education at Bradfield College. Both of his parents had died before he reached his sixth birthday so that his upbringing was entrusted to Dr Edwin Beale, his maternal uncle, who was the throat and chest specialist at both Victoria Park and the Great Northern hospitals.

He went to Dartmouth as a naval cadet on the training ship HMS *Britannia*, and watched in March 1902 as King Edward VII laid the foundation stone for the college buildings. In September Bell-Davies joined HMS *Diana* on the Mediterranean station and on 1 April 1903, after having been discharged from the hospital in Malta when recovering from Malta fever, he was sent to the Royal Hospital Haslar, 'a gloomy place', to complete his convalescence.

Bell-Davies was on board HMS *Dominion*, in Mounts Bay, Cornwall, with the fleet when, during the summer manoeuvres of July 1902, his attention was caught by the sound of cheering spreading from ship to ship with all the crew looking towards the shore. The subject of their attention was a Farman biplane flown by Claude Grahame-White, flying over the fleet which circled the flagship HMS *Dreadnought* at about 300ft before heading back to land. Grahame-White had qualified as a pilot three months earlier and had also taken out an option for the purchase of 207 acres of land for an aerodrome between Colindale and Hendon.

Passed fit for duty in August 1903, Richard joined the battleship HMS *Magnificent* of the Channel Squadron. Over the next six years he served on various ships and in 1909 was on the battleship HMS *Swiftsure* when she sailed to Mersina on the Armenian coast where a massacre of Armenian Christians had largely been averted by Colonel Doughty-Wylie, the British Consul.

Early in the next year Francis Maclean offered to place at the disposal of the War Office and Royal Navy two of his machines for officers wishing to be instructed in the art of piloting. The War Office declined, but the Admiralty accepted his offer. Richard paid for the instruction (£50 plus a deposit of £25 against damages) that gained him British Empire Flying Certificate No. 90 in May 1911.

A posting to the cruiser *Minotaur*, flagship of the China Station, then followed, with instructions to make his own way to Manchuria via the Trans-Siberia Railway, so with help from Thomas Cook & Son he caught the *Nord Express* from Flushing to Moscow, changing trains there, eventually arriving at Dalny in Manchuria. From there he went by destroyer to join the *Minotaur* at Weihaiwei. An exciting and varied period of service in the areas around Hong Kong, Canton and Japan followed, but as Bell-Davies was still very keen to resume his flying he had put in a request for transfer. Eventually he received a letter from the Admiralty, confirming his appointment at the Naval Flying School at Eastchurch, which he joined in February 1913.

Acting-Commander Charles Rumney Samson was in command and Richard later wrote of him, 'His manners were brusque, he was frequently quite rude and he had no tact, but as a friend he was absolutely loyal.' It was late in April when Bell-Davies was appointed flying officer, and shortly after, flight lieutenant. In September the First Lord of the Admiralty, Winston Churchill, had sent the Admiralty yacht *Enchantress* to Sheerness for his use on his occasional visits to Eastchurch at weekends to see the flying, and he occasionally brought visitors with him. Bell-Davies had the privilege of giving Sir Ian Hamilton his first flight.

In January 1914, Bell-Davies was promoted to squadron commander at Eastchurch, and in April he was sent to Somaliland to work with the Airship Section and the Camel Corps in attempts to suppress the 'Mad Mullah'. He returned to Eastchurch a few weeks before the outbreak of war and was taken ill with jaundice at Portsmouth and sent to Haslar where he found the conditions much improved since his 1903 visit. While on sick leave he was recalled to Eastchurch where, as his regular craft had been 'written off' by another aviator, it was necessary for him to have his old aircraft, No. 33, rebuilt in time for a trial flight on 4 August, the first day of the war.

The unit was formed as a mobile squadron and flew reconnaissance patrols from the Humber south to Great Yarmouth until 24 August when it returned to Eastchurch. On 27 August, the collection of different aircraft which made up 'Samson's Aeroplane Party', soon to be designated No. 3 Squadron RNAS, flew to Ostend in support of the newly formed Royal Marine Brigade. Initially based at the racecourse the squadron moved to a better site east of the town near a ruined fort. After only three days the marines, and Samson's party, were ordered back to England but Samson 'decided there was going to be a bad fog in the Channel which would force us to land at Dunkirk' and a landing was made near St Pol.

Samson became very involved in the producing, and patrolling, of armoured cars, leaving Bell-Davies to organise many of the aircraft reconnaissance flights which watched for German troop movements from Lille to Amiens. During September 1914, the squadron was advised by the Admiralty of the arrival of an inspecting officer at dawn the following day, to be collected from Dunkirk Harbour. Richard drove 'a small four-seater tourer' from St Pol. The boat which came to the mole steps contained not one, but four persons: Winston Churchill (First Lord of the Admiralty), Admiral Hood (commanding Dover Patrol), Admiral Lambert (naval secretary) and Commander Murray Sueter (director of the Air Division)! By using both running boards, the senior officers were transported to the landing ground for the inspection and after also making a surprise inspection of the French garrison and the Dunkirk defences, the party was later returned to its cruiser. Following this visit some royal marines were added to Samson's armed car patrols.

The squadron moved to Antwerp on 5 October, where it was to work with the Naval Division, but the aircraft were not very effective here, managing only to drop a few bombs on artillery batteries.

The armoured cars had been in action, with Samson being slightly wounded. On 6 October the withdrawal from Antwerp commenced with all stores and aircraft leaving except Flight Lieutenant Reginald Marix and his Sopwith Tabloid, whom Samson had delegated for an attack on the Zeppelin sheds at Düsseldorf. This attack was very successful, destroying airship LZ25 and its shed before marix had 'an adventurous time reaching Antwerp' after his plane ran out of fuel.

By 13 October, Ostend needed to be evacuated and Bell-Davies made the arrangements for the remaining serviceable aircraft to be flown out. The squadron was involved in many flying tasks over the following weeks, including the delivery of messages to Sir John French, commander in chief, BEF, at St Omer and to Lieutenant-General

Sir Henry Rawlinson GOC IV Corps, in the Cloth Hall at Ypres. The squadron returned to Dunkirk in the first week of November where a French squadron was based at the time and Bell-Davies had the opportunity to see a tractor aeroplane fitted with a machine gun which fired through the airscrew developed by Roland Garros.

Reports came in to Admiralty of enemy submarines based at Zeebrugge and Bruges and also of an airship shed at Brussels, so on 20 December 1914 Commander Samson sent a Maurice Farman pusher, No. 1241, piloted by Bell-Davies with a load of twelve bombs to attack the airship shed. After the release of his bombs Bell-Davies considered that his 'stick of 20lb bombs certainly crossed the shed diagonally and much smoke appeared'.

The inclement weather grounded many flights during January and it was not until 23 January that, flying over Ostend, towards Zeebrugge, Bell-Davies spotted a new German landing field with enemy aircraft visible on the ground. After spotting two submarines in Zeebrugge harbour and returning to base he saw that the enemy aircraft near Ostend were taking off, and he reported both items on landing. Flight Lieutenant Richard Peirse was sent out in the Farman to attack the submarines, which he did on an approach from the sea and was subjected to heavy anti-aircraft fire. He straddled one submarine with his 20lb bombs but was not sure he had hit it. On his return it was decided that there was time to make another attack before the light went. Reloaded with bombs, Bell-Davies flew off in the Farman with Flight Lieutenant C.H. Butler as observer. To avoid the heavy gunfire which had greeted Peirse, Bell-Davies turned inland near Nieuport, only to find that the anti-aircraft fire was, 'the heaviest barrage I had met ...' and went back out to sea again. The aircraft had been holed in several places though not badly damaged, but Bell-Davies had been hit on the right knee by, 'something feeling exactly like a well hit hockey ball ...' He was still able to fly east and approach Zeebrugge harbour from landward where Butler accurately dropped the stick of bombs astride the submarine. Landing just before dark, Bell-Davies sought medical attention for his now stiffened leg and the squadron medical officer Hardy Vesey Wells discovered he had been hit with a shrapnel bullet and sent Richard to the hospital ship *Magic* in Dunkirk Docks. Bell-Davies spent a few days on board after the removal of the bullet before returning to England on sick leave.

Changes were afoot for No. 3 Squadron which, now enjoying the status of a wing, was withdrawn from Dunkirk to England and ordered to the Dardanelles. Its chief responsibility here was to provide cover for the forthcoming Allied landings on the Gallipoli Peninsula.

Bell-Davies rejoined his former colleagues shortly before sailing from Plymouth on the SS *Inkosi*, their aircraft and transport on board SS *Moorgate*.

The squadron arrived at Tenedos in early April 1915 and it was on this Aegean island, close to the Turkish coast, that news of his previous bravery was published in the *London Gazette* of 10 April. Both Squadron Commander Richard Bell-Davies and Flight Lieutenant Richard Edmund Charles Peirse had been admitted to the Distinguished Service Order 'For Services rendered in the aerial attack on Dunkirk [sic] on 23rd January, 1915'. The joint citation stated:

> These Officers have repeatedly attacked the German submarine station at Ostend and Zeebrugge, being subjected on each occasion to heavy and accurate fire, their machine being frequently hit. In particular, on 23rd January, they each discharged eight bombs in an attack upon submarines alongside the mole at Zeebrugge, flying down to close range. At the outset of this flight Lieutenant Davies was severely wounded by a bullet in the thigh, but nevertheless he accomplished his task, handling his machine for an hour with great skill in spite of pain and loss of blood.

On the evening of 24 April Bell-Davies sat on a cliff overlooking the sea north of the island where the *River Clyde* and numerous smaller vessels were anchored prior to the landings of the next day. He was soon to hear first-hand stories from survivors of the terrible scenes on the beaches and also of the death of Colonel Doughty-Wylie at W beach, whom he had met in 1909.

The aircraft of No. 3 Wing were much used as artillery spotters for the battleships. They also carried out reconnaissance and occasional bombing missions. Four months later, at the beginning of August, a move was made to the island of Imbros, less than 2 miles from the Turkish coast, in preparation for their role in supporting the coming landings at Suvla Bay.

On 4 August, Bell-Davies returned from a reconnaissance flight over the area inland from Suvla Bay and reported the lack of new Turkish preparations beyond the Salt Lake and Chocolate Hill. Waiting for him was Commander Martin Nasmith VC of the submarine E11 who was to commence a patrol up 'the mined and obstructed Straits ... that night' and wanted to 'have a look at the narrows at Chanak where the Turks had tried to lay anti-submarine obstructions ...' Richard flew the commander over the straits in a Maurice Farman and Nasmith's patrol commenced that night and lasted until 3 September. The operation was as successful as his first, after which he was awarded the Victoria Cross.

This time he sank a number of enemy vessels including the battleship *Barbarossa* on 8 August.

On 6 August, on the eve of the Suvla Bay landings, Bell-Davies was in command of No. 3 Wing as the CO, Commander Samson, was on leave. He received conflicting orders regarding the role of his aircraft the next day. The navy had scheduled a 'full programme in spotting for ships' gun-fire' whilst orders from military headquarters also committed the wing to what would be a full day's work. Admiral de Robeck, commanding the naval force at Gallipoli, had informed Bell-Davies that the aeroplanes would 'be entirely under military control', but it appeared that such instructions had not been completely understood by naval officers below him.

Richard tried to persuade the chief of staff of Sir Ian Hamilton's Mediterranean Expeditionary Force, General William Braithwaite, to sort out the problem with the navy, but he was 'reluctant to comply'. Bell-Davies was then sent to see de Robeck's chief of staff, Commodore Roger Keyes, on board HMS *Triad*, and succeeded, after a 'rather stormy interview', in getting his orders which he confirmed back to Keyes as, 'I am to give priority to the general's orders carrying them out in full, and if, after doing so, I have any aircraft available, I am to carry out as much of the Inshore Squadron's orders as I can.'

That evening Bell-Davies dined with Sir Ian Hamilton who 'appeared full of confidence'. Amongst the other dinner guests was Major Jack Churchill, Naval Liaison Officer for the Mediterranean Expeditionary Force, whom he had met when his brother Winston visited Eastchurch.

On 7 August, following a reconnaissance flight at dawn during which he noted no forward movement of British troops across the Salt Lake and little visible sign of Turkish soldiers, Bell-Davies again met Jack Churchill who was fuming over a delayed boat carrying drinking water which was only just leaving harbour for Suvla Bay.

During August, new aircraft started being delivered to the wing, including Henry Farmans with more powerful 120hp engines and Nieuports powered by 80hp engines. Much of the month was spent on reconnaissance and spotting for ships' gunnery and it was on the former, flying one of the new Farmans, that the rare view of an enemy aircraft occurred. A German Ettrich Taube was sighted while flying over Australian troops. Several rifle shots were fired by Second Lieutenant Jupp, Richard's observer, and the aircraft went into a very steep dive. Bell-Davies later heard that the Australians watching below had cheered the encounter, believing that the German machine had been shot down.

Following the entry of Bulgaria into the First World War in October 1915, on the side of the Central Powers, Germany was sending supplies to Turkey both by road and rail passing through Bulgaria, so long-range bombing attacks were planned. One of the best places at which to attack and disrupt supply trains was Ferejik rail junction, close to the Turkish–Bulgarian border, so on 8 November Commander Samson opened the series of attacks that were to follow by bombing the rail bridge where it crossed the River Maritza with a pair of 100lb bombs dropped from a converted Maurice Farman which had been fitted with an extra fuel tank. This operation was repeated two days later when Bell-Davies dropped a similar weight of bombs from 2,000ft on a four-hour mission. His return was delayed by a broken throttle wire and bad weather.

Five of the Nieuport 12 two-seaters had been sent out from England, Samson and Davies each having one for their personal use, this aircraft was originally built as a two-seater, but some were converted by to single-seaters.

Flying towards Ferejik station on 13 November, through the heavy clouds and rain, Bell-Davies saw his target and was to be first to go in, followed by Samson, also in a Nieuport. Bell-Davies dropped three 20lb bombs and climbed away. Samson was able to observe one bomb actually explode on the line before he made his own attack. Then as the rifle and machine-gun fire increased, the two set course for home, only to encounter a downpour en route.

In the following five days the same target was subjected to two further raids by Commander Samson alone, during which periods reports of the line being ripped up and one of the buildings roofless were confirmed, as was the belief that the defending fire had been augmented. In the attack planned for 19 November each pilot was to concentrate on a specific target at one of two points – Burgess Bridge and Ferejik Junction. Samson and Bell-Davies again flying the Nieuports, were to be supported by Sub-Lieutenant Gilbert Smylie and Sub-Lieutenant Barnato in the two Henry Farmans. Last to attack was to be Sub-Lieutenant Heriot, with Captain Edwards as his observer, in a Maurice Farman.

The first to take off a little after 10 a.m. hours was Bell-Davies in the converted Nieuport 12, 3172 and his load consisted of six Hales 20lb bombs, high-explosive missiles on which Bell-Davies later wrote, 'I did not think these little bombs could do much harm'. Having arrived over Ferejik simultaneously with Samson and Smylie he made the first bombing attack and was turning for home when he saw Smylie's Farman on the ground, seemingly undamaged. What had happened was that his engine had been hit and had stopped but it had proved possible to glide down to a landing in a dry watercourse about a mile from the target. Clambering out, Smylie at once saw a party of Bulgarians approaching, but still some distance off. He decided to set fire to his machine and make for Turkish territory on foot, the prison camps of the latter being the lesser of two evils, he reckoned.

Smylie had gone only a little way when he was astonished to see Bell-Davies' Nieuport circling, the pilot clearly looking for a suitable landing spot. He decided that a dry watercourse offered the best hope of success and he at once prepared to set his aircraft down on it, but before he could do so there was 'an almighty shock' as the burning Farman exploded. The bomb remaining in the rack had been deliberately set off by Smylie with the third shot from his revolver on realising Bell-Davies' intention, a precaution against it exploding when the Nieuport was alongside. In fact the detonation delayed the rescue attempt, giving the soldiers time to get closer. Ignorant of how many bombs remained on the Farman's racks, Bell-Davies climbed slightly and made a circuit until the situation appeared to have settled down. Now he brought 3172 carefully in, although the rough ground, baked to a concrete-like surface, set the little aeroplane pitching and rolling as the wheels touched the ground. Bell-Davies had the presence of mind to retrace his landing run, with Smylie giving a helpful heave at the wing tip to turn the aircraft to position it for an uninterrupted take-off.

Meanwhile, fitting the 6ft Smylie into the single-seat aircraft proved difficult. Had the machine been designed from the first to accommodate pilot only it would have proved impossible, but the fact that the alteration from twin-seat configuration had been largely effected by little more than adding a panel to blank off the position of the second occupant offered the chance of a solution. Bell-Davies later described how it was accomplished: 'He had to climb over me, slide under the cowl and crouch on all fours between the rudder bar and engine bearers with his head bumping on the oil tank.'

Smylie removed his bulky flying coat the better to fit into the cramped space, and was finally installed. Seizing their last chance the Bulgarians, some kneeling while others stood to shoot over the heads of the front rank, commenced to pour a torrent of fire at the machine, now gathering speed and finally rising into the air.

Back at the Imbros base, Bell-Davies was long overdue. At almost 12.20 p.m., the sound of an aeromotor was heard heralding the return of the missing aircraft. Onlookers were astonished when, after the little machine had rolled to a stop, two men were found to be aboard the single-seater. Smylie was very difficult to extract from the aircraft. The whole operation from take-off to touch-down had taken two hours and fifteen minutes.

Both officers were recommended for the Victoria Cross by Commander Samson, although in the event Smylie, whose cool head had considerably contributed to the success of the operation, was to receive the DSC. However, there was no question of the skill and devotion exhibited by Bell-Davies, the citation for the Victoria Cross being gazetted on the first day of 1916:

> The King has been graciously pleased to approve of the grant of the Victoria Cross to Squadron Commander Richard Bell Davies, D.S.O., R.N., and of the Distinguished Service Cross to Flight Sub-Lieutenant Gilbert Formby Smylie, R.N., in recognition of their behaviour in the following circumstances. On the 19th November these two officers carried out an air attack on Ferrijik [sic] Junction. Flight sub-Lieutenant Smylie's machine was received by very heavy fire and brought down. The pilot planed down over the station, releasing all his bombs except one, which failed to drop, simultaneously at the station from a very low altitude. Thence he continued his descent into the marsh. On alighting he saw one unexploded bomb, and set fire to his machine, knowing that the bomb would ensure its destruction. He then proceeded towards Turkish territory. At this moment he perceived Squadron Commander Davies descending, and fearing that he would come down near the burning machine and thus risk destruction from the bomb, Flight Sub-Lieutenant Smylie ran back and from a short distance exploded the bomb by means of a pistol bullet. Squadron Commander Davies descended at a safe distance from the burning machine, took up Sub-Lieutenant Smylie, in spite of the near approach of a party of the enemy, and returned to the aerodrome, a feat of airmanship that can seldom have been equalled for skill and gallantry.

No. 3 Wing RNAS was withdrawn from Gallipoli and in January Bell-Davies, Samson and another pilot were at Malta travelling home when Richard heard of his promotion to wing commander RNAS. They sailed across to Marseilles and from there to Paris for a night at the Ritz – where they were recognised by the head waiter, who had previously worked at a hotel in Ostend, resulting in 'a wonderful dinner'.

In January Bell-Davies was appointed district commander of RNAS stations in the north of England. He had been promoted to wing commander at the New Year.

On 15 April Richard Bell-Davies was invested with the Victoria Cross by King George V at Buckingham Palace.

Bell-Davies was advised, in early June, that No. 3 Wing, which had disbanded after its return to England, was to be re-formed for service in

France. He was appointed commander of this unit based at Manston, Kent, and in July the first squadron, flying 1½ Strutters, flew out to France and were based at Luxeuil, 70 miles south of Nancy. Long-range bombing raids were later made, often in conjunction with French squadrons, against industrial targets in Germany. Earlier training in close-locked formation flying was found to be very worthwhile as most British aircraft 'usually met with ... half-hearted interference from German aircraft'. Bell-Davies remained in France with No. 3 Wing until a directive was issued 'by the Air Department' banning operational flights by 'officers of wing commander rank and above', at which point he applied to the Admiralty for a naval posting.

Consequently he took up a new appointment at the beginning of January 1917 as senior flying officer of the Grand Fleet in command of air operations aboard HMS *Campania*, once a fast Cunard liner and now converted to a seaplane carrier. He was very involved in aircraft carrier development during the months that followed and in July of the next year he helped plan the first raid on a land-based target by carrier-based aircraft. This occurred on the 18th of that month when Sopwith Camels took off from the carrier *Furious* and successfully bombed the Zeppelin sheds at Tondern, in Schleswig-Holstein. Zeppelins L54 and L60 and their sheds were destroyed in this raid, and the gas plant badly damaged so that no further airship flights took place from here.

Bell-Davies continued with his involvement in aircraft carriers and their aircraft until the end of the war. He was appointed a lieutenant colonel in the RAF on its formation in April 1918, and was later given a permanent commission in this rank, but he was determined to remain with the Royal Navy. On 7 May 1919 he relinquished his RAF commission and was appointed to serve on HMS *Lion*.

In recognition of his pioneering work with aircraft carriers Bell-Davies was awarded the Air Force Cross, gazetted on 7 October 1919 after having being made a Chevalier of the Légion d'Honneur avec Palme gazetted on 22 August of the same year.

He married Mary Montgomery on 29 September 1920 and they had one daughter and one son, Lancelot, who followed his father into the Royal Navy.

From 1920 until early 1924 Bell-Davies was in charge of the Air Section of the naval staff at the Admiralty. From then on he held a variety of posts, both sea-going and shore-based rising to the rank of rear-admiral in 1938 prior to his retirement on 29 May 1941. He had been appointed CBE in the King's Birthday Honours of 1939. Following his retirement from the RNAS he joined the Royal Naval Reserve with the lower rank of commander and served as commissioning captain on the carriers HMS *Dasher* and *Pretoria Castle*. He retired from the Royal Naval Reserve in 1944.

Vice-Admiral Richard Bell-Davies died at the Royal Naval Hospital, Haslar on 26 February 1966 and he was cremated at Swaythling Crematorium, Southampton (ref 39765) and his ashes were strewn from the admiral's launch off the Knab Tower.

Bell-Davies completed his autobiography shortly before his death and it was published in 1967 under the title *Sailor in the Air*. Typically, said those who knew him, it makes no mention of the award of the Victoria Cross.

Bell-Davies attended the garden party at Buckingham Palace for recipients of the VC given by King George V, on the afternoon of 26 June 1920. On 31 July 1932 he was present when Lord Trenchard unveiled the Memorial to the Missing at Arras.

There is a road named after him at Manston Airport (Kent), which was originally an RNAS Station, and roads with this name can also be found at Fareham and Lee-on-the-Solent.

His VC, with its blue ribbon, is displayed at the Fleet Air Arm Museum, Royal Naval Air Station, Yeovilton, Somerset, where an oil painting entitled *Richard Bell-Davies, VC, Rescues Gilbert Formby Smylie at Ferrijik Junction, Bulgaria, 19 November 1915* by Kenneth A. McDonough can also be seen.

The medal entitlement of Vice-Admiral Richard Bell-Davies, No. 3 Squadron, Royal Naval Air Service is: VC, CB, DSO, AFC, 1914–15 Star, British War Medal (1914–20), Victory Medal (1914–19) 1939–45 Star, Atlantic Star, Defence Medal (1939–45), War Medal (1939–45), King George V Silver Jubilee Medal (1935), King George VI Coronation Medal (1937), Queen Elizabeth II Coronation Medal (1953), Knight, Legion of Honour (5th Class (France)), Order of Michael the Brave (Romania), Croix de Guerre (France).

His name, together with the other members of the RFC, RNAS and RAF awarded the VC, is listed on the roll of honour in St Clement Danes Church, the Strand, London.

L.W.B. REES

Double Crassieurs, France, 1 July 1916

The preparations for the Allied 'Big Push' of 1916 were lengthy and involved both ground and air forces. From the middle of 1915, British and Commonwealth troops were gradually moved south to make ready the fortifications, camps, hospitals and airfields needed for the thousands of men, machines and horses required for a major attack. The areas behind the British front line became one enormous military camp which included several airfields and their squadrons.

One such group of aircraft was No. 32 Squadron, the first equipped solely as a 'fighter' squadron with the DH2, a small single-seat pusher biplane armed with one machine gun on a flexible mounting which initially did not endear the design to the squadron pilots who took it to France on 28 May 1916, staying for a few days each at St Omer and Auchel, both in Northern France, before arriving at Treizennes, Aire-sur-Lys, on 7 June. The squadron commander, Major Lionel Wilmot Brabazon Rees MC, proved the antithesis of a 'chairborne' commander. He repeatedly flew, since, in the words of a colleague, Gwylim Lewis, 'He has permission to go out as a flying squadron commander, and he can teach every member of the squadron how to fly.' The philosophy for the squadron was always to have a go at the enemy!

The Battle of the Somme began on 1 July 1916, after a seven-day artillery bombardment, and No. 32 Squadron's first responsibility was to deny the enemy reconnaissance behind the British lines. However at 3.40 a.m. six of their DH2s were ordered off to act as escorts to British bombers attacking the railway station at Don, south-west of Lille, and to disrupt enemy troop concentrations. Later, at 5.55 a.m., two further

DH2 machines took off, carrying Lieutenant John Clark Simpson from Ontario in aircraft 7856 and Major Rees in 6015. Simpson was to patrol the la Bassée-Loos-Souchez area while Rees, in his position as squadron commander, forbidden to cross the front lines, would fly along the front line and watch out for the return of the bombers. The two aircraft quickly became separated. Then Simpson saw an enemy formation of ten German aircraft and immediately attacked. Three of the enemy aircraft left their formation and quickly fired at Simpson whose DH2 was hit when at about 8,000ft. For a while it looked as if the plane was under control and then, about 3,000ft from the ground, it went out of control and crashed. Later inspection revealed that Lieutenant Simpson died from bullet wounds to the head. He is buried in Vermelles British Cemetery, about 6 miles north-west of Lens, Pas de Calais, IV.F.24.

At 6.15 a.m. Rees, flying at 9,000ft over the Double Crassiers near Loos – two large mining slag heaps which are still prominent landmarks – sighted a group of aircraft which from a distance he believed to be returning British bombers flying west. He therefore flew towards them in order to provide some protection. In fact what he was about to become escort to was *Kagohl* 3, an enemy unit commanded by Leutnant Erich Zimmerman, made up of ten two-seaters, mainly Rumpler CIIIs but with some Albatroses, the same group which had accounted for Simpson. Not knowing this, Rees climbed toward the formation, which was at about 11,000ft, and when nearer, was able through his binoculars, to see that the machines were German.

Adhering to his own maxim of attacking whatever the odds, Rees kept flying upwards towards the enemy aircraft and, in his own words: 'at about Annequin, the ... machine turned ... and dived towards me firing his gun. I waited until he came within convenient range and fired one drum ... after about the 30th round I saw the top of his fuselage splinter ... the machine turned round and went home.' He then attacked a second machine which fired red Very lights which attracted three more enemy aircraft who 'fired an immense amount of ammunition', but the range was too great. Rees then manoeuvred into an attacking position and fired another drum, during which 'a big cloud of blue haze came out of the nacelle'. This aircraft then dropped down towards the front lines. He then saw five more enemy craft quite close together at about 9,000ft, which fired at him from extreme range. Rees waited until he was nearer and fired yet another drum into the group which quickly scattered.

Rees followed three of the enemy westwards, quickly catching them as the lower of the aircraft dropped its bomb and the German observer opened fire at him from long range. The distance decreased and shortly before Rees was ready to fire his Lewis gun he was hit in the left leg, 'putting the leg temporarily out of action'. He fired another drum with his machine only partially under control, and 'finished firing about ten yards away and saw the observer sitting back firing straight up in the air instead of at me'. Rees then grabbed his pistol, intending to finish off this enemy aircraft, but dropped it on the floor, out of reach. It was then that he recovered the use of his leg, and seeing the formation leader going back towards the front line he used up his last drum of ammunition at long range. As Major Rees later reported, 'Having finished my ammunition I came home.'

Rees landed at Treizennes at 6.50 a.m., 'in the usual manner taxied in' and the ground crew brought out the steps for the pilot to get down. He did so, but immediately sat on the grass and calmly told them to bring a tender to take him to hospital where examination revealed how lucky he was that the shot had missed an artery. He is alleged to have commented, '[I] would have brought them all down, one after another if I could have used my leg!'

The action had been seen, in its entirety, by soldiers of the 22nd Anti-Aircraft Battery who reported what they had witnessed: 'A single de Havilland Scout appeared to have completely broken up a raid of 8–10 hostile aircraft. Of these two were seen to retire damaged ...' It was later confirmed that the German observer Rees had seen firing upwards had been killed and his pilot wounded. Their plane crashed not far from la Bassée; the observer was Leutnant Erich Zimmerman, Staffelfuhrer of *Kaghol 3* who is buried at Görlitz, near Dresden.

Rees was recommended for the DSO but this was later amended by Major-General Hugh Trenchard, GOC RFC, to, 'I am of the opinion that Major Rees' action is well worthy of a higher award and he should be granted a VC'. Trenchard's opinion was respected and the award of the Victoria Cross to Rees was gazetted on 5 August 1916. It is important to note here that this was the only VC awarded to the RFC during the Battle of the Somme, which continued until November, and also the effect that this attack had on the German bombers, 'whose attempts at daylight raiding afterwards were few'.

Rees, meanwhile, after immediate treatment in a CCS, was hospitalised and in due course sent to the Duchess of Pembroke's Hospital, Wilton House near Salisbury to receive further treatment and recuperate from his injury. It was here that he heard the news of the VC award. Major Lionel Wilmot Brabazon Rees MC was presented with the Victoria Cross by King George V at a Buckingham Palace investiture on 14 December 1916.

❖ ❖ ❖

Lionel Wilmot Brabazon Rees was born at at Plas Llanwnda, 5 Castle Street, Caernarfon, on 31 July 1884, the son of Lieutenant Colonel Charles Herbert Rees, VD, and his wife Leonora Maria. His father was a solicitor, newspaper proprietor and commanding officer of the 3rd Volunteer Battalion, Royal Welsh Fusiliers. Lionel was educated at The Elms Colwall Malvern Preparatory School before moving to Eastbourne College in the spring of 1898. At Eastbourne, where he was in Blackwater House, Rees played rugby for the school and also excelled in running and shooting. He also held the rank of sergeant in the College OTC. In 1901 he entered the Royal Military Academy at Woolwich as a gentleman cadet and was later gazetted as a second lieutenant in the Royal Garrison Artillery on 23 December 1903 when he was 19 years old. He was very successful at Woolwich and in addition to taking first place in the commissions and winning other prizes, he also won the Tombs Memorial Prize, awarded to the senior cadet.

Immediately before being posted to West Africa with No. 9 Company RGA, Lionel had shown a growing interest in flying. During the next few years he served with various RGA companies in Gibraltar, Sierra Leone and Cork and was promoted to lieutenant on 23 December 1906 and adjutant when serving at the School of Gunnery in April 1913. When on leave, Rees took flying lessons at the Bristol School, Larkhill and on 7 January 1913 qualified with Royal Aero Club Certificate no. 392. When war was declared in August the following year Rees was on active service with the West African Frontier Force from where, having requested this earlier, he was seconded to the RFC. After completing a course at the Central Flying School at Upavon, Wiltshire, he was posted to No. 7 Squadron at Farnborough, Hampshire.

Rees was later sent to form an aircraft acceptance park at Bruges, Belgium, but the rapid German advance through Belgium stopped such plans, and with No. 6 Squadron, to whom he had also been delivering stores, he moved bases rapidly, arriving at Bruges on 6 October. The next day he moved to Ostend and on the 13th to St Pol before leaving there for St Omer on 21 October. Rees returned to England having seen some service as an observer. He was promoted to captain at the end of October and posted to the Central Flying School as an instructor.

On 14 February 1915 Rees was posted as flight commander to No.11 Squadron at Netheravon, Wiltshire. This newly formed squadron was intended to be a unit focusing on the specific task of air fighting, a new idea at the time. The aircraft was the two-seat Vickers FB5, a pusher carrying an observer in the front seat of the nacelle with a 0.303 Lewis gun on a troublesome pillar mounting, so that the squadron soon devised their own. The squadron flew to St Omer, France, on 25 July and from there the aircraft moved to Vert-Galand airfield, 'a sloping little field ... to the south of Doullens on the main road down to Amiens'. Rees had gone ahead to make arrangements for the squadron's arrival and when they arrived his colleagues discovered him, 'covered in oil and as happy as Larry', working on his machine which had been damaged in an engagement with a German aircraft the day before. Rees had been on patrol alone when he spotted a Fokker monoplane which he then attacked. Despite the fact that his machine received damage to both spars of the lower port wing he continued the fight, and having hit the enemy plane he watched as it disappeared downwards through clouds behind enemy lines. This 'kill' was not confirmed but it seems highly likely that this first combat between a 'fighter pilot' and the enemy was a victory for Rees.

Rees was such a good shot that he could hit a business card held aloft by a colleague, with shots at a range of 25yd from a service revolver held in either his right or left hand, a skill which demonstrated superb eyesight and above average physical co-ordination.

Their first unified operational patrol was made on 29 July. Apart from Rees one of the pilots was Lieutenant G.S.M. Insall, who on 7 November 1915 also won a Victoria Cross.

The first day of August found Rees in Vickers 1649 with Flight Sergeant James Hargreaves in front as gunner when a two-seat LVG was spotted at some range. This was probably a BII variant, an excellent type which had been used since the spring for scouting and reconnaissance duties. Hargreaves opened fire but the distance separating them was too great and the enemy escaped. Later, on 31 August, Rees, again with Hargreaves, was flying between Bucquoy and Bapaume at 7,000ft when another LVG was sighted on a reconnaissance flight. When it became clear that the German pilot was too far from home to turn for safety Rees turned, having decided to fight it out.

A running battle ensued, with the observer in the German aircraft opening fire at about 200yd. Hargreaves returned fire, but the German aircraft, with its superior speed, flew out of range. Similar tactics lasted for a full forty-five minutes, with the both observers exchanging fire several times. Eventually Hargreaves had expended all four drums of ammunition so Rees broke off contact with the German plane and returned to Vert-Galand airfield where he kept the aircraft engine running as more drums of ammunition for the Lewis gun were loaded aboard.

After take-off Rees flew the aircraft back to the area where the German aircraft had last been seen and a blue LVG was spotted, flying about 1,000ft beneath them, seemingly unaware of their presence. Rees quickly dived, enabling Hargreaves to fire a complete drum of forty-seven rounds at the enemy aircraft, which dived very steeply down into clouds. It was witnessed falling down beneath the clouds in spirals by Second Lieutenants H.A. Cooper and his observer A.J. Insall (brother of Gilbert), also members of No.11 Squadron. Ground reports later confirmed an enemy aircraft crashing.

On 21 September, shortly before the start of the Battle of Loos, Rees and Hargreaves were flying on a photographic mission between Esterre and Péronne to obtain up-to-date information on the enemy front line. As usual, the observer would be taking the photographs – eighteen glass plates – in addition to manning the Lewis gun. In order to get the best quality photographs of the various objectives and owing to the time needed to change the photographic plates it was necessary for the British aircraft to retrace their route twice over the enemy trenches, which inevitably attracted anti-aircraft fire. When the photography task was completed, Hargreaves was about 'to collect the scattered plates from the floor of the nacelle' when Rees alerted him to an enemy aircraft climbing up towards them.

Rees glided down 2,000ft until they were about 200yd away from the enemy whose craft Hargreaves later described as, 'a new bus and vastly different from anything we had encountered before' with 'an excellent distribution of gun power …' The German fired several bursts without any obvious damage and when the range was less than 100yd Hargreaves fired about twenty shots which 'must have resulted in some damage' as the aircraft turned and glided towards the German lines 'where she apparently crashed on landing'. The photographic plates were later safely delivered to army headquarters.

A week later Rees and Hargreaves attacked an Albatros two-seater near to Gommecourt. Hargreaves fired a complete drum from the Lewis gun and then Rees gave chase to the diving aircraft enabling another drum to be used, causing the Albatros to 'spiral and nose-dive'. British anti-aircraft shells then began to explode around the enemy craft. The starboard wing was damaged and became detached from the body, causing the aeroplane to crash behind the British lines. The artillery claimed the destruction of this machine from *Flieger Abteilung* 23, but the pilot, Leutnant Kölin, was found to have been killed by a machine-gun bullet, so Rees and Hargreaves were given this victory. The pilot and the observer, Oberleutnant Leonhardi, of the Albatros are buried in Forceville Communal Cemetery Extension.

The *London Gazette* of 29 October published the citation for the Military Cross:

For conspicuous gallantry and skill on several occasions, notably the following:

On 21st September 1915, when flying a machine with one machine gun, accompanied by Flight-Serjeant Hargreaves, he sighted a large German biplane with two machine guns 2,000 feet below him he spiralled down and dived at the enemy, who having the faster machine, manoeuvred to get him broadside on and then opened fire. In spite of this Captain Rees pressed his attack and apparently succeeded in hitting the enemy's engine for the machine made a quick turn, glided some distance and finally fell just inside the German lines near Herbecourt.

On 28th July, he attacked and drove down a hostile monoplane in spite of the fact that the main spar of his machine had been shot through and the rear spar shattered.

On 31st August, accompanied by Flight-Serjeant Hargreaves, he fought a German machine more powerful than his own for three-quarters of an hour, then returned for more ammunition and went out to attack again, finally bringing the enemy's machine down apparently wrecked.

The author has found occurrences which include the action of 28 September amongst those in the Military Cross Citation, but this is not correct.

Flight sergeant James McKinley Hargreaves was awarded the Distinguished Conduct Medal, which was gazetted on 16 November, for the actions on 31 August and 21 September 1915.

On 7 November he was sent out by the commanding officer, Major G. Dawes, with spare parts and mechanics to fit a new petrol tank to an aircraft some 15 miles away, just inside the French lines. This work was carried out at night using screened lights and enabled the pilot, Flight Lieutenant G.S.M. Insall to fly the plane back to base at dawn. By the end of November Rees had returned to England to take command of the Central Flying School, and was promoted to temporary major on 1 December. His time at Upavon was short, and Major Rees was posted to Netheravon in February as commanding officer of No. 32 Squadron, which was being formed from the surplus personnel of No. 1 Squadron.

Lionel Rees gave his men lectures on such subjects as the Monosoupape rotary motor and aerial fighting tactics and some of his extensive knowledge was published in a special monograph published about this time dealing with rigging the new de Havilland scout. Another of his publications was *Fighting in the Air*, a carefully formulated work on all spheres of contemporary air warfare. In a letter home dated 9 May, one of his pilots, Second Lieutenant Gwylim Lewis, had prophetically observed, 'I shouldn't be surprised if he comes home with a VC.'

In early 1917, following his VC award and a period of further convalescence in Scotland, Rees was a War Office delegate on the Hon. Arthur Balfour's Military Mission to America in April when the Foreign Secretary was seeking American aid and co-operation following the USA declaration of war on 6 April. Because of his very respected abilities he was asked to remain in the United States as a technical advisor and was very influential in setting up the embryonic US Air Force, travelling extensively within the country to this end.

After his return to England in January 1918, Lieutenant Colonel Rees (he had been promoted to this brevet rank on 1 May 1917) was appointed to command No. 1 School of Aerial Fighting at Turnberry, Ayrshire, a post he held until the end of the war. Here his experience and ability to impart his knowledge were fully utilised.

An incident here was typical of the commander's ability, taking place as it did after a spate of crashes suffered by the temperamental Sopwith Camels. Realising that morale would certainly be affected, Rees, without comment to anyone, took off in a Camel. He climbed to no more than 500ft and performed almost every known aerobatic manoeuvre of the period for ten minutes before landing, having silenced the Camel's critics.

On the formation of the RAF on 1 April 1918, Rees was appointed temporary lieutenant colonel, and on 2 November the *London Gazette* announced the award of the Air Force Cross for his work as a flying instructor. On 26 July 1919 Rees was given a permanent commission with the rank of lieutenant colonel and on 27 August he was promoted to wing commander. He had also, as published in the *London Gazette* dated 31 May, been made a member of the OBE.

Rees secured second place in the newly constituted Gordon Shephard Memorial Prize Essay Competition. This was established in memory of Brigadier-General Gordon Strachey Shephard DSO MC by his father. It was an annual award for essays on reconnaissance by RAF officers and airmen. Shephard was a friend of the author Erskine Childers and an early aviator who flew a BE 2 to France with the first contingent of the BEF on 13 August 1914. He survived until fatally injured in an accident in his Nieuport Scout at Auchel Airfield on 19 January 1918. Brigadier Shephard was the highest-ranking RFC/RAF officer to be killed in a theatre of war in the First World War and he is buried at Lapugnoy Military Cemetery, Pas de Calais, France, VI.B.15.

On 15 January 1920 Rees's native Caernarfon honoured him with a presentation of the freedom of that borough and also bestowed upon him a beautiful sword of honour which was later placed in the care of the RAF Museum at Hendon. As a gesture of thanks Rees paid for all the Caernarfon children 'to go to the pictures'.

Wing Commander Rees took command of the flying wing at the newly established RAF College at Cranwell on 21 June 1920, and after nearly three years there, became assistant commandant on 26 March 1923. Having vacated his position at Cranwell, Rees was involved in the intensive work necessary to lay the foundations on which the new RAF was to be based. In 1925 he was appointed to the Air Ministry in the Directorate of Training, at the same time being honoured by being selected as ADC to His Majesty King George V.

Posted to RAF Transjordan at Amman on 6 May 1926, Rees assumed command of AAA British forces, both army and RAF, in Palestine and Transjordan on 1 October 1926. Apart from his military duties, which included RAF intervention to stop the Druze from using a refugee camp at Azrak as a base for incursions into Syria, he was able to further his two main interests, Biblical history and aerial photography. He had developed an excellent knowledge of the desert and had became a respected writer on the archaeology of the Old Testament as well as being one of the early pioneers in the use of aerial photography in furtherance of this work. It was not unknown for him, when on an exploratory desert flight and having seen something which piqued his interest, to tell the pilot to organise lorry transport for him. He would then parachute from the aeroplane! Such habits 'failed to endear him to his immediate superior in Egypt', AVM Tom Webb-Bowen. (Coincidentally this officer had been OC No. 2 Squadron at Merville when Rhodes-Moorhouse was awarded the first VC for the RFC in 1915.) Although it was not generally known amongst his colleagues, Lionel Rees, whilst in this post, and possibly others, had his pay donated directly to RAF charities. On his return home in 1929, he took command of RAF Uxbridge and later No. 21 Group before retiring in 1931. Also, after his retirement, he donated his VC and service medals to Eastbourne College, where they remain to this day although they have been loaned, on occasion, to Firepower, The Royal Artillery Museum, Woolwich.

At about this time, Rees took up sailing and became a member of the Royal Welsh Yacht Club. In 1933, after receiving an invitation from some friends in the West Indies, he decided to sail to the Bahamas from Great Britain in his 34ft, 8-ton ketch *May*. This single-handed feat took him over two months and when he started his journey from the river Hamble in Hampshire on 2 July no one had sailed the Atlantic from east to west. Another sailor achieved this shortly before Rees arrived at Nassau on 21 October 1933, but the Blue Water Medal given by the Sailing Club of America for the most outstanding feat of seamanship in that year still went to Rees.

In 1940, Lionel Rees volunteered for service with the RAF with the rank of wing commander, having voluntarily given up his rank of group captain. He served as OC RAF Helwan, Egypt, until he was invalided out in 1942. To avoid flying over occupied Europe an air route had been organised from Cairo via Khartoum and other staging posts to Takoradi, Gold Coast (Ghana), a journey in excess of 3,500 miles, much of it over the desert. Here, on his way home, he found a group of men from the RAF Regiment who had no commanding officer and 'he felt that was a shame, so he said he would do it himself'. One suspects that as the RAF base here was much concerned with the unpacking and assembly of aircraft destined for action in the Western Desert, Rees would have relished this opportunity to get involved. He received no pay for this unofficial post and allegedly it took the RAF bureaucrats six months to discover what he was doing!

In 1943 Rees again retired from the RAF and returned to his new home on the island of Andros in the Bahamas where he spent his time farming and sailing. In 1947 his housekeeper, 18-year-old Sylvia Williams, became pregnant, and their mixed-race marriage on 12 August of that year caused gossip in the white community. The couple lived in Mangrove Cay and had two sons and a daughter. A grandson, Nick Rees, at a college in the USA, swam for the Bahamas in the 2000 and 2004 Olympics, and was pictured with the flag of the Bahamas tattooed on his chest.

Lionel Rees died of leukaemia in Princess Margaret Hospital, Nassau, aged 71, on 28 September 1955. He was buried in Nassau War Cemetery for United Nations Airmen, previously known as the Royal Air Force Cemetery. The cemetery contains, near the lychgate, two non-World War graves, those of Hilary St George Saunders CBE MC, the official RAF historian, and beside him Group Captain L.W. Brabazon Rees, VC, OBE, MC, AFC. His complete medal entitlement is: VC, OBE, MC, AFC, 1914 Star and clasp, BWM (1914–20), Victory Medal (1914–19) and MiD oak leaf, 1939–45 Star, Africa Star, War Medal (1939–45), King George VI Coronation Medal (1937), Queen Elizabeth II Coronation Medal (1953).

An oil painting by Norman Arnold showing the action of Rees winning the Victoria Cross is in the custody of the Imperial War Museum, Lambeth, as is a portrait by C. Dobson. Other portraits of him hang in the Council Chambers, Caernafon and at the RAF College, Cranwell. His name appears in the ruined St George's garrison church,

Woolwich, along with other VC winners from the Royal Artillery and also on the roll of honour of air VC winners in St Clement Danes Church, the Strand, London. A plaque is affixed to the outside wall of the Royal Welsh Yacht Club at Porth-yr-Aur, Caernafon where his Blue Water Medal is also housed.

It was the deep knowledge he had of aircraft engines that made a lasting impression on many of his contemporaries so that one, writing twenty years after, was to describe those who 'could not be kept away from their engines' as 'a Rees'. His air gunner during the much of the First World War, Flight Sergeant J.M. Hargreaves, described him as 'a gentleman, a real gentleman, a rare species'.

W.L. ROBINSON

Air Operation over Cuffley,
Hertfordshire, 2–3 September 1916

Zeppelin night attacks intended to focus on military establishments and docks began on the night of 19–20 January 1915 when naval Zeppelins L3 and L4 reached England and dropped bombs in Norfolk killing four people, and injuring sixteen more, of whom two were children. Many houses, a church and a power station were damaged. Significantly, the official report stated, no anti-aircraft action was taken, either by guns or aeroplanes.

Both of the naval airships used in this attack were lost in a snowstorm off the Jutland coast on 8 February, which 'imposed caution on the airship command', and no subsequent raids took place until mid April. However, further air attacks on England resumed and anti-aircraft defences were quickly increased including the deployment of mobile units of searchlights and anti-aircraft guns. More landing fields for aircraft were established along the East Coast and close to London, for use by the expanding RNAS and RFC squadrons.

It became quite clear that the main use of Zeppelin raids was to terrorise the British public and the government was accused of not taking the raids seriously enough. It appeared to some of the population that the giant airships were attacking English towns and cities with impunity. It was possibly true as, by the end of August 1916, casualties, mainly civilian, from air raids had totalled more than 1,400, including over 400 fatalities. Seventy of the victims were children and the term 'Baby Killers' become popular usage in some sections of the popular press. Wealthy businessmen advertised substantial rewards for the destruction of a Zeppelin.

The Germans had selected 2 September 1916 for what would be the largest assault by airships so far on targets in England, the main target being London. No fewer than sixteen vessels had been assembled, twelve supplied by the navy and four by the army. The weather was 'generally fair, but there was a good deal of cloud and some mist, especially in the London area ... Conditions were therefore very favourable for an air raid ...' So said a later official British report. Two of the airships, however, returned to their bases before reaching the English coast.

The Admiralty had intercepted radio messages from the airships while they were still over the Continent and ten RFC machines from No. 39 (Home Defence) Squadron had been sent up to carry out patrol duties. One of these aircraft, BE2c biplane 2693, flown by Lieutenant William Leefe Robinson, had taken off just after 11 p.m. and was to patrol an area between his home base at Sutton's Farm near Hornchurch, Essex, and Joyce Green across the Thames in Kent. The climb to the operational altitude of 10,000ft usually took about fifty-three minutes.

The raiders, on the other hand, had not yet appeared over the English coast. The defences, aircraft, fixed anti-aircraft guns – and those of the mobile section – and searchlights had been alerted by the Admiralty, which had intercepted the airships' messages while they were still over the Continent.

By the time Robinson had reached 12,000ft, the enemy vessels were over Britain, as he later reported: 'I saw nothing till 1.10 a.m. when two searchlights picked up a Zeppelin about S.E. of Woolwich ... which was being fired on by a few anti-aircraft guns.' He lost sight of this airship, LZ98, as it rose high through clouds over Gravesend, Kent.

Shortly before 2 a.m. he headed towards the glow of fires and searchlight beams north-east of London and after a few minutes spotted an airship. Robinson now made towards this ship and with his earlier encounter in mind, he flew his BE2c at about 800ft lower than the airship. After firing a red Very light to alert the ground artillery to his presence, he flew along its length from bow to stern firing all the way with his Lewis gun and used up a complete drum of alternate New Brock and Pomeroy incendiary ammunition. This appeared to have no effect so he repeated the process. Now at a range of only some 500ft, Robinson concentrated his fire at a single point, and expended a third drum, aimed at an area beneath the stern, and shortly after he saw flames in the rear of the airship. Robinson would have been unaware that crowds of excited, cheering, people, heedless of the danger of falling bombs and shrapnel, thronged the streets to see the spectacle.

The airship had flown south from Tottenham, dropping bombs on the way, and was under heavy fire from most of the anti-aircraft defences of North and Central London, even including those guns at Regent's Park, Paddington and Green Park which were out of range. This gunfire possibly contributed to the change of direction by the Zeppelin at Finsbury Park, when it turned northwards but then again came under fire from other guns at West Ham, Clapton and Temple House. Official reports show that some 120 shells were fired at the airship before it changed course and in excess of sixty as it headed northwards. A few hits were claimed by anti-aircraft units, but due to the extreme range, this was unlikely. Six planes had ascended in the London District with Lieutenants Robinson (Sutton's Farm), MacKay (North Weald Bassett) and Hunt (Hainault Farm) all sighting this particular airship. Robinson, being the nearest pilot to the aircraft, had caught up with it between Enfield Highway and Turkey Street.

Robinson headed for his home airfield at Sutton's Farm and eventually made a perfect landing at 2.45 a.m. The exhausted and very cold pilot was helped from the aircraft by his colleagues and carried shoulder high to the flight office where he wrote his report before finally retiring to bed. When one of his fellow airmen asked if it was indeed he who had downed the Zeppelin he responded, 'Yes, I've strafed the beggar this time.'

The crash of the Schütte-Lanz airship SL11, for such it was, came north of Enfield in a farmer's field of beet, behind The Plough public house, near Cuffley, Hertfordshire, with a sunset-like glow. The fire was visible from miles around and, first witnessed at close quarters only by a farmer and a policeman, burned for over two hours.

The police retrieved sixteen charred bodies from the wreckage including one wearing an officer's coat thought to be that of the airship commander, Hauptmann Wilhelm Schramm. All were then covered with a tarpaulin. It appeared, from the nature of his injuries, that one of the crew had jumped, or fallen, from the burning airship before the crash. Among the wreckage, pieces of three Iron Crosses were discovered together with a revolver. Hundreds of people started arriving at the crash site before dawn and, despite a number of military and police guards around the wreckage, opportunistic souvenir hunters grabbed scraps of scorched cotton, wood, wire and anything they could find, with no shortage of buyers. The roads around the crash site quickly became clogged with every type of road transport, mechanical and horse-drawn, as excited Londoners headed towards Cuffley. It was into this melee that a tender full of RFC officers arrived during the morning. Once it was discovered that William Robinson was with this group further chaos ensued, as happy, cheering people clamoured for a handshake or autograph from the bemused pilot. He had been roused earlier from his rest by fellow RFC officers and driven the 20 miles from Sutton's Farm to the crash site. Robinson left the site later but returned during the afternoon, this time in civilian clothes in an attempt to escape the over-enthusiastic attention of the crowds. Unfortunately, as some of the morning arrivals were still present, he was recognised very quickly and embarrassed by the attention he received, not least from young girls throwing flowers at him.

Many in the crowds had expected to see at least a great skeleton and were surprised that so little remained of the giant airship, and on that wet and thundery Sunday they found only ash, scattered piles of splintered, charred wood and hundreds of feet of bracing wire, which was rolled into gigantic masses to be carted away.

The Schütte-Lanz airship was of plywood construction (Zeppelins used aluminium), 570ft long, with her maiden flight having taken place a month earlier on 1 August. The four Maybach motors, now scorched and dispersed across the muddy field, had been capable of giving the craft a top speed of almost 60mph. This was her first, and only, operational flight.

Many visitors to the site had not allowed for the wet weather and, after a thunderstorm and torrential rain during the morning, found their light summer clothing inadequate. Chaotic seems an apt description of the whole scene when over 10,000 passengers arrived from London in special trains within forty-eight hours – so heavy was the influx of arrivals at Cuffley Station that additional ticketing staff were drafted in. Cars were abandoned beside many narrow roads as drivers sought petrol; exhausted sightseers had to walk miles to other rail stations as return trains from Cuffley were, at times, insufficient; taxis ferried people back and forth to London – when they could be acquired. There were no refreshments to be had at The Plough. All food and drink was sold in the early morning on 'Zepp Sunday', as it quickly became known. Added to these difficulties the actual field was now a quagmire with remaining wreckage of any size closely guarded by soldiers and police. Not all visitors were content with a glimpse of the charred wreckage and scorched engines and on more than one occasion military guards had to forcibly move those more morbid sightseers who attempted to lift the tarpaulins covering the dead German crew. One woman who fainted after managing to sneak a look at the charred remains was rudely brought to her senses by a bucket of water tipped over her by one of the guards. The remains of the sixteen German crew were later moved to St Andrew's Church, Cuffley where, in their wooden coffins, they were guarded by police.

This enemy airship raid had been the largest to date but the relatively small loss of life – four civilians killed and twelve injured – and material damage later officially estimated at £21,000, were much less than the enemy might have hoped for. In addition the actual monetary value of SL11 was over £90,000 and this, together with the loss of an experienced airship commander and crew, very adversely affected the enemy morale, with the exact opposite effect for the British. Undoubtedly the incredibly fast award of the VC to Robinson – announced in the *London Gazette* dated 5 September – was partially for propaganda purposes, as was the deliberate incorrect naming of the airship as 'Zeppelin L21' in press releases. Papers were found on some of the crew which assisted with the identification of the airship and later research in official archives has ascertained that Zeppelin L21 was tracked on her return journey back out to sea. Perhaps in some senior government and military circles the attitude was 'the public want it to be a Zeppelin so we will give them one'. Whatever the reason, this news of a 'Baby Killer' being shot down was a refreshing change from the long daily casualty lists from the Western Front.

There was little delay either, with the inquests, both of the airship crew and of the fatalities caused by the raid. The Plough was used for the Monday evening inquest into the dead German airmen and after hearing a number of witnesses the coroner revised his original opinion that anti-aircraft guns were responsible for the airship's demise and concluded by stating that 'The Zeppelin was brought down by the fire of a British aeroplane manned by a pilot, Lieutenant Robinson, Royal Flying Corps.'

The War Office ordered that the Germans were to be given a military funeral and that the service should be organised by the RFC. This decision, together with the graphic reporting of the deaths of two sisters at Essendon, near Hatfield, Hertfordshire, when another of the attacking Zeppelins, L16, had dropped bombs near a searchlight, caused much controversy locally with unsurprisingly little sympathy for the Germans.

At the heavily policed funeral for the German airmen, on 6 September at Mutton Lane Cemetery, Potters Bar, the fifteen crew were interred in a mass grave while the remains thought to that be of the commander were buried separately. Only this coffin was identified as, 'An unknown German officer, killed while commanding Zeppelin L21 3rd Sept 1916.' Ironically, the commander of SL11, Hauptmann Wilhelm Schramm, had been born not many miles away at Old Charlton, Kent where his father had worked for Siemens before the family returned to Hameln, Germany, in 1900.

The investiture at Windsor Castle which included Robinson's award took place on Friday 9 September and huge crowds arrived at the railway station before daybreak to welcome the 'Hero of Cuffley' off the train on which he, together with others to be decorated by the King, would be passengers. They arrived on this train and were driven the short distance to the castle but Robinson was not one of them. Just before half past three that afternoon Robinson arrived at the stationmaster's house in a borrowed car as his had broken down 3 miles away. He was quickly driven to Windsor Castle where a late lunch was provided for him in the state dining room before he was received by the King and invested with his VC. The King, and later the Queen, Princess Mary and Prince Albert expressed 'more than a little interest in the pilot's attack [on the airship]'. Robinson had to endure enthusiastic shouting crowds when he departed from the castle and yet more when he later met his sister, Kitty, at a Windsor hotel.

William Robinson received rewards totalling more than £4,200, as promised by wealthy businessmen for the first pilot to destroy a raiding airship over Britain. He used some of the 'prize' money to acquire a brand new Prince Henry Vauxhall, a 4-litre, 70mph sports car in which he and his RFC colleagues were frequently pictured. A local newspaper reported seeing him driving, with other RFC officers, to Billericay, Essex, with the intention of viewing the wreck of a Zeppelin (LZ32) which had been shot down by his colleague Second Lieutenant Frederick Sowrey in the early hours of 24 September. For this action Sowrey was awarded only a DSO, as was Second Lieutenant Wulstan Tempest for a similar feat with Zeppelin LZ31 at Potters Bar on 1 October, although both these officers received a silver cup from the Hornchurch residents. The military authorities frowned upon the monetary 'prizes' which Robinson had received and speedily regulated against such practices in the future.

Robinson also received invitations to a large number of social and official functions and, embarrassing to the modest officer, a tide of public adulation. Gifts both large and small were bestowed upon Robinson, one of which was a silver cup from grateful residents of Hornchurch. Another was an engraved gold watch donated by the Overseas Club.

He was promoted to flight commander and temporary captain, backdated to 1 September 1916, and it was not until 9 February 1917 that Robinson was rescued from this unwelcome publicity when he was posted to No. 48 Squadron at Rendcomb, near Cirencester, where the squadron was in training for overseas operations before it moved to Bertangles, near Amiens on 8 March 1917. The squadron was now equipped with the new Bristol F2A and these machines were thought to be fast and manoeuvrable enough to outfly the Albatros DIIIs.

On 5 April 1917, while the Battle of Arras was fought, six of the aircraft, led by Robinson in A3337 with Lieutenant E.D. Warburton as observer, made the unit's first offensive patrol using these new aircraft. Having hardly crossed the lines near Douai, the Bristol formation was set upon by five Albatros DIII scouts of *Jagdstaffel 11*, *Leutnant* Manfred Freiherr von Richthofen, 'The Red Baron' in the lead.

The advantage lay entirely with the enemy. Not only were the British pilots flying unfamiliar new machines, and in a tight formation which Robinson had been advised against, but also, acting on orders, they made the cardinal error of attempting to use their Bristols in the manner of conventional two-seaters. The pilots were manoeuvring to give their gunners a wide field of fire instead of fighting back in the manner of single-seaters. The outcome of the engagement was that four Bristols were brought down, two personally accounted for by von Richthofen. Robinson and Warburton escaped unhurt and were then taken prisoner, when they were forced down, with a bullet damaged engine, near Douai, by Vizefeldwebel Sebastian Festner.

Several weeks elapsed before Robinson's fate was known by his family, for although he wrote a card to his fiancée on 5 April, from Karlsruhe, where he had been taken after his capture, delivery to England via the Red Cross took some time. For Robinson it was the start of nearly two years of captivity starting off with imprisonment in the camp at Freiburg-in-Breisgau, where he was later involved in a number of failed escape attempts. In mid September, Robinson, with Second Lieutenants C.M. Reece and Arthur Baerlin, travelled within 4 miles of the Swiss border near Stühlingen before they were recaptured and sent back to camp. Robinson was punished with a court martial and a month in solitary confinement at Zorndorf.

Robinson was moved at the beginning of May 1918 to the Clausthal camp where another escape attempt was thwarted. At this camp the commandant was Heinrich Niemeyer, who had a reputation for coarseness and cruelty. He was known to the prisoners as 'Milwaukee Bill', due to his American accent and slang. The German took an instant dislike to Robinson and later had him transferred to the more secure POW camp at Holzminden. This was commanded by Karl Niemeyer, twin brother of the Clausthal commandant. The treatment of Robinson here is summed up in a letter from fellow prisoner Geoffrey Hopkins to Peter Cooksley in September 1973:

Robinson was of more than usual interest as he'd won the Victoria Cross and there were, of course, people who thought he had been unduly highly decorated for what he did. However, he was the lucky one (with respect) and public opinion made him a national hero. Whatever the Germans may have thought about the affair privately, they obviously had to make out he was a superman to have shot down one of their marvellous airships! Their mentality would lead them to believe that a superman of that sort would be able to escape from a POW camp in some way impossible for ordinary mortals, so that they took very stringent precautions to see that he didn't get away.

We were very sorry for him in that the Boche harried and badgered him, bullying him in every way possible ... they were always having special roll calls for him, waking him up at night to see if he was still there etc. All this must have worried him a good deal.

Robinson's harsh treatment so incensed other inmates that a detailed report was written and smuggled out to the War Office, hidden in the handle of a tennis racquet. Two other VC holders were incarcerated in Holzminden at various times, Commander Edward Bingham of the Royal Navy and Lieutenant Edward Bellew of 7th Battalion CEF.

Robinson was repatriated to England and disembarked at Leith on 14 December 1918. After passing through the reception camp at Ripon in North Yorkshire he travelled, on Christmas Eve, to join his friend Captain Edward Clifton and his wife Nancie at Lavender Cottage, in Gordon Avenue, Harrow Weald, where his sister Kitty and fiancée Joan also awaited his arrival. Robinson also visited his old station at Sutton's Farm en route to Harrow Weald and those who remembered him there were shocked at his appearance, which found him 'bent over' and walking with the support of a stick.

Robinson had contracted a strain of Spanish influenza that was sweeping across the world at the time, and tragically died from the effects of it on the night of 31 December 1918 while still staying with his friends at Lavender Cottage.

His funeral took place at All Saints Church, Harrow Weald, in the early afternoon of 3 January 1919, and before the service a flypast of fighter aircraft flew over Lavender Cottage. One of them dropped a large laurel wreath in front of the cottage. This wreath was sent from 6th Brigade RAF, and was placed on the coffin.

The funeral cortège was led by the band of the Central Royal Air Force, and when, at the church gates the coffin was carried, the pall-bearers were six RAF officers including Major Frederick Sowrey and Major Edward Clifton. William Leefe Robinson was laid to rest in the south-west corner of All Saints churchyard extension, Harrow Weald, in a plot chosen since it was nearest to where 'he had spent many happy hours'.

❖❖❖

Horace and Elizabeth Eshe Robinson (née Leefe) had seven children, of whom five were born in India including the youngest, William, born on 14 July 1895 at Kaima Betta in the South Coorg of India, near Mercara, where William's grandfather had purchased a coffee estate. All the children were given their mother's maiden name of Leefe as a second Christian name but it was usual for the family only to use this as an initial letter. Owing to a downturn in the Indian coffee market, the family returned to England in 1901 when they stayed at their English home, Tennyson Villa, Boscombe, Bournemouth. After a while the family moved to Oxford where William and his elder brother Harold were enrolled as day boys at the Dragon School. However, as the situation in the coffee industry proved less alarming than had been thought, the family returned to India in 1903.

While in India, William's education was at Bishop Cotton School, and in the autumn of 1909 he and Harold were sent back to England so that their education might be completed at St Bees School in Cumberland, where they enrolled in September of that year.

William later became head of his house (Eaglesfield), a prefect and sergeant in the School OTC, and during holidays he travelled in France and Russia. The latter trip extended three weeks into the autumn term, which had a detrimental effect on that year's academic results. By early 1913 he had made up his mind to join the armed services and told his mother this in a letter. He thought he should have a private coach who would prepare him for entry into Sandhurst as an army cadet. After this preparation he entered Sandhurst on 14 August 1914 – ten days after war had been announced.

He left the Royal Military College in December 1914 when commissioned into the 5th Militia Battalion, Worcestershire Regiment, and posted to Plymouth. This allowed him to visit Boscombe and Bournemouth when off duty. He was hoping for more active service, and also applied to join the Royal Flying Corps. He was duly accepted, and on 29 March 1915, posted to St Omer as a member of No. 4 Squadron as a gunner/observer. He would be flying in a BE2c to be engaged mainly on reconnaissance and artillery ranging.

Robinson found much of this work tedious, but an event late in the afternoon of 8 May changed this. The squadron, now flying from

Baillieul, was covering the heavy fighting taking place around Ypres and obtaining important sightings of German troop movements as Allied troops, in particular the British 28th Division, came under severe enemy attacks. His aircraft was the object of a near miss by an anti-aircraft shell over Lille at about 4.50 p.m. As this shell exploded the machine was sent bucking and whirling in the blast, observer Robinson felt a violent blow to his right arm. He had sustained a wound which was bleeding heavily, and later, in No. 7 Stationary Hospital, Boulogne, two pieces of shrapnel were extracted from his arm. He later left France for twenty-eight days sick leave in England.

On 29 June Robinson was ordered to report to South Farnborough, there to commence flying training. He made his first solo flight nineteen days later and qualified for the Royal Aero Club pilot's Certificate No. 1475 in a Maurice Farman after a further ten days' instruction. On 14 August he went to the Central Flying School, Upavon, flying solo there in a twenty-minute flight on the next day in BE8 693. Six days later he was posted to No. 19 Squadron based at Castle Bromwich, a few miles from Birmingham, which had only recently been formed and was currently engaged in training crews for service in France, using BE12s.

Robinson was posted on Christmas Eve 1915 to the home of No. 10 Reserve Aeroplane Squadron at Joyce Green, Kent, 'on loan to the London defences'. The squadron's task was to defend the capital against aerial attacks. At the time the raiders were almost exclusively airships, vessels against which there was, in the minds of many British citizens, little defence.

A number of BE2c biplanes, twin-seaters now converted for a pilot alone, were distributed in pairs at ten fields on the periphery of London. The twenty machines involved were regarded as the strength of No. 19 Reserve Squadron until 15 April, 1916, when they became No. 39 Squadron. Robinson was moved about to various bases during this time before ending up at Sutton's Farm at Hornchurch in early 1916 where he was given command of B Flight, No. 39 (Home Defence) Squadron.

In the same year he received the sad news that Second Lieutenant Arthur Limnell Robinson, his brother-in-law attached to 173rd Tunnelling Company had, on 25 February, died of wounds received eight days earlier. This was followed by a second blow when he heard that Harold, his brother and second lieutenant attached to the 103rd Mahratta Light Infantry, had died on 10 April 1916 of wounds sustained in Mesopotamia during the attempted relief of Kut-el-Amara.

❖ ❖ ❖

After the Armistice in November 1918, Robinson's parents left India to return to England and settled at a large house, called Dalnabreck, 83 Woodcote Road, Wallington, Surrey. Formerly it had been the home of their daughter Katherine (Kitty) and her husband, and it was Kitty's daughter Regina who became custodian of the memorabilia linked with the life and deeds of her uncle William. Elizabeth died on 23 February 1929 and was buried at Bandon Hill Cemetery, Beddington. Her husband, Horace, was interred in the same grave following his death a few weeks later on 11 April.

After his death, Captain William Robinson was commemorated in many ways. On 9 June 1921 a memorial stone was unveiled at East Ridgeway, Cuffley, close to the SL11 crash site. The 17ft-high obelisk had been paid for by subscriptions from *Daily Express* readers, and like many other references named the airship as L21 – this was later corrected to SL11 in the 1960s. The monument was renovated in 1986 and again in 2009, the latter occasion being to correct movement caused by subsidence. The site of the crash has now been replaced with the houses of Bacons Drive and Cranfield Crescent. Also at Cuffley a model of the airship was displayed in the village hall and the local football team were nicknamed 'The Zeps'. Cuffley Masonic Lodge was consecrated On 13 November 1980 and their Lodge Badge incorporated, amongst other emblems, an image of SL11. On 27 April 2010, the railway company First Capital Connect named a Class 313 locomotive *Captain William Leefe Robinson* to celebrate the centenary of the Great Northern route extension connecting Grange Farm to Cuffley.

William's old school, St Bees, published its First World War *Roll of Honour and Record of Service* in 1921, which details the service of 987 Old St Beghians of whom 184 died. Three VC winners are included: Captain W.L. Robinson, VC, RAF, Captain J. Fox-Russell, VC, MC, RAMC and Captain R.W.L. Wain, VC. The name of Robinson's brother Harold also appears on the roll. A memorial to the fallen was dedicated in this year and 'Memorial Field' officially opened in 1925. In 1932, on Speech Day, a memorial to the three Victoria Cross winners was unveiled in the school chapel and, on Armistice Day each year, a poppy wreath from St Bees is placed on Robinson's grave.

Robinson's grave was, for many years, maintained by the staff of the inn named after him near the cemetery. This inn has since had a number of ownership and name changes, but in February 2009 the name Leefe Robinson VC reappeared on the sign outside.

On 9 April 1962 RAF Hornchurch, as Sutton's Farm had later become, was closed and now most of the old airfield site is occupied by a housing estate, but the airmen and airfields of the past survive in the local road names. Amongst the many names can be found Robinson, Tempest and Sowrey. His name also appears with those other VC winners of the RFC, RNAS, and RAF on the wall in St Clement Danes Church in the Strand, London.

The remains of Hauptmann Schramm and his crew of SL11 were transferred to Cannock Chase German War Cemetery, Staffordshire, which was dedicated in June 1967. Here, in a small separate section, they are commemorated along with the crews of three other airships – LZ32, LZ31 and LZ49 – brought down in the First World War.

In November 1988 Regina, Katherine's daughter, put the greater part of the family collection linked with her uncle William for sale by auction at Christies. The proceeds went to fund the Medal for Life charity, which aids children suffering from leukaemia. The Victoria Cross medal group alone realised £99,000.

The Victoria Cross awarded to Captain William Leefe Robinson is displayed in the Lord Ashcroft Gallery at the Imperial War Museum, Lambeth. His medal entitlement is VC, 1914–15 Star, BWM, Victory Medal and oak leaf (MiD 25 January 1915 and 16 December 1919).

A portrait of Robinson and also the Lewis gun from BE2e 2693 are still in public ownership, preserved by the Ministry of Defence. The Imperial War Museum, Lambeth, has a number of items connected to Robinson and the Cuffley airship crash, which include a portrait medal by Mary Gillick with a depiction of Robinson on the obverse and a biplane flying over St Paul's Cathedral on the reverse, presented by The Imperial Air Fleet Committee in 1917. A number of items from the crash site, including photographs and souvenirs sold to raise money for the British Red Cross, are also held in the museum.

A tunic which belonged to Robinson, together with other items of memorabilia, are held at Thurrock in the Purfleet Gunpowder Museum. The propeller from BE2e 2693 is displayed in the armoury at Culzean Castle, Ayrshire.

One of the last surviving witnesses to the shooting down of SL11 was Arthur Crumper, a 7-year-old schoolboy from Woolwich, who watched the spectacle among the crowds. Arthur died on 20 April 2013 and a contemporary photograph of the crash site appeared with his obituary in *The Times*.

The airship is still identified as 'L21' in the inscription on Robinson's grave.

T. MOTTERSHEAD

Ploegsteert Wood, 7 January 1917

Having just completed two weeks' home leave over Christmas 1916, Acting Flight Sergeant Mottershead was posted to No. 20 Squadron, based at Clairmarais, 3 miles north-east of St Omer, Pas-de-Calais. He quickly realised that the new unit's FE2ds were more powerfully engined than those of his previous unit as they used Roll's Royce Eagle motors of 250–275hp instead of 160hp Beardmores.

On Sunday 7 January 1917, two of the squadron's FE2ds were ordered to take off for routine patrols but after the first machine became airborne Mottershead's take-off was delayed. The first aircraft was away at a little before midday, but A39, flown by Mottershead, with Lieutenant W.E. Gower as his gunner, was late taking off. A last-minute change of crew had been necessary when the FE intended for this pair had proved unserviceable, but eventually some hard flying enabled the second crew to rendezvous with the other at an altitude of about 10,000ft. Their mission was to patrol in the vicinity of Ploegsteert Wood, a little over 3 miles north of Armentières.

Here their first adversaries of the day were encountered in the form of a pair of Albatros scouts, probably DIIIs. The first of these lost little time in closing in for the kill, but in point of fact it was he who would, in a matter of seconds, become the victim of the encounter. Gower, twisting in the narrow confines of his cockpit, remained calm, and, lining up the bright fuselage of their attacker carefully in his sights, let go a long burst. It sent the Albatros over on to one wing, before going down steeply, and plainly out of control, the dark-clad silhouette of the pilot visible as he attempted to halt the descent of his seemingly doomed aircraft.

There was no time to observe its ultimate end, as the second Albatros, flown by Vizefeldwebel Göttsch – from *Jagdstaffel 8*, as was no doubt the first – closed to a surprisingly short range beneath the undefended blind spot behind the tail of the British pusher and put in a hail of fire from its synchronized twin Spandau machine guns. The burst was not long but it was accurate, making its mark on the fuel tank which immediately exploded into flames. Very quickly this had spread to the ply of the nacelle. Having lost 1,000ft in the opening minutes of the encounter, the aircraft began slowly descending. Reacting swiftly to the situation, Gower seized a fire extinguisher and began to spray its contents not on the flaming timber but over his pilot, whose clothing was now alight at the back where his seat flanked the engine.

Mottershead attempted to bring his blazing machine into a normal landing, but as soon as the wheels touched the earth, the partially burnt undercarriage collapsed. The momentum took the FE2 forward for a few yards until its nose dug in, flinging the tail unit spectacularly skywards and throwing Gower upwards and outwards, to land safely, but leaving Mottershead trapped in his seat.

The activity had attracted a large number of soldiers to the crash site and, guided by a shaken, bruised and cut Gower, they immediately set about lifting the perilously balanced pilot from his seat, a rescue made the more difficult by the fact that the machine was still on fire. However the rescuers did succeed and Mottershead was despatched with all speed to receive medical attention at No. 8 CCS, Bailleul, for the first-degree burns he had sustained. These included severe injuries to his back, hands and legs. Sadly his injuries were too severe and he died on 12 January.

This extremely courageous pilot was given a funeral with full military honours at and buried in Baillieul Communal Cemetery Extension, III.A.126. the following day. Every available man from his squadron followed the flag-draped coffin in the cortège.

The authorities decided to award a posthumous VC to Mottershead and the citation was published a month later on 12 February. It read as follows:

1396 SERGT. THOMAS MOTTERSHEAD, LATE R.F.C.

For most conspicuous bravery, endurance, and skill when, attacked at an altitude of 9,000 ft., the petrol tank was pierced and the machine set on fire. Enveloped in flames, which his observer, was unable to subdue, this very gallant soldier succeeded in bringing his aeroplane back to our lines, and though he made a successful landing, the machine collapsed on touching the ground, pinning him beneath the wreckage, from which he was subsequently rescued. Though suffering extreme torture from burns, Sergeant Mottershead showed the most conspicuous presence of mind in the careful selection of a landing place, and his wonderful endurance and fortitude undoubtedly saved the life of his observer. He has since succumbed to his injuries.

His widow Lilian was presented with the decoration by the king during an open air investiture in Hyde Park on 2 June 1917. Lieutenant William Edward Gower received the Military Cross at the same ceremony.

❖ ❖ ❖

Thomas Mottershead was a son of Thomas Mottershead and his wife Lucy (née Hawkins) and born on 17 January 1892. They lived at 6 Vine Street, Widnes, Lancashire, a short road in the centre of the town with rows of terraced houses on either side. Thomas Junior, followed by five boys and four girls, was to prove not only highly intelligent but also capable of applying his skills to engineering problems. This fact was soon realised at Simms Cross Council School in the town centre, and in 1907 he became a student at Widnes Technical School where he took a three-year course. Successfully completing the course, studying engineering practice and theory both at home and school, he became an apprentice fitter and turner at the local United Alkali Company works where his father was a horse-keeper. He regularly played football, first with the local junior team and later with the town's Wesley Guild and was also a Bible reader at St Paul's Sunday school.

Soon Tom took new employment at the Birkenhead works of Cammell Laird, and married Lilian Bree, a childhood friend, on 10 February 1914. The couple had a son the following year, whom they named Sydney Thomas, and their home was 12 Market Street, Widnes.

Believing that the south of England offered greater employment opportunities, Tom took on temporary employment as a motor mechanic in Andover, Hampshire. Then, together with a friend from Widnes, he went to Portsmouth where work at the naval dockyard promised permanent employment. However the outbreak of war changed their plans and they enlisted in the Royal Flying Corps on 10 August.

No. 1396 Air Mechanic Thomas Mottershead was posted to the Central Flying School, Upavon, Wiltshire where he served on the maintenance staff. He was promoted to corporal on 15 September 1915 and acting sergeant on 1 January 1916, achieving the substantive rank of sergeant only three months later on 1 April.

Mottershead had strong ambitions to take up flying, and in May 1916, his application for pilot training was accepted. He had an immediate aptitude for piloting and obtained his First Class Pilot's Certificate on 9 June, followed by almost a month as a flying instructor at Upavon before he was posted to the RFC Pilot's Pool at St Omer, north-west of Lille. Three other NCO pilots flew to St Omer that day, 5 July 1916: Flight Sergeant J. McCudden MM and Sergeants H. Pateman and E. Haxton. Tom Mottershead was posted the following day to No. 25 Squadron at Auchel (Lozinghem), some 8 miles west of Béthune.

This squadron was equipped with FE2b and FE2d two-seater pusher machines and was designated as a reconnaissance squadron. However, the division of work to operational groups was arbitrary, and other activities included bombing raids and aerial fighting. The Battle of the Somme had started on 1 July and after only two short flights with an experienced gunner/observer to familiarise him with the area, Mottershead was sent out on his first operational sortie. This was a low-level attack on an enemy anti-aircraft battery which he bombed successfully from 1,000ft.

Further operational sorties followed over the next two months, culminating in his award of a medal for an action on 22 September. Flying FE2b, 6998, with Second Lieutenant C. Street as observer/gunner, Mottershead was detailed to bomb the railway station at Samain. By diving to 1,500ft he destroyed a stationary ammunition train with bombs followed by a very low pass over a second train, enabling Street to rake it with gunfire from the guard's van to the locomotive. As he climbed away, Mottershead was attacked from behind by an enemy Fokker. Its pilot's first burst of fire failed to accomplish a victory and he was immediately outmanoeuvred and sent down himself by a well-placed burst of fire from Street's front gun. This action resulted in the award to Mottershead, shortly to be promoted to the rank of flight sergeant, of the Distinguished Conduct Medal which was gazetted on 14 November.

❖ ❖ ❖

Naturally proud of their gallant son, the people of Widnes opened an appeal fund to benefit the widowed Lilian and her 2-year-old child, 'The Mayor of Widnes Memorial Fund to Thomas Mottershead'. Its many fundraising activities realised at its closure a total approaching £1,000. Sadly none of this money was to reach Lilian, who continued to live in straitened circumstances, and it is difficult to explain why Lilian was not given the funds due to her.

Minute books of the charity were rediscovered in the early 1970s, which record the decision of the fund's trustees to decline an application for assistance made by Mrs Mottershead. But the discovery came too late, and, disgusted that his father's memorial fund had been handled in an incompetent manner, Sydney Thomas sold the medal that his father had so courageously won. However, in a seeming gesture of recompense, the fund was finally used, with the considerable interest it had accrued, to establish the current 'Mottershead Scholarship' at Halton College of Further Education in Widnes, which is awarded to promising students who go on to university.

In March 1995, a VC 10 aircraft of 10th Squadron RAF, serial no. XV 106, was one of fourteen named after flying services ecipients of the VC and carried the name of Thomas Mottershead VC. Over time the squadron aircraft were replaced and the name-bearing scroll was finally affixed to VC 10 C1K XR 808 beneath the names of Kenneth Campbell VC and Hugh Malcolm VC, both Second World War airmen. This latter aircraft was on display at the Waddington Air Show in early July 2013 before its final flight a few weeks later.

Tom's cap and goggles are in the care of the Imperial War Museum, Lambeth, London, as is a painting of him by Cowan Dobson. His home town perpetuates his name in Mottershead Road in the Simms Cross area, near the centre of the town, and it is of course inscribed on the memorial to all the fallen of Widnes in Victoria Park. Also in this park is a memorial to the town's three winners of the Victoria Cross: Private Thomas 'Todger' Jones VC DCM Cheshire Regt 26 October 1916, Sergeant Thomas Mottershead VC DCM Royal Flying Corps 12 February 1917, and Lieutenant Thomas Wilkinson VC Royal Naval Reserve 17 December 1946. This memorial, together with another outside the Royal British Legion HQ at Walton, was unveiled on 13 August 2006 in the presence of surviving family members. His medals, VC, DCM, BWM and Victory Medal, are displayed in the Lord Ashcroft Gallery at the Imperial War Museum. Together with other Victoria Cross winners from the RFC, RNAS and RAF, the name of Flight Sergeant Thomas Mottershead appears to the left of the altar in St Clement Danes Church, the Strand, London.

1396 Mottershead, Sergeant Thomas, was the only non-commissioned officer of the air war during 1914–18 to be awarded the supreme decoration for valour.

F.H. MCNAMARA

*Near Tel el Hesi, Palestine,
20 March 1917*

In March 1917, British and Commonwealth forces were planning an attack on Gaza, Palestine, and an important Turkish supply centre known as Junction Station, 40 miles west of Jerusalem, was during that month subjected to repeated bombing attacks by No. 1 Squadron of the Australian Flying Corps and No. 14 Squadron of the RFC. On 20 March two BE2cs from No.1 Squadron, piloted by Captain Rutherford and Lieutenant Drummond, set out to bomb railway lines crossing Wadi Hesse, at Tel el Hesi, 20 miles north-east of Gaza, and were accompanied by Lieutenants McNamara and Ellis flying Martinsydes. Each of the four aircraft carried six bombs, which were actually modified 4.5in howitzer shells fitted with forty-second delay fuses! The BE2Cs dropped their bombs, followed closely by Ellis who, after releasing his bombs, flew off chasing a German aircraft he had seen. McNamara, in Martinsyde 7486, flew in low over a train and released three of his bombs, followed by two more on railway lines. Unfortunately the last 'bomb' exploded almost immediately and jagged pieces of shell cut through the aircraft structures, one piece wounding McNamara. He dropped two smoke bombs to act as positional guides for other aircraft and made to return back to base.

He then saw Rutherford's aircraft on the ground with a group of Turkish cavalry heading in its direction. Despite his injury, McNamara cut the engine and glided down to land about 200yd away from the grounded machine. As he taxied over the rough terrain towards Rutherford, who was trying to set his machine on fire, McNamara, who was unable to get out of his machine unaided, shouted for him to hurry.

Rutherford left his aircraft still intact, ran to the Martinsyde and climbed up onto the cowling in between the struts, as this was only a single-seater aircraft. McNamara gave his engine full throttle and attempted take-off, but when he reached a speed of about 35mph the weight of Rutherford on one side of the aircraft, combined with his lack of control due to the numbness of his right leg – or, in McNamara's own words, 'right leg pretty dud' – caused the machine to tip and swing to the left.

The undercarriage collapsed, the nose dipped and the aircraft turned over on its side, smashing the propeller and port-side wings. After both men had extricated themselves, McNamara set fire to the wreckage by shooting a hole in the petrol tank and then igniting the spilled fuel with his Very pistol. As the two airmen then made for Rutherford's machine, rifle bullets started hitting the sand nearby. Turkish horsemen were now within range. While their attempted take-off in the Martinsyde had been taking place, both Drummond and Ellis had made repeated machine-gun strafing attacks on the enemy horsemen from the air.

When the pair had reached the BE2c, the remaining bomb in McNamara's aircraft exploded in the fire, which made the Turkish troops a little less ambitious in their approach. The damage to the BE included several snapped wires, a detached tyre, and spare Lewis gun drums jammed under the rudder bar. McNamara was helped into the pilot's seat by Rutherford, who now swung the propeller before clambering up into the observer's seat, via the lower wing, as the machine prepared to take off, while at the same time McNamara took shots with his revolver at the enemy. More than once the soft sand threatened to stop the take-off but eventually the aircraft was airborne and McNamara set course for the nearest airfield which was Kilo 143, near El Arish, some 70 miles distant. He was weak through loss of blood and although almost passing out at times, he landed the Martinsyde eighty minutes after take-off and it was then discovered that three of the aircraft's bombs were still in the bomb rack!

McNamara, who had now lost consciousness, was quickly given medical treatment including a routine tetanus injection to which he had a near fatal allergic reaction. In an attempt to restore blood circulation after his flight, hot bricks were also placed close to his feet but, due to an accidental displacement of a blanket while he was unconscious, his legs were badly burned. He was sent by hospital train initially to No. 24 Stationary Hospital at Kantara East, 30 miles south of Port Said, before transfer to No. 14 Australian General Hospital at Abbassia, Cairo, on 23 March. It is interesting to note that his records show due to the injuries to his buttock he 'would be considered wounded in action'.

On 26 March 1917 his courageous actions were noted when the recommendation for the award of the VC to 'Lieutenant Frank Hubert

McNamara, 5th Wing No. 67 (Aust.) Squadron, R.F.C.' (sic), was made by GOC Middle East Brigade RFC, Brigadier-General Geoffrey Salmond. His recommendation was strongly reinforced by written statements by his fellow airmen, Drummond, Ellis and Rutherford.

Whilst in hospital McNamara's promotion to captain and flight commander in No. 71 Squadron AFC was announced on 20 April, and the *London Gazette* of 8 June 1917 carried the citation for the award of his Victoria Cross.

❖ ❖ ❖

Francis (Frank) Hubert McNamara was born at Waranga, near Rushworth, Victoria, Australia on 4 April 1894, the first of eight children of William Francis McNamara, an officer of the Department of Lands, and his wife Rosanna (née O'Meara). Frank was educated at Rushworth and Shepparton Schools and later attended teachers training college in Melbourne. After graduation he was appointed to temporary teaching posts at Shepparton and Melbourne. His parents, with the rest of the family, moved to Melbourne in 1910.

McNamara joined the militia in the shape of the 46th Infantry Battalion of the Brighton Rifles in 1912, and in July 1913 he was offered a second lieutenant's commission. After the outbreak of war in 1914 he served on garrison duties with the Brighton Rifles, who were for a brief period organised for home defence at Queenscliff and Point Nepean, Victoria. Between February and May 1915 he was an instructor at the Broadmeadows AIF Training Depot.

In July 1915 McNamara was selected to undertake training with the flying school at Point Cook, near Melbourne, which he began in a Bristol Boxkite. On 20 October he was awarded Royal Aero Club Certificate No. 2254, and, following further instruction, posted as adjutant to No. 1 Squadron, Australian Flying Corps, in January of the next year. His records show that when this posting was made he was 5ft 10in tall and weighed 11 stone.

No. 1 Squadron embarked from Port Melbourne in the transport *Orsova* for service in Egypt on 16 March 1916. The only technical equipment taken by the squadron was 'two motor-cars and seven motor-bicycles'. All other equipment, including aircraft, would be supplied by the RFC in Egypt. The officers and other ranks – 223 in total – arrived at Port Said, Egypt, on 14 April 1916, but their aircraft would not be arriving for six weeks. The unreadiness of the squadron is illustrated by a recorded note which states, 'When No. 1 Squadron arrived in Egypt in April 1916, many of the personnel had never seen an aeroplane or an aeroplane-engine'. The pilots and observers had received no training at Point Cook in gunnery, armament, photography, or bombing; consequently many of the squadron personnel, including McNamara, were sent to England for operational training. McNamara underwent this further training at Filton, near Bristol Upavon, Wiltshire and Reading in Berkshire and then returned to Egypt on 24 August.

The last two weeks in England were enlivened by visits to the Royal Opera House, clubs and restaurants in London, while the War Office sorted out a mix-up with his papers. He returned to Egypt for further training, this time in desert conditions, at No. 3 School of Military Aviation, Aboukir, a few miles north-east of Alexandria. From 8 September until 3 October he was confined to No. 3 General Hospital, Abbassia, where he was treated for orchitis. McNamara rejoined No. 1 Squadron in December at Mustabig, a new airfield immediately west of the Mazar Oasis on the coastal caravan route from the Suez Canal to Palestine.

The operational area No. 1 Squadron had to patrol was vast, calling for lengthy patrols which took crews over a large expanse of desert surrounding the Suez Canal. The squadron was equipped with a mixture of BE2c and Be2e machines and a few Martinsyde G100 Scouts, popularly referred to as 'Elephants' on account of their comparatively large size when compared with other scouts. These single-seaters were intended to provide protective escorts for the two-seat BEs when the latter were used as bombers.

McNamara made his first operational flight on 22 December in BE2c 4475, when he was one of thirteen aircraft sent to bomb Turkish positions at Magdhaba, a strong point on the Wadi El Arish, which was to be attacked by the ANZAC Mounted Division on the following day.

During this period, aerial activity was comparatively slight, in part due to the small numbers of aircraft available to both sides, but this was balanced by the demanding nature of the operations. These consisted of daily reconnaissances over isolated and inhospitable country, where the danger of emergency landings, as likely due to engine failure as to enemy action, presented a very real danger of death by exposure. In addition, there was the fear of encountering tribes of hostile Arabs or being taken prisoner by the Turks – the poor treatment of prisoners by the Turks prompted more than one 'rescue' of Allied airmen by German flyers!

During the first two months of 1917 McNamara flew in many of the air-support operations, general reconnaissance and photographic sorties undertaken by the squadron. At the end of this period he was sent to the flying school at Aboukir for a rest, acting as an instructor.

After he returned to his squadron he occasionally had to make attempts to rescue stranded colleagues from the desert and McNamara became victim to this himself on 29 December 1916 when his propeller was broken at an advanced landing ground. His friend, Lieutenant Roberts, was sent out with a new airscrew and a mechanic in the late afternoon, but the trip was made through violent rainstorms which had partially flooded the emergency strip, and it was dark before the work was completed and a return to base could be attempted.

After winning the VC in March 1917, and after four months in hospital, he was discharged and embarked on board HT *Boorara* which sailed from Egypt on 23 August. Australian newspapers of 28 September reported that McNamara had arrived at Melbourne the previous day: 'Conspicuous among the returning soldiers was Capt. F. McNamara VC who was wounded in Palestine. As he came ashore from the ship today on crutches three cheers were called for the Victoria Cross hero.'

The Oriental Hotel, Melbourne, was the venue for a dinner for Captain Frank McNamara VC by his former unit, 46th Infantry, Brighton Rifles. This was held on 5 November and 'the distinguished guest, who still walks with the aid of a stick ... was presented with a very handsome gold wristlet watch'. Fulsome tributes were paid to 'the hero of the Ballarat' before the final toast to 'absent comrades'.

McNamara was discharged from No. 5 Australian General Hospital, Melbourne when declared 'fit for light duty' on 5 December 1917 with instructions to report to the Central Flying School at Laverton on 17 December, although it was still necessary for him to attend a medical board in early January. At the end of January his appointment with the AFC was officially terminated and from 1 February – the next day – he was appointed as an instructor at the Central Flying School.

As if to emphasise the dangers still very inherent in flying at this time, a Tasmanian newspaper reported, in June of this year, that:

> Captain McNamara, V.C., of the Flying Corps, who is at present instructing at the Laverton Flying School, bumped back to earth very unceremoniously the other day and wondered what part of the map he had landed on. It was the sleepy little town of Yarram, away up in Gippsland [140 miles east of Melbourne]. No bones broken – just a shake.

On 9 September 1918, McNamara was reappointed to the AFC with the rank of captain, and was in command of the aerial reconnaissance unit based in South Gippsland, east of Melbourne. On the first day of January 1919 the secretary of state for the colonies, writing from Downing Street, Whitehall, to the governor-general of Australia, advised that the Victoria Cross awarded to Lieutenant F.H. McNamara had been forwarded to the Administrative HQ of the AIF in London 'for transmission to Australia in order that it may be formally presented on His Majesty's behalf, and I have to request that you will be good enough to arrange for its presentation accordingly'. This letter was 'signed' with a rubber stamp, L.S. AMERY. In later correspondence the governor-general suggested to the Department of Defence that the presentation 'should be postponed until the arrival of H.R.H. The Prince of Wales', who was scheduled to visit Australia and New Zealand the following year.

Consequently on 27 September 1920, at Federal Government House, Melbourne, the Prince of Wales invested Captain Frank McNamara with his Victoria Cross, over three years since the citation had been published in the *London Gazette*.

On the inauguration of the Royal Australian Air Force in March 1921 McNamara was given a permanent commission with the rank of flight lieutenant and for a time was working on the staff at RAAF HQ. During the following years McNamara held a number of posts, most of these linked with the establishment of the new service. Occasionally his duties brought him to England with postings to the RAF's No. 5 Flying Training School and the Air Ministry.

In 1924 he married Hélène Bluntschli, a Belgian national who had been born in Egypt where her Swiss father worked. Frank McNamara had originally met his future wife in Heliopolis, Egypt, in September 1916. In due course, they had two children, Robert and Anne.

He was promoted to group captain in 1936, and received a CBE on 1 January 1938. He became an Air Commodore in May 1940. On 25 August the King's brother, the Duke of Kent, was killed in a flying accident when the Sunderland flying boat in which he was a passenger crashed in the Scottish Highlands. On the 29th, the six pallbearers at his funeral at St Georges's Chapel, Windsor, comprised two air marshals and four vice-marshals, including Frank McNamara VC.

McNamara served with the RAF throughout the Second World War and became AOC British Forces, Aden in 1942, from which post he returned to England in March 1945. The year 1945 was a traumatic one for McNamara, for although he was made a Companion of the Order of the Bath (CB) in the New Year Honours list, later in the month he received news that a younger brother, Maurice, serving with the RAAF, had been posted missing following a bombing raid on Germany. Later in the year it was confirmed that 429719 Flight Sergeant Maurice McNamara, RAAF, had died on 14 January. He is buried in Choloy War Cemetery (II.D.2.), 20 miles west of Nancy, Meuthe-et-Moselle, France. McNamara's good friend Peter Drummond, who had helped in keeping back Turkish horsemen in the VC-winning desert rescue of 1917, was lost when his plane, a B-24 Liberator, did not arrive in Canada, having gone missing over the sea near the Azores. All aboard were presumed to have died. Sadly, Frank McNamara had to break this news to Drummond's widow. Also in this year a new appointment at the Ministry of Defence had to be delayed, as the hot and dusty conditions in Aden had adversely affected his health.

After the war ended McNamara, among many other senior officers, was retired from the RAAF, discharged on 11 July 1946, officially 'to make way for the advancement of younger and equally capable officers'. In May the British Government offered him the post of senior education control officer in Westphalia, Germany, and later deputy director of education with the British Occupation Forces. This work was completed by October 1947 when he joined the National Coal Board until his retirement in 1959.

Frank McNamara died of heart failure following a fall in his garden at Gerrards Cross, Buckinghamshire, on 2 November 1961. His funeral took place on 6 November at St Joseph's Priory, Gerrards Cross, and was very well attended including by many representatives of the RAF, RAAF and the USAF. He was survived by his wife and their two children.

His headstone, which records the achievement of being 'The first and only Australian Air VC of the First Great World War' also bears the name of his wife, Hélène Marcelle Emma, who survived him by over thirty years, 'happily reunited' with him on 12 February 1996.

McNamara insisted that his Victoria Cross should not go to Australia after his death. Consequently this and his other awards, together with his full dress uniform, were donated by his family to the Royal Air Force Museum in Hendon, London. He had been disappointed over his treatment by the Australian Government when he was dismissed from the RAAF and with what has been described as a 'meagre severance'.

His full medal entitlement is: VC, CB, CBE, BWM (1914–20), Victory Medal (1914–19), 1939–45 Star, Africa Star, Defence Medal (1939–45), War Medal (1939–45), King George V Silver Jubilee Medal (1935), King George VI Coronation Medal (1937), Queen Elizabeth II Coronation Medal (1953).

A display and a painting by Septimus Power, depicting the dramatic escape of the two pilots, is in the Australian War Memorial collection at Canberra. The Frank McNamara VC Club at Oakey Arms Aviation Centre, Queensland, Australia is named after him, as is a leisure park in Shepparton, Victoria. His name appears, with other recipients of the Victoria Cross in the RFC-RNAS-RAF, on the walls of St Clement Danes Church (left of the altar), the Strand, Central London.

One of the eleven Victoria Cross holders to die in 1961, Frank McNamara has been described by one of his contemporaries as 'quiet, scholarly, loyal and beloved by all'.

A. BALL

France, 25 April to 6 May 1917

On 7 April 1917 at 11 a.m., the thirteen SE5 aircraft of No. 56 Squadron RFC took off from London Colney airfield and flew to the RFC Depot at St Omer, France. Shortly afterwards the squadron took off again and flew to its base airfield, Vert-Galand, close to the Amiens–Doullens road, 11 miles north of Amiens where they were part of No. 9 Wing, RFC. The airfield was shared with the Spad S7 aircraft of No. 19 Squadron and No. 66 Squadron with its Sopwith Pups, and in the impending Battle of Arras, No. 9 Wing was responsible for air cover on the right flank of this Allied offensive. These fighter squadrons were to patrol an area centred on Cambrai which extended to le Cateau–Busigny–Solesmes–Denain.

The flight commander of No. 56 Squadron's A Flight was T/Captain Albert Ball DSO and 2 Bars and MC, who had over thirty victories to his credit. He was already a household name having established himself as the leading fighter pilot in the RFC by September of the previous year during the Battle of the Somme. Ball accepted his praise and awards with genuine modesty although his letters home reflected the real pleasure he felt at receiving his 'prizes'. Although not a particularly social person he was not rude and had individual traits such as flying wearing neither helmet nor goggles. His sole objective was to shoot down as many 'Huns' as he could, but Ball admitted that, 'I only scrap with them because it is my duty ... it is either them or me.'

Ball had returned to England early in October on a home posting as it was felt by senior RFC commanders that he needed a rest and that it would be only a short time before his fearless style of aerial combat would lead to his demise. Ball considered the undemanding postings in

England a waste of his abilities and had constantly agitated for a return to a fighting unit.

Since an earlier test flight of the SE5, Ball had volubly expressed his dislike of the aircraft in his letters home and had expressed his desire to again fly a Nieuport Scout. Consequently his father had exerted pressure wherever possible and in particular with Major-General Hugh Trenchard, GOC, RFC, to achieve this. Ball was able to write that he 'had tea at the General's house today ...' and consequently Nieuport 17 B1522 was delivered to Vert-Galand on 13 April.

Although most of the pilots had been hand-picked by the squadron commander Major Richard Blomfield, many lacked combat experience and, allied to their unfamiliarity with the SE5, No. 56 Squadron was instructed to fly no operational patrols for two weeks. During this period Blomfield arranged for many modifications to be made to the SE5s similar to those made to his own machine by Ball.

On the day after the arrival of his Nieuport, Ball took the aircraft up on a two-hour 'practice flight', but in a letter to his fiancée, Flora, dated 14 April, he wrote, 'I had my first two fights this morning.' This combat is not in the squadron records, but another pilot, Arthur Rhys Davids, comments on this flight in a letter of the same date, also that Ball was going up alone again that evening.

No. 56 Squadron began operational flying on 22 April and on the previous day Ball was recorded as flying a 'test flight' in his Nieuport, but he told Flora that he had flown near St Omer and engaged two Albatros scouts which 'cleared off'. At 10.18 a.m. on the 22nd, Ball, flying SE5 A4850, led A Flight towards the front lines with orders to fly high and not to cross the front line. At 11,000ft Ball spotted an Albatros two-seater over Adinfer Wood at which he fired from 150yd, but caused no apparent damage.

He took off at 6 a.m. the following day in his Nieuport and less than an hour later attacked two Albatros CIII machines over Cambrai. The first aircraft turned away eastwards but Ball fired into the second which crashed near the Tilloy-Abancourt road. Shortly after, in an engagement with another Albatros south-east of Arras, its gunfire badly damaged Ball's aircraft in a number of places. As this machine was now out of action for a few days, Ball flew SE5 A4850 on his next lone patrol two hours later and attacked an Albatros two-seater, but his Lewis gun jammed after five rounds. Ball landed at Filescamp Farm where the gun was repaired and he took off, flew towards Cambrai and attacked a formation of five pale green Albatros Scouts over Selvigny and shot one down in flames. He later attacked an enemy two-seater, which fell away and landed north of Cambrai.

It was two days before Ball increased his number of victories. When flying A4850 on a lone evening patrol he accounted for two Albatroses, but with widespread bullet damage to his own machine. On 28 April Ball led three of his flight on patrol and claimed a further two victories although his SE5 was very badly damaged by shellfire. The first four days of May brought him five more victims and two days later, on 6 May, Ball shot down an Albatros of *Jasta 20* near Sancourt. It was in early May that Ball met up with William Bishop and the two men discussed Ball's proposal to carry out a two-aircraft attack on a German airfield.

The following morning, 7 May, Ball was part of an escort for nine aircraft of No. 70 Squadron on a photographic reconnaissance flight. Later, at 5.30 p.m. flying SE A4855, he led a fighting patrol of eleven SE5 scouts towards Cambrai where formations of enemy aircraft had been reported. In less than an hour they were in action with the red Albatros DIIIs of *Jasta 11*, part of von Richthofen's flying circus, led on this occasion by his brother Lothar. Dog fights developed over a large area, with casualties on both sides, and continued until nearly dark. Ball was last seen chasing and firing at a red Albatros as both aircraft disappeared into a large cloud. A German pilot, Wilhelm Allmenroeder, later claimed to have seen the two aircraft and described Lothar von Richthofen in action against a British machine which 'dived down to the ground'. This witness did not see the British plane crash as he was more concerned with the fate of von Richthofen who had dived away steeply at the same time. Evidently the German's machine had incurred engine damage and made a forced landing.

Leutnant Franz Hailer of *Flieger-Abteilung* A.292 described how, through binoculars, he saw Ball's SE5 emerge from low cloud, upside down with its propeller stopped and trailing black smoke. The aircraft then vanished from his sight behind trees and crashed close to Fashoda, a ruined farmhouse, a little over a mile from the village of Annoeullin, 6 miles east of la Bassée. When Hailer and his three companions arrived at the crashed machine they found that Ball had been lifted from the wreckage and laid nearby by a local French girl. Apparently Ball was still alive when she reached the crash, but died moments later. Hailer was able to identify the British airman by personal items on the body and a later medical examination confirmed that Ball's death was caused by the crash. Later, however, the credit for the victory over Ball was officially given to Lothar von Richthofen by the German authorities. This is very questionable as he, and other witnesses found to corroborate this victory, claim it was a British tri-plane which von Richthofen attacked. RNAS triplanes were in action nearby, but no losses were recorded. A possible scenario is that Ball became disorientated in the cloud and was too low to correct the alignment of his aircraft, which may also have been damaged, when he emerged.

Two days later, on 9 May, Ball was buried by the enemy and given a military funeral with honours in Annoeullin Communal Cemetery, German Extension, Grave 643. The funeral was attended by representatives from a number of German military units, some British POWs and many local French inhabitants.

Meanwhile, at Vert-Galand airfield, five aircraft from the sortie had landed by 8.30 p.m. on 7 May and confirmation was later received that two more pilots were down safe within Allied lines. Of the remaining pilots, two were wounded and treated in hospitals, but of Ball and Lieutenant R. Chaworth-Musters there was no news.

Five days later on 12 May, not having received any definite information, Major Blomfield was authorised to drop messages behind the enemy lines requesting news of both Ball and Chaworth-Musters, but it was not until three weeks after his death that the German authorities confirmed Ball's death and burial. This information was quickly sent via the War Office to the MP for Nottingham who broke the sad tidings to Ball's family. The Germans also reported that Lieutenant Chaworth-Musters had been shot down and killed by Verner Voss, a notable enemy pilot.

The supplement to the *London Gazette* of 8 June 1917 carried the posthumous VC citation and on the same day Ball was made a Chevalier of the Légion d'Honneur:

LT. (TEMP. CAPT.) ALBERT BALL, D.S.O., M.C., LATE NOTTS. AND DERBY. R., AND R.F.C.

For most conspicuous and consistent bravery from the 25th of April to the 6th of May, 1917, during which period Capt. Ball took part in twenty-six combats in the air and destroyed eleven hostile aeroplanes, drove down two out of control, and forced several others to land.

In these combats Capt. Ball, flying alone, on one occasion fought six hostile machines, twice he fought five and once four. When leading two other British aeroplanes he attacked an enemy formation of eight. On each of these occasions he brought down at least one enemy.

Several times his aeroplane was badly damaged, once so seriously that but for the most delicate handling his machine would have collapsed, as nearly all the control wires had been shot away. On returning with a damaged machine he had always to be restrained from immediately going out on another.

In all, Capt. Ball has destroyed forty-three German aeroplanes and one balloon, and has always displayed most exceptional courage, determination and skill.

On 10 June, crowds waited in Nottingham city centre to pay their last respects to the young airman born in Nottinghamshire as a large procession passed through on its way to a memorial service in St Mary's Church. Representatives of many local and national organisations together with senior military figures, as well as Ball's father, brother and sister, were present at the service, but his mother was too grief-stricken to attend.

Nottingham City Council agreed to open a fund for the purpose of erecting a memorial to Ball and subscriptions quickly came in from all walks of life. In the following month, at 4 King Edward's Road, Hackney, East London, the Eccentric Club Hostel for disabled ex-servicemen was opened and dedicated to Albert Ball.

The family had yet further reason for concern when Ball's brother Cyril was shot down on 5 February 1918 when flying an SE5a of No. 60 Squadron, and it was some time before news was received that he had been made a prisoner of war.

❖❖❖

Albert Ball was born on 14 August 1896 to Albert and Harriett Mary (née Page) at 32 Lenton Boulevard (now Castle Boulevard), Nottingham. He had an older sister Lois Beatrice, born in 1892, and Arthur Cyril, his brother, was two years his junior. The first-born daughter, Hilda, had not survived infancy. Albert Senior was a master plumber by trade and by the end of 1899 was a Nottingham city councillor and an estate agent and property dealer.

The family moved a number of times and finally settled at Sedgley House, 43 Lenton Road, Nottingham. The young Albert had a wooden hut in the extensive gardens of this house where he conducted experiments with Morse radio equipment and electrical items in addition to stripping and repairing various engines. His father taught him to handle firearms and he became a first-class shot. The Ball family had strong religious beliefs, which Albert Junior shared. He always tried hard to please his family and when away from home he kept in regular contact by letter.

Albert and his brother Cyril were educated at Lenton Church School and later as boarders at Grantham Grammar School before gaining places at Nottingham High School in September 1907. They enrolled at Trent College, Long Eaton, in January 1911, where strict discipline was enforced and a strong emphasis made on ideals such as a sense of duty. Albert did not achieve good academic results but much involved himself with such diverse interests as playing the violin, photography, technical machine drawing, carpentry and electric boat building, in all of which he was quite accomplished. In the summer of 1913 the 17-year-old Ball, then 5ft 6in tall, began work at Universal Engineering Works near his home in Castle Boulevard, Nottingham, with moral and financial support from his father.

Following the declaration of war a year later, Ball volunteered for military service at a recruiting meeting addressed by the Duke of Portland and the Mayor of Nottingham, Ball's uncle Frederick, and had put his name forward before the speeches. Consequently it was announced at the meeting that the son of a prominent citizen had already joined up. He was enlisted in the 7th (Robin Hood) Battalion, Sherwood Foresters (Nottinghamshire and Derbyshire Regiment), TF, on 21 September 1914, and posted to 1st Platoon, A Company. Within a few days he was promoted to sergeant, and on 28 October commissioned second lieutenant.

Ball was impatient to see action and to this end he requested a transfer and was seconded to the North Midlands Division Cyclist Company on 1 January of the following year. Unfortunately his new unit remained in England and was sent to Bishop's Stortford, Hertfordshire and then, in early March, to Luton, Bedfordshire. Ball had inherited his father's business acumen and he did many 'deals' with his comrades including the sale of motorcycles and cars. He much preferred living on his own and obtained permission to lodge in Hightown Road, Luton.

In June, Ball was sent to Perivale, Middlesex, on an officers' training course. He was about 4 miles from Hendon aerodrome which meant Ball could take flying lessons there at the Ruffy-Bauman School, and he drove there on his motorcycle for lessons just after dawn. Ball was still taking flying lessons in August when he returned to his unit at Shefford's Farm, St Alban's, Hertfordshire, and he often returned to Hendon for further instruction in the evenings. The inherent dangers in learning to fly these early aircraft was highlighted when he wrote that his flying was 'going on fine' and later describing, with almost brutal detachment, the death of a fellow trainee in an accident.

Eventually Ball received his Royal Aero Club Certificate, No. 1898, on 15 October 1915. (This certificate, incorrectly, gives his date of birth as 21 August 1896.) A little over a week later, Ball was seconded to the RFC and posted to No. 9 Reserve Squadron at Mousehold Heath, Norwich, Norfolk. His initial billet was the Royal Hotel, Norwich, but as he much preferred his own company, Ball obtained permission to stay in a private house and after finding a Riverside Road address not to his liking he moved to 68 Thorpe Road.

In early November, Ball turned down the chance of a posting to France where he would have been an observer in a Vickers FB5, as he reasoned that the £75 spent on his flying lessons would have been wasted if he gave up pilot training. He was posted to the Central Flying School, Upavon, Wiltshire on 19 December and a few weeks later sent a telegram to his father: 'Got Wings plus three days leave. Please wire £10.' On 29 January 1916 he was posted to No. 22 Squadron, stationed at Fort Rowner, Gosport, Hampshire as an instructor before embarking for France on 17 February.

Ball reported for duty at the RFC Depot, St Omer, the following day and was posted to No. 13 Squadron, stationed at Marieux, 20 miles north of Amiens. The squadron was equipped with two-seater BE2c and BE2d aircraft and was mainly employed on reconnaissance and artillery spotting duties. Two days later he took up BE2c 4352 for a short familiarisation flight and the next day flew on an artillery observation patrol.

By the end of February Ball had flown BE4352 on five varied operational sorties and in early March, when 5 miles behind the enemy front line, he was attacked by a Fokker, but managed to return safely. The squadron moved to Savy Aubigny, 9 miles north-west of Arras, on 19 March, and the next day Ball and his observer Second Lieutenant S.A. Villiers survived a bad crash when BE4352 suffered engine failure immediately after take-off and was wrecked. Fortunately the two airmen escaped serious injury. A week later Ball was on patrol in BE2c 4200 when the engine was damaged by anti-aircraft fire and he was forced to crash-land near Aubigny, but again, neither he nor his observer was injured.

On 30 March, Ball, accompanied by Villiers in BE2c 4200, was in action with two enemy Aviatiks between Vimy and Givenchy and the following day, he exchanged fire with an Albatros two-seater above Gavrelle resulting in minor damage to his aircraft. Less than two weeks later, on 10 April, Ball and Villiers were returning after escort duties when they saw and attacked an enemy observation balloon and forced the ground crew to quickly haul it down.

Although Ball was flying the BE2c aggressively whenever he could, he was under no illusions about its capabilities and recorded that 'the BE2c is not a fighting machine'.

During the few weeks he had been on operational duty, Ball had regularly flown patrols through heavy anti-aircraft fire and survived crash landings and attacks by enemy aircraft, all of which had affected the highly strung young man. Consequently when he wrote home at the end of March he asked his father, 'Please tell Cyril that perhaps he had better stick to his regiment. I like this job, but nerves do not last long, and you soon want a rest.' (His brother had enlisted in the Sherwood Foresters and intended to transfer into the RFC.)

On 29 April Ball and Villiers were on an artillery shoot in Be2c 4070 when they were attacked by an Albatros CIII two-seater. After only a few shots from Villiers at point-blank range, the enemy observer/gunner slumped in his cockpit and the Albatros dived down to safety near Rouvroy. That same day Ball had his first flight in the squadron's Bristol Scout No. 5316 and later flew it over the front lines, where he was impressed by the light controls, agility and speed of this machine.

On 7 May, after over forty operational patrols with No. 13 Squadron, Ball was posted to No. 11 Squadron, based at the same airfield, and reported to the adjutant, Lieutenant A.J. Insall, who later wrote in his autobiography that Ball had 'more self-assurance than his experience justified'. Ball constructed a wooden hut close to the Bessoneau hangar and made a productive garden there where he could relax after sorties. He slept in the hut ready for a quick take-off and, as his hangar was some distance from the squadron mess, he often ate there too.

On 16 May when flying a Bristol Scout at 13,000ft over Givenchy, Ball spotted an Albatros two-seater below him. He dived and chased this aircraft towards Beaumont, then attacked and wounded the observer. The Albatros then made a forced landing. Less than a week later, on 22 May, Ball attacked and drove down an enemy two-seater near Moyenville and later an LVG two-seater suffered the same fate. On patrol in Nieuport 5173, he attacked an LVG two-seater over Moyenville on 29 May and fired half a drum at the enemy machine which then dived away vertically. Later on the same patrol Ball waited high above another LVG until its escort of two Fokkers departed before he attacked and fired at 50yd range. The LVG dived and force-landed but not before the enemy gunner had hit the Nieuport, which also incurred further damage from anti-aircraft fire during the return flight.

Ball flew the Nieuport over a German airfield at Douai on 1 June and circled at 10,000ft for half an hour before two enemy aircraft, an Albatros CIII and a Fokker Scout, took off to attack him. He attacked the Albatros but after he had only fired a few shots this two-seater dived back to its airfield. Meanwhile the Fokker attempted an attack, but Ball manoeuvred and fired at the enemy machine which dived and landed in a field 2 miles from the airfield.

Ball was given almost two weeks' home leave and returned to France on 23 June. Two days later an aircraft attack was ordered against fifteen kite balloons in an attempt to limit enemy observation. Flying in Nieuport 5173 Ball attacked an enemy observation balloon with phosphor bombs but failed to destroy it. He returned later that day in Nieuport A134 and while under very heavy and accurate anti-aircraft fire destroyed the balloon with Le Prieur rockets, but his engine was hit and he was forced to fly back to base at a very low height. For this attack, as well as his actions over the preceding weeks, Ball was awarded the Military Cross (gazetted on 27 July 1916).

The Battle of the Somme began on the morning of 1 July with the squadron fully engaged, and Ball wrote home, 'I'm OK but oh so fagged ... Things are on full steam just now, 2.30am to 9.30pm.' On this day the squadron commander, Major T. O'Brien Hubbard, presented Ball with some MC ribbon to sew on his tunic. The following afternoon, flying in Nieuport A134 with other British aircraft, he attacked a formation of six Roland CIII machines, of which one was shot down by an FE and crashed near the Arras-Mercatel road while Ball fired at another which crashed near its companion.

Thirty minutes later Ball attacked an enemy two-seater over Lens when he dived under the enemy aircraft, lowered the Lewis gun on its rail and fired into the underside of the Aviatik which fell and crashed in pieces. This was the first occasion he had employed such an attack method. The next day, 3 July, Ball attacked a kite balloon at Pelves with Le Prieur rockets, which missed, and then fired with Buckingham incendiary bullets from 15yd which hit, but the balloon did not ignite.

Heavy rain showers began on 4 July. Consequently only local test flying was possible, so Ball spent the time making adjustments to his aircraft including some to the Lewis gun rail which had been adapted by Sergeant R.G. Foster of No. 11 Squadron and named after him. This modification allowed the pilot to lower his gun from above the upper wing for insertion of ammunition drums and also to fire it vertically, which Ball now did to great effect.

The RFC flew as many missions as the weather allowed in support of the ground offensive, and on 5 July Ball had twelve sorties from early morning onwards. The stress of almost continuous combat flying, together with the frequent casualties occurring to his colleagues, began to take its toll on him and on 16 July he asked Major Hubbard if he might have a 'brief rest' from flying. The next day he was posted to No. 8 Squadron at la Bellevue airfield, 9 miles east of Doullens, who flew the slow and vulnerable BE2c. Ball regarded this move as a 'retrograde' step for him. However, as he became involved with the regular formation patrols, this did much to calm his nerves, as did the shorter flying hours.

A task for which Ball later volunteered was the night landing of an Allied agent behind enemy lines. This had twice been attempted but mist had prevented a landing. After brief night flying practice Ball in BE2c 4138, with 'M. Victor' in the observer's seat, left la Bellevue airfield at 8.15 p.m. on 28 July. Ball evaded three enemy aircraft which attempted an attack when he crossed the front lines, but later the BE2c was subjected to very heavy anti-aircraft fire which fortunately caused no serious damage. After dark he set the plane down in the designated field, but the agent refused to get out, and despite making further landings his passenger still refused to disembark. Consequently Ball returned to base and landed just before 10 p.m. The consequences of this mission were that he received congratulatory messages from the RFC commander Major-General Hugh Trenchard, but more importantly for Ball, assurance that he would return to No. 11 Squadron after he had completed a month with No. 8 Squadron.

By 8 August Ball had taken part in more than ten bombing raids and artillery shoots with No. 8 Squadron and the next day, with his flight commander Captain G.A. Parker, he attacked two observation balloons. On 12 August he flew his last sortie with No. 8 Squadron in a successful bombing raid on Beugny. On the return flight he attacked and forced down an Albatros two-seater. Two days later, on his twentieth birthday, he returned to No. 11 Squadron at Savy Aubigny where a new Nieuport Scout 16, A201, awaited him.

On 16 August, Ball spotted four enemy aircraft escorted by a Roland CII over St Leger. He exchanged fire with the Roland, which eventually made a forced landing. Ball then used all his remaining ammunition in attacks on the remaining enemy machines, two of which he forced to dive down to safety.

Ball flew eight sorties on 21 August with no close enemy contact. However, in the early evening of the following day near Warlencourt, he dived and attacked a formation of seven enemy machines. He approached from their rear and fired at the last Roland at very close range and this aircraft fell vertically and crashed west of Bapaume. Ball climbed back upwards, and spotting five further Rolands flying over Vaux, he again came up under the rearmost aircraft, and fired a complete drum of ammunition vertically into the fuselage. He replaced the drum and again fired into the aircraft from below and the Roland turned and dropped down, issuing flames and smoke. Ball was then attacked by three of the other enemy machines but flew to the same height as one of his attackers and again at a few yards' range, fired into this two-seater. He wounded the gunner and this aircraft also fell, out of control, and crashed in a village.

Ball managed to land at a British airfield where he was re-armed, and he then attacked three more Rolands over Vaux and forced them to return eastwards; his plane was hit in a number of places and he also ran out of fuel, but achieved a landing near Senlis. He sent a message to his airfield for a maintenance crew who refuelled and repaired his aircraft during the night while Ball slept nearby. This was his last action with No. 11 Squadron and on his return to base at 8.30 the next morning he learned that he was to join No. 60 Squadron the following day.

No. 60 Squadron was based at the large airfield at Filescamp Farm, Izel-lès-Hameau, 10 miles west of Arras where it had recently moved from St André-aux-Bois. The squadron was equipped with Nieuport Scouts and Ball took Nieuport A201 with him and was allotted to A Flight with permission to patrol independently. Two days after his arrival he attacked a formation of Roland CII machines over the Cambrai-Bapaume road and forced down two out of control and a third which crashed. Ball patrolled alone for most of the following two days with no enemy contact, and it was not until 28 August that he was again in action. South-east of Bapaume he manoeuvred unseen beneath one of two Roland CIIs and fired over 100 rounds into its underside, which killed the pilot, but the observer managed to land the aircraft near Transloy. Later in the evening, near Loupart Wood, he forced down an enemy two-seater near Grevillers and another near Beugny and later shot down a Roland which crashed near Ayette.

In late August, when his squadron commander requested a list of actions from him, Ball reckoned he had been in eighty-four combats. When he related the figures to his sister, he wrote, 'So it is not so bad, and I have done my best.'

During the early evening of 31 August Ball spotted twelve Rolands forming up over their own airfield near Cambrai. He dived and scattered the formation, he then manoeuvred under one machine and fired a burst of fifty rounds into it from 15yd. This Roland spun down and crashed south-east of Cambrai. Ball flew amongst the other scattered aircraft and fired at whichever target presented itself, and at least one more enemy aircraft went down south-east of Bapaume. Ball's Nieuport was hit in several places and one burst of fire cut his ignition leads. He was also out of ammunition, but managed to glide his Nieuport across the front lines through enemy ground fire before a landing at Colincamps. He was exhausted and slept by his machine and did not return to Filescamp Farm until the following morning.

Ball was greeted at his home airfield with the news that he had been awarded the DSO (gazetted on 26 September) for his actions on 22 August. Later that day the squadron moved to Savy Aubigny and that evening Ball was given a leave warrant, to begin the next day.

Brigadier-General J.F.A. Higgins, commander of 3rd Brigade RFC, issued an official summary of Ball's fighting record to date:

> Lieutenant Ball has had more than 25 combats since 16th May in a single-seater scout. Of these 13 have been against more than one hostile machine. In particular, on 22nd August he attacked in succession formations of 7 and 5 machines in the same flight, on the 28th August, 4 and 10 in succession, on the 31st August, twelve. He has forced 20 German machines to land, of which 8 have been destroyed, one seen to be descending vertically with flames coming out of the fuselage, and 8 have been wrecked on the ground. During this period he has forced two hostile balloons down and destroyed one.

There was little opportunity for Ball to relax during his leave in Nottingham as accounts of his exploits appeared in newspapers following the award of his MC. As a result he was the centre of attraction wherever he went.

Ball returned to France on 11 September and was made commander of A Flight. Two days later he received a telegram advising him of the award of a Bar to his DSO for his actions on 31 August (also gazetted on 26 September). Two days later he was notified of the Russian Order of St George (not gazetted until 16 February 1917) and was officially awarded this decoration on 24 September.

The balance of power in the air war had shifted against the Allies with the formation of German fighter squadrons, *Jastas*, equipped with the latest single-seat scouts, and by late September these aircraft were taking a heavy toll of British machines. The Albatros DI biplane, with its two fixed machine guns firing through the propeller arc, was now the most heavily armed fighter on the Western Front.

Whenever possible, Ball flew solo patrols in his Nieuport, now fitted with a bright red nose cone, or spinner, which was soon recognised by the Germans, as recounted by a fellow pilot who flew this machine while Ball was on leave, stating, 'I couldn't get near a Hun! As soon as they saw the red spinner they dived away east.'

In an attempt to prevent the Germans from observing preparations for the forthcoming use of tanks during the Battle of the Somme, an all-out effort to destroy enemy observation balloons was ordered by Major General Trenchard. Eight of these were in No. 60 Squadron's sector, and on 15 September, Ball and Second Lieutenant A.M. Walters, both flying Nieuports armed with Le Prieur rockets, took off on their particular mission. Unfortunately their target balloons had been winched down before the pilots' arrival, so the Nieuports climbed and later spotted enemy aircraft below them, north-east of Bapaume. Ball dived at one and fired his rockets, but these missed, so he then fired half a drum from his Lewis gun from 50yd, hitting the tail section of the enemy aircraft which spun down and crashed east of Beugny. Meanwhile Walters hit an LVG two-seater with his rockets, which then caught fire and crashed near Bapaume.

On a later patrol in Nieuport A212, Ball attacked an Albatros two-seater over Bapaume and injured the pilot, but when he pulled the Lewis gun down for reloading it hit his head and he was temporarily stunned. When he recovered, the Albatros had flown down to land. Two hours later, in Nieuport A201, again armed with rockets, Ball was flying in another attempt to destroy enemy observation balloons. He spotted three Rolands over Bapaume, dived and fired his rockets at them, which broke up the formation. Ball then manoeuvred under one aircraft and fired a complete drum of ammunition, which wounded both of the crew. This machine fell out of control to crash east of Bertincourt.

From the beginning of September, Ball was involved in at least twenty-four combats and in his final action on 1 October he claimed three more victories. He was notified of leave followed by a home posting and two days later was congratulated by Brigadier-General Higgins and then given lunch by his Wing Commander. Ball gave his gramophone and records to his ground crew, and that evening he received a traditional send-off in the mess.

Ball arrived at Nottingham railway station on 5 October where he was collected by his sister Lois, and the smiling airman was photographed being driven by her to the family home, Sedgley House, in an open top car. Outside the house he was mobbed by the press and Albert Ball Senior had arranged for a local photographer, Charles Shaw, to visit Sedgley House where he took many images which later appeared in publications worldwide. Any hopes Ball might have cherished of a restful leave were quickly dispelled as, in addition to constant attention from well-wishers, he was pressed into attending several formal functions. However, he made time to visit the families of a number of airmen and officers he had served with in France, as he knew from personal experience the importance of such visits.

During this home leave Ball visited the Austin Motor Company and had discussions with them concerning his ideas for the design of a fighter aircraft which eventually led to the War Office approving the construction of a prototype of 'The Austin Ball Scout'.

On 18 October Ball reported for duty at Orfordness, Suffolk, where he was posted as a fighting instructor to No. 34 (Reserve) Squadron.

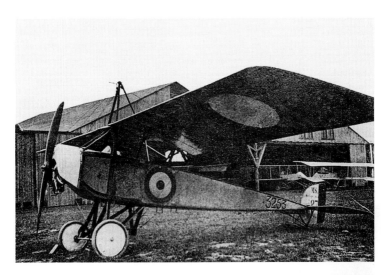

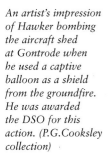

Morane 'L' 3253 at St Pol (JMB/GSL collection)

An artist's impression of Hawker bombing the aircraft shed at Gontrode when he used a captive balloon as a shield from the groundfire. He was awarded the DSO for this action. (P.G.Cooksley collection)

The Bristol 'C' Scout 1611 used by Lanoe Hawker in the action of 25 July 1915, for which he was awarded the Victoria Cross. Its obliquely mounted Lewis gun is clearly seen. (Lt.Col. T.M. Hawker)

Manfred von Richtofen collected souvenirs of those he had vanquished in combat. To the right of the roundel is a rectangle of fabric bearing the serial number 5964 – that of the DH2 in which Lanoe Hawker died. (Bruce Robertson collection)

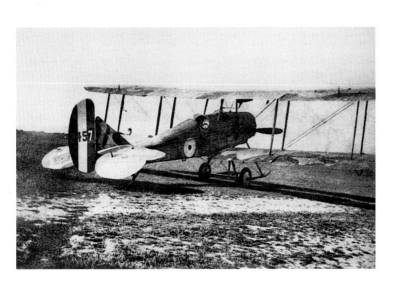

The RE5 2457 in which, with Second Lieutenant R.H. Peck, Captain Liddell participated in the action which was to earn him a Victoria Cross. (Lt. Col Sir Piers Bengough

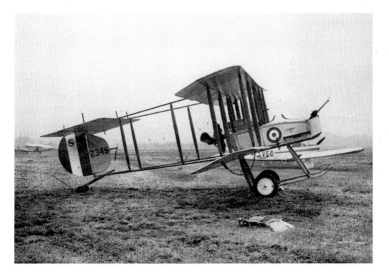

A modern replica 'Gun Bus', or Vickers FB5 (I.J. Dickson)

An artists impression of the action against the submarine station at Zeebrugge by Squadron Commander Richard Bell-Davies, accompanied by observer Flt. Lt. C.H. Butler, for which Bell Davies was awarded the DSO. The artist has erroneously included two RNAS machines in the attack. (P.G. Cooksley collection)

An artist's impression of Bell-Davies' rescue of Lt. Smiley. (P.G. Cooksley collection)

Home Defence pilots in jubilant mood. Left to right: Lieutenants W.J. Tempest, F. Sowery, and C.C. Dunston, Caprain R.S. Stammers, Lieutenant W.L. Robinson and Major A.H. Morton. In the background is the BE2c used by Robinson to bring down the SL.11. (Bruce Robertson collection.)

Base of the memorial obelisk at Cuffley, which was completely restored on the seventieth anniversary of Robinson's feat and rededicated in September 1986. Sadly, the bronze RFC wings were stolen in the early 1990s, but have been replaced with a black marble slab. (B.J. Grey)

T/Captain W.A. Bishop photographed in his Nieuport scout aircraft B1566 early in 1917, while serving with No. 60 Squadron RFC. (Bruce Robertson collection)

Opposite top: *Mottershead proudly displays his new pilot's brevet with his hand on the airscrew of a BE2c. (Cheshire County Council).*

Opposite bottom: *McNamara is on the far left of this group No. 1 Squadron's C Flight, photographed at Kantara in late 1916 or early 1917. They are in front of a Martinsyde G100 with the CO, Captain R. Williams in the centre while McNamara's friend, Lt. E.G. Roberts, is on the right in his forage cap. (Australian War Memorial P05340)*

The Christmas card of No. 60 Squadron RFC was designed by Roderic Hill, Commander of A Flight. The colour original showed Ball's original Nieuport scout 5173 with a red spinner in the foreground. (P.G. Cooksley collection)

Ball, centre, with Ross Hulme and Parker stand in the entrance of a Bessoneau hangar of No. 8 Squadron, sheltering BE2d 5779 within. (JMB/GAL collection)

Albert Ball's memorial in Nottingham. (B.J. Grey)

Jerrard in the cockpit of SPAD S.VII A8825, constructed by the Air Navigation Company at Scampton, Lincolnshire. He was seriously injured on 5 August 1917 while flying a similar machine. (JMB/GSL collection

McCudden in the cockpit of (probably) the Bristol M1C at Turnberry (JMB/GSL collection)

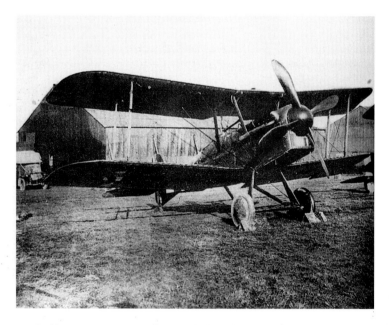

McCudden's SE5a, B4891, fitted with the red spinner from an LVG CV. (Bruce Robertson collection)

West (right) and his observer in front of Armstrong Whitworth FK8, C8594, which was used in the action for which he was awarded the VC. (JMB/GSL collection)

A heavily clad Barker, far left, in front of Sopwith F1 Camel B6313. (JMB/ GSL collection)

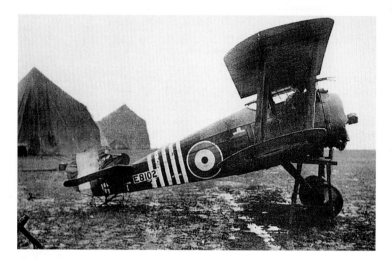

The Sopwith 7F1 Snipe E8102 flown by Major W.G. Barker during the action which won him the VC. The damage caused by turning over on landing is evident. (JMB/GSL collection)

Lt-Col. W.G. Barker adjusts the sling for his right arm before a flight, while in the centre, Edward, Prince of Wales, dons a flying helmet. A two-seater Sopwith Dove stands in the background and Thomas Sopwith looks on. (Bruce Robertson collection)

The diminutive figure of Beauchamp-Proctor is dominated by his colleagues, including, on his left, Joseph E. Boudwin who himself was only 5ft 4in tall. (JMB/GSL collection)

Mannock in the cockpit of a No. 40 Squadron Nieuport scout. (JMB/GSL collection)

Mannock in the cockpit of an SE5 of No. 74 Squadron. The photograph is identified as, 'Taken at London Colney, England, just before the Sqn flew to France.' (Keith Caldwell via Bruce Robertson)

Memorial Plaque to Grp Gapten Lionel B. Rees VC at Porth yr Aur, Caernarfon. (W.Alister Williams)

Warneford wearing his Cross of the Légion d'Honneur, outside the Ritz Hotel, Paris. (Fleet Air Arm Museum)

British Air Services Memorial at St Omer (Peter Batchelor

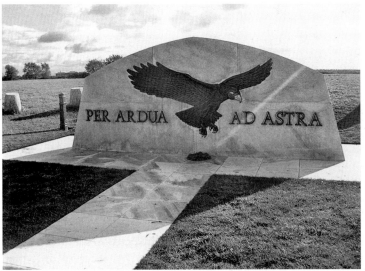

PER ARDUA AD ASTRA

Lord Trenchard, Marshal of the Royal Air Force at the unveiling of the Flying ServicesMemorial at Arras on 31 July 1932. (CWGC

The unveiling of the Flying Services Memorial to the Missing at Arras on 31 July 1932. On the right is pictured Lord Trenchard, Marshal of the Royal Air Force and to his right Sir Edwin Lutyens the architect and Major General Sir Fabian Ware founder of the Imperial War Graves Commission. Also present is Vice Admiral Richard Bell-Davies VC representing the Admiralty. (CWGC)

He found the work undemanding, but was even less impressed by his next appointment on 7 November at the RFC School of Aerial Gunnery, Hythe, as a weapons instructor. Ball considered it was a waste of his talents and experience and began a campaign to be posted to a fighting squadron again. He discovered that his requests for a posting through normal military channels were rebuffed, as were attempts to use the 'old boy network' using his father's connections.

Meanwhile Ball, accompanied by his parents, brother and sister to a Buckingham Palace investiture on 18 November, was presented by the King with the DSO, two Bars (the second Bar to his DSO was gazetted on 25 November) and the Military Cross. Less than a week later, on 24 November, Nottingham City Council passed a resolution to make Albert Ball a Freeman of the City. On 19 December, in the Albert Hall, Nottingham, at a formal civic gathering, he was presented with an illuminated address and also, as a tribute from the citizens of Lenton, an inscribed silver rose bowl.

Two weeks later Ball received another instructional posting, to No. 7 Wing RFC at King's Lynn, Norfolk. He continued agitating for an overseas posting and on 17 February he was advised of a posting to No. 56 (Training) Squadron based at London Colney, Hertfordshire and was forming up for overseas duty. He was given leave before he took up this posting and on 19 February Ball was made an Honorary Freeman of the city of Nottingham where his illuminated freedom scroll was presented to him in a silver gilt casket surmounted by a model Nieuport Scout.

Ball arrived at No. 56 Squadron on 25 February and was appointed commander of A Flight. The aircraft, SE5 single-seat scouts, began to arrive on 13 March, and Ball selected A4850 as his personal machine, which was then very extensively modified to his requirements.

On 25 March, Ball was first introduced to Flora Young, an 18-year-old living in St Albans. He took her up for a flight in an Avro 504 on their first meeting, and over the next two weeks he spent much of his spare time with her and gave her a small silver and diamond brooch in the shape of RFC wings. The squadron was mobilised on 1 April and became an RAF unit, as this was the day when the RAF was formed from the RFC and RNAS. Four days later, the Thursday before Easter, Ball became unofficially engaged to Flora and gave her his gold identity bracelet in lieu of a ring, while she gave him a small book of prayers.

The squadron left for France on 7 April 1917 and during the following four weeks Albert Ball enhanced his reputation even more before his luck finally ran out a month later.

After the Armistice, Albert Ball Senior visited his son's grave in Annoeullin Communal Cemetery and arranged for the wooden cross, erected by an RAF squadron in 1919, to be replaced with a marble headstone and surround. For the continued maintenance of the grave he created a fund and also arranged for the erection of an engraved memorial stone to mark the position of the crash site. He later purchased this field, which is located a little over half a mile from the cemetery on the D41C between Carnin and Allennes-les-Marais. Albert Senior wanted his son's remains brought back to Nottingham for burial, but the policy of the Imperial War Graves Commission forbade that, so when the remains of the other twenty-three British casualties were removed to Cabaret Rouge British Cemetery, Souchez, Ball remained at Annoeullin Communal Cemetery, German extension, grave No. 643.

After lengthy delays and a shortfall of funds, the Memorial to Albert Ball VC was finally unveiled by the chief of air staff RAF, Sir Hugh Trenchard, on 8 September 1921. The ceremony took place in the grounds of Nottingham Castle in the presence of Ball's family and a large crowd. A year later, on 17 September 1922, the Albert Ball Memorial Homes, or Pensioners' Homes, were officially handed over to trustees by Albert Ball Senior and his wife, the original purpose being that the occupiers would be widows and mothers of Lenton servicemen killed during the war. The eight houses were designed to resemble an aircraft with the actual homes forming the wings and the central porch the cockpit. A cupola on white pillars was topped by a weather vane carrying a model of Albert Ball's Nieuport.

Seven years later, in 1929, the bronze statuette model by Henry Poole for the Ball part of the Nottingham Castle monument was presented by Ball's father to the National Portrait Gallery in London. Sir Albert Ball (he had been knighted in 1924) threatened legal action against the author and publisher of a biography of his son (*Captain Albert Ball, VC, DSO* by R.H. Kiernan, 1933) for 'a slur on my son'. The author had investigated the facts behind the wording of the VC citation, which stated that Ball had *destroyed* forty-three German aircraft, and had then carefully detailed the results. No legal action followed.

Sir Albert Ball served as Lord Mayor of Nottingham in 1936–37, his fourth term as mayor, and died in 1946. His wife had pre-deceased him in 1931. Fifty years after his death, in 1967, the Albert Ball VC scholarships were instituted at the Trent College, Long Eaton.

Ball is particularly remembered in Annoeullin with an annual ceremony every Armistice Day, and when the new high school was opened there in 1999 it was named Le Collège Albert Ball, the name selected by the students. The Royal Mail issued a set of six postage stamps on 1 September 2006 to commemorate the 150th anniversary of the VC, and an image of Albert Ball was featured on one of the 72p stamps.

Four years later, a memorial to Nottinghamshire's twenty recipients of the VC was unveiled in the grounds of Nottingham Castle on 7 May 2010, and the following year, on 17 May, a memorial blue plaque was unveiled in honour of Ball at King's School, Brook Street, Grantham.

Numerous artefacts connected to Albert Ball exist, and the more significant of those held in public collections include:

The Imperial War Museum, Lambeth, London – service dress with Captain's insignia, leather flying helmet and gloves, medal ribbons, and an oil painting by Edward Newling. Oil paintings of Captain Ball VC by Captain Denholme Davis may be found at the Royal Air Force museum, Nottingham Castle Museum and at Trent College.

The Royal Air Force Museum, Hendon, Middlesex – medals ribbon Bar, one pound sterling treasury note (found on his body) and a gold, silver and diamond brooch in the shape of pilot's wings (given to his fiancée Flora Young).

Nottingham Castle Museum – complete set of medals and awards (Ball's medal entitlement is: VC, DSO and two Bars, MC, BWM, Victory Medal and MiD oak leaf, Chevalier Légion d'Honneur 5th Class (France), Cross, Order of St George, 4th Class (Russia)), Royal Aero Club Certificate, Freedom of Nottingham scroll and casket, gold identity bracelet, framed combat reports, various letters and photographs. Included wiht his medals is a gilded 1914–15 Star with CAPTAIN BALL VC engraved on the reverse. He was ineligible for this medal as he arrived in France on 18 February 1916, and it was added to the medal group by his father prior to its presentation to the museum.

Trent College, Long Eaton, Nottinghamshire – in the college chapel is the original German-made wooden cross from his grave at Annoeullin, and a propeller from one of his Nieuport Scouts is mounted in the dining hall. A. Ball is the first of the ninety-four names on the college roll of honour.

No. 56 Squadron has Ball's full RFC dress uniform along with engine and airframe logbooks for SE5, A4850 and various photos, letters and documents. A clock mounted in the hub of the propeller from A4850 was presented to the squadron by Sir Alfred Ball. No. 11 Squadron hold his original combat reports.

Ball's name is inscribed on the Nottingham War Memorial, the Lenton War Memorial and also in Holy Trinity Church on the Ball family memorial plaque. His name also appears with other VC winners of the RFC, RNAS and RAF, on the wall left of the altar, in St Clement

Danes Church, the Strand, London. One of the houses at Nottingham High junior school is also named after Ball.

In March 1995 it was announced that No. 10 Squadron's complement of fourteen VC 10 aircraft would carry the names of selected RAF recipients of the Victoria Cross. The name of Albert Ball VC was inscribed on aircraft serial number XV105 and later transferred to machine number ZA147.

In less than a year this young man, still under 21 when he met his death, had been credited with forty-four victories over enemy aircraft and was then the highest scoring airman in the RFC. Ball was a sensitive, gentle man who spent much of his off duty time tending a little garden which he had created near his hut, and he was often to be seen there at night playing his violin by the light of a flare. Ball was a contradiction in terms as he admitted that he abhorred actual killing but enjoyed the aerial combat into which he threw himself wholeheartedly. Although he was aware that the fighting was taking a severe toll on his nerves he contrived to be in action with his fellow pilots, and in the words of a contemporary (Captain Archibald James), 'Ball was bound to be killed as he had absolutely no regard for his own safety; whatever the odds, he went bald-headed into the attack.'

W.A. BISHOP

Near Cambrai, France, 2 June 1917

During the early months of 1917, Allied casualties among both aircraft and crew had been very heavy, particularly after the start of the Battle of Arras in early April when the ground forces' need for air cooperation was at its height, culminating in 'Bloody April' when German aircraft were much in the ascendency. The combining of more than one *Jasta* to make large formations of Fokker aircraft, such as that headed by Manfred von Richthofen, the Red Baron, was a very successful German tactic, and it was not until the the Arras offensive was over in May that the tide began to turn again in favour of the RFC.

Canadian born T/Captain William A. Bishop was the commander of B Flight, No. 60 Squadron, RFC, and he had returned to France on 22 May after spending two weeks' leave in England. Since late March he had accumulated some sixteen victories over enemy aircraft and had been nominated for a Military Cross (gazetted on 26 May). The squadron was based at Filescamp Farm, near Izel-lès-Hameau about 13 miles north-west of Arras, and equipped with Nieuport 17 Scouts. This small rotary-engined biplane was very manoeuvrable, with sensitive controls, and armed with a Lewis gun firing above the propeller arc.

Four days after his return, Bishop shot down a German Albatros and the following day a two-seater Aviatik. The enemy tactics had recently changed and their two-seater reconnaissance aircraft now often flew in threes and would fly over anti-aircraft guns. When British machines appeared, these decoy two-seater machines would dive away and the enemy anti-aircraft guns would open fire on the British aircraft. Bishop proposed to his commanding officer Major A.J.L. Scott that an attack on aircraft on the ground at an enemy aerodrome would be a suitable retaliatory action, and he was given outline permission for carrying out such an action.

The initial idea had been for two aircraft to make an attack and was suggested to Bishop by Captain Albert Ball whose feats and very impressive number of victories had made him an inspiration for the Canadian. The two had discussed the possibilities of such a raid when Ball visited the squadron during the first few days of May, but after Ball had been killed on the 7th, Bishop was unable to persuade any of the rest of the squadron pilots to accompany him.

Not to be outdone, Bishop was more than usually careful in preparations for his flight and, with his mechanic, ensured that the aircraft engine and his Lewis gun were in particularly good working order. Bishop took off at 3.57 a.m. on 2 June 1917 flying Nieuport B1566, and headed towards Arras and the Cambrai road, but after nearly half an hour he lost his bearings and found himself well inside enemy-held territory. He descended through the clouds and spotted an enemy airfield, but as this appeared deserted he flew on south-east for a further 3 miles before locating another aerodrome near Cambrai. He could see activity below him as six Albatros Scouts and a two-seater aircraft had been run out of their hangars and were being prepared for flying.

Bishop dived down low and amidst heavy ground fire attacked the line of aircraft, firing as he passed over the machines. He then turned for an attack from the opposite direction and spotted that one Albatros had begun to taxi. It was about 10ft from the ground when Bishop fired a short burst which caused it to hit the grass and break up as it slid along the field. A second Albatros was also attempting to take off. Bishop's fire missed the aircraft but the enemy pilot swerved and crashed into a tree at the edge of the airfield, ripping off its starboard wings. Bishop now turned to fly home, but as he climbed away to 1,000ft two more aircraft took off, but in opposite directions, a difficult tactic to oppose, and he was left with little alternative than to fight.

One Albatros climbed and closed in behind the Nieuport while the other waited at some distance. Bishop turned and fired before beginning to circle, a manoeuvre that eventually placed him under the tail of the Albatros. As it came into view he fired a complete drum into the machine and the enemy fell away to crash near the airfield perimeter.

In his hurry to get back to his home airfield, Bishop had overlooked the other Albatros and was suddenly made aware of its presence as it dived in with guns firing. He returned fire and expended a complete drum from his Lewis gun before the enemy machine dived down towards the airfield. Bishop now headed west at full speed and flew low to avoid a formation of four enemy aircraft near Cambrai. He crossed the front lines near Bapaume, where his aircraft received further damage from enemy anti-aircraft fire, before arriving back at Filescamp Farm airfield at 5.40 a.m.

Bishop circled over the airfield and fired several Very lights before he landed; he held up three fingers to his mechanics to indicate his latest victories as he taxied in. The Nieuport was 'full of holes caused by machine gun fire' and had torn fabric on the wings and fuselage. Shortly after he landed Bishop made his combat report, in which he stated that the airfield he had attacked was either Esnes or Awoignt, both not far from Cambrai. Major Scott reported the sortie to the RFC Wing HQ and the news rapidly spread, which resulted in many messages of congratulation for Bishop including one from Major-General Hugh Trenchard GOC RFC, who described the sortie as 'the greatest single show of the war'.

Bishop continued with the normal duties of a scout pilot, and his victory tally continued to increase. When flying one of the newly issued SE5 Scouts on 28 June he attacked two enemy two-seater machines over Monchy-le-Preux and his engine was hit by anti-aircraft fire. He attempted to fly back to Filescamp Farm, but the engine caught fire and in an attempted landing he crashed into poplar trees. He was left unconscious, hanging upside down while his machine was on fire, but fortunately some nearby infantry rescued him. This experience was his closest brush with death.

On 9 August Trenchard informed Bishop, by telephone, that he was to receive the Victoria Cross for his raid on 2 June, and two days later the supplement to the *London Gazette* No. 30228 of 11 August 1917 published the citation:

Captain Bishop, who had been sent out to work independently, flew first of all to an enemy aerodrome. Finding no machine about, he flew on to another aerodrome about 3 miles south-east, which was at least 12 miles the other side of the line. Seven machines, some with their engines running, were on the ground. He attacked these from about 50ft, and a mechanic, who was starting one of the engines, was seen to fall. One of the machines got off the ground, but at a height of 60ft Captain Bishop fired fifteen rounds into it at very close range, and it crashed to the ground.

A second machine got off the ground, into which he fired thirty rounds at 150yds range, and it fell into a tree.

Two more machines then rose from the aerodrome. One of these he engaged at the height of 1,000ft, emptying the rest of his drum of ammunition. This machine crashed 300yds from the aerodrome, after which Captain Bishop emptied a whole drum into a fourth hostile machine, and then flew back to his station.

Four hostile scouts were about 1,000ft above him for about a mile of his return journey, but they would not attack. His machine was badly shot about by machine gun fire from the ground.

Bishop left No. 60 Squadron for England late in August, and on the 28th was promoted to major. The following day he was invested with his VC by the king at Buckingham Palace.

Bishop was disappointed when news of his home-based posting had reached him earlier in the month as he had become slightly obsessed with the number of his victories and wanted to be the top 'ace' in the RFC. From his return to No. 60 Squadron in May to his departure in August, his accredited score of victories was twenty-eight. Bishop's new posting was as chief instructor at the School of Aerial Gunnery, but he was granted two months' extended leave in Canada from 15 September before taking up this new post.

Following his investiture and many celebrations in London, Bishop sailed for Canada, but not before the award of a Bar to his DSO, the citation appearing in the *London Gazette* No. 30388 of 25 September:

> For conspicuous gallantry and devotion to duty when engaging hostile aircraft. His consistent dash and great fearlessness have set a magnificent example to the pilots of his squadron. He has destroyed not fewer than forty-five hostile machines within the past five months, frequently attacking enemy formations single-handed, and on all occasions displaying a fighting spirit and determination to get to close quarters with his opponents, which have earned the admiration of all in contact with him.

Bishop arrived in Montreal where he was greeted by large crowds and much front-page press coverage. He had arrived home in Owen Sound, Ontario, by 6 October and on 17 October he married his fiancée, Margaret Eaton Burden, at Timothy Eaton Memorial Church, Toronto (named in memory of Margaret's grandfather, the department store founder). Thousands of people lined the streets to catch a glimpse of the couple.

Bishop was attached to the British War Mission in Washington and with his new wife travelled across North America on a number of very successful public relations tours. Canada was dealing with a crisis on conscription and the ever-present long casualty lists, so the appearance of Bishop, the VC and multi-award-winning airman, was a tonic much needed and recognised by the Department of Militia and Defence. They, along with the Office of Public Information, encouraged Bishop in the writing of his autobiography, which was published under the title *Winged Warfare*. The book's introduction was worded as a thinly veiled recruitment drive and also includes a fictional combat with von Richthofen, 'The Red Baron'.

Bishop was promoted to major on 13 March 1918 and returned to England with his wife, where he expected to be appointed to the School of Aerial Fighting at Loch Don, Scotland. Instead he was given the command of No. 85 Squadron at Hounslow, Middlesex. This new squadron was initially equipped with Sopwith Dolphin aircraft, but these were replaced by the SE5a Scout. Bishop was given virtually a free hand in the selection of his pilots and over 200 applications were received.

The RAF was formed on 1 April when the RFC and the RNAS combined so it was No. 85 Squadron RAF which flew to France on 22 May 1918. The squadron was based at Petite-Synthe, near Dunkirk, and five days later Bishop recorded his 48th victory with the destruction of an enemy two-seater over Passchendaele. The following day, when on patrol near Ypres, he made a lone attack on a formation of nine enemy Albatros and shot down two of them.

By the following month Bishop had added a further five victories and on 4 June he was credited with four more. Four days later the squadron moved to St Omer and it was not until 15 June that Bishop achieved another victory. This was a Pfalz DIII destroyed near Estaires, and was followed the next day by victories over two more Pfalz machines near Amentières. Three more enemy aircraft were added to his list of victories on 17 June and claims made for another two the next day.

The rapid increase in Bishop's rate of victories since his return to operational flying was not unconnected with his ambition to become the highest-scoring British flyer. Although he had exceeded Albert Ball's final total of forty-four, the flyer with the most victories was then Captain James McCudden, with fifty-seven. Bishop was also aware that the Canadian Government and Military High Command wanted to withdraw him from operational flying as he was much more useful for propaganda purposes. Bishop's fears were realised on 18 June when orders were received at St Omer for his return to England by midday the next day. On the 19th Bishop decided to have 'one last look at the war' and took off on a lone mid-morning sortie. It took no more than fifteen minutes of combat for him to bring down four more Pfalz DIII aircraft and an LVG two-seater, only three of which were officially credited to him, but it still brought his official total to seventy-two.

In recognition of his last tour of duty, in which he had twenty-five victories in twelve days of actual combat, the *London Gazette* of 3 August announced the award of the Distinguished Flying Cross.

On 5 August, Bishop was promoted to the rank of lieutenant colonel in the Canadian Cavalry and posted to Canadian Forces HQ in England. Here his work was to supervise the formation of the Canadian Corps Wing (later to become the Royal Canadian Air Force), but by the end of September this wing was not ready for operations and Bishop travelled to Canada on 3 October to update the Canadian Prime Minister. Bishop arrived back in England on 17 November having heard the news of the Armistice when on board ship.

Before the war ended he had received the recognition of the French Government in the form of Croix de Guerre with palms and Croix de Chevalier, Légion d'Honneur. Both honours were gazetted on 2 November.

❖❖❖

William Avery Bishop was the third of four children of William A. Bishop and his wife Margaret Louise (Green) He was born on 8 February 1894 at Owen Sound, Grey County, Ontario where his father, a lawyer, was the county registrar.

Bishop could not achieve the entrance requirements for university so he followed in the footsteps of one his brothers, Worth, who had earlier graduated from the Royal Military College (RMC), Kingston, and entered the college on 28 August 1911. The treatment meted out to first year cadets by their seniors who abused their position of authority was at times brutal and sadistic, so it is unsurprising that Bishop was involved in a number of episodes resulting in disciplinary procedures, which included rustication at the end of his first year for failing examinations. Three years later, when the outbreak of war was announced, Bishop had commenced his final year at the RMC and been promoted to corporal. Like many of his contemporaries he did not want to miss the expected excitement and adventure of a European war. Consequently on 30 September, No. 943, Gentleman Cadet William Avery Bishop was granted a discharge from the RMC. His RMC discharge paper records that he was 5ft 6in tall and that his conduct had been 'good'.

He was commissioned in the 9th Mississauga Horse with the rank of lieutenant but was in hospital suffering from pneumonia when his regiment embarked for England in October 1914. After he recovered he was transferred to 7th Canadian Mounted Rifles (CMR) stationed in London, Ontario, and on 9 January 1915 he was commissioned as a lieutenant. Bishop's shooting skills served him well and in particular he excelled with the machine gun. He was admitted to Victoria Hospital, London, Ontario on 6 April for less than a week, with injuries to his eye, wrist and hand after a horse riding accident.

Before he was posted overseas, Bishop became engaged to his long-time girlfriend Margaret Beattie Eaton Burden, whom he had met at Owen Sound where her wealthy parents took their summer holidays.

A Squadron, 7th CMR, designated as 2nd Canadian Division Mounted Troops, embarked on the SS *Caledonia* and sailed for England on 9 June 1915. On a rough crossing which caused the death of some of the 700 horses on board, the convoy came under U-boat attack off the coast of Ireland. Two of the ships were sunk, with the loss of Canadian lives, but the *Caledonia* arrived safely and Bishop disembarked at Plymouth on 23 June.

The 7th CMR were based at Shorncliffe, Kent, for training camp. In July, after Bishop had witnessed an RFC machine land and later take off from a nearby field, he wrote, 'the only way to fight a war; up there above the mud and the mist'. He was hospitalised again on 24 July, this time with pleurisy and, following his discharge from the Helena Hospital at Shorncliffe on 1 August, Bishop began his efforts to transfer into the RFC.

Bishop had learnt from acquaintances in the RFC that Lord Hugh Cecil at the War Office could facilitate transfers to the RFC and on his next leave Bishop presented himself at the War Office. He was able to put in a transfer request but was informed that a wait of six months was to be expected for pilot training. On the other hand an immediate transfer would be available to an observer trainee. After talking this over with his CO, Bishop put in his application for a transfer and on 1 September 1915 he was accepted into the RFC and posted to No. 21 (Training) Squadron at Netheravon, near Salisbury, Wiltshire.

His training continued until the beginning of 1916 and his skill at aerial photography was such that he soon trained others in this task. No. 21 Squadron was posted to France and arrived at Boisdinghem airfield near St Omer on 18 January 1916. The squadron was equipped with RE7 machines and the daily work was reconnaissance, aerial photography, artillery spotting and bombing sorties. The flying conditions for the crews in these early aircraft were hard and Bishop was admitted to No. 10 Stationary Hospital at St Omer for a few days in February, suffering with slight frostbite to his face.

Bishop appears to have been accident prone, as in the first few months of his time in France he was involved in an accident in a lorry, injured when part of an aircraft fell on him, and later suffered a knee injury when his regular pilot, Roger Neville made a crash-landing. Despite the pain from his knee he continued on sorties until 2 May when he proceeded to London on leave. The injury to his knee did not improve and on 11 May, the last day of his leave, he was admitted to Lady Carnarvon's Hospital for Officers at at 48 Bryanston Square, London, diagnosed as suffering with synovitis. While there he met and was befriended by the philanthropic Lady Susan St Helier, widow of Baron St Helier, who was a socialite with a circle of very influential friends.

When discharged from hospital Lady St Helier arranged for Bishop to convalesce at her house, 52 Portland Place and later, when his father suffered a minor stroke, she used her influence to have Bishop returned to Canada to complete his recuperation. In so doing he missed his squadron's activity in the Battle of the Somme, when their casualties were very high. Bishop returned to England in September 1916 but a medical board did not pass him as fit for pilot training as he had a heart murmur, his knee still troubled him and he had been affected by an earlier bout of pneumonia. It would seem likely that Lady St Helier's influence enabled Bishop to have a subsequent, less stringent medical examination when he was passed fit and on 1 October he reported to Brasenose College, Oxford, for initial ground training. On 15 November he was posted to the Central Flying School at Upavon, Wiltshire to begin flying instruction.

At Upavon his instructor was a Norwegian pioneer aviator, Captain Trygve Gran, and it was due to his perseverance that Bishop, whose training was interspersed by more than the usual number of crashes and heavy landings, finally gained his pilot's brevet. His first solo flight was in a Maurice Farman 'Shorthorn' and he was appointed a flying officer in the RFC on 8 December 1916. Following night flying training at Northolt, Bishop was posted to No. 37 (Home Defence) Squadron at Sutton's Farm, Hornchurch, Essex (this is the airfield from which Lieutenant W. Robinson VC flew when he shot down airship S11 on 3 September 1915), for advanced training in night flying and patrols attempting to locate enemy airships. Bishop missed the activity of the operational squadron and applied for a transfer back to the Western Front.

On 7 March 1917 he was posted to No. 60 Squadron, equipped with Nieuport 17 Scouts and based at Filescamp Farm airfield near Arras. His commanding officer, Major A.J. Scott, allotted him to B Flight.

Bishop's first patrol was on 22 March when he had difficulty coping with the sensitive controls of his machine and became separated from the remainder of the patrol. His next flight, two days later, concluded with an especially heavy-handed landing of his Nieuport, which was witnessed, at close hand, by a group of important visiting officers including the brigade commander. Bishop was later informed he would be sent back to England for further flying instruction, but that he would remain with the squadron until a replacement pilot arrived.

The following day, Bishop was on patrol in Nieuport A306 with three other aircraft, between St Leger and Arras, when they engaged three Albatros DIII scouts, one of which attempted to fly under the tail of the leading Nieuport and in so doing came into Bishop's view. He fired about fifteen rounds and hit the enemy aircraft in the cockpit. The Albatros dived down and Bishop followed for about 7,000ft, his guns still firing at about 20yd range. The Albatros flattened out and Bishop did likewise and fired a series of long bursts which sent the other machine down to crash on the ground. After he had pulled up out of his dive his engine stalled at 1,500ft above the ground but he managed to glide down and surprisingly made a good landing close to the front lines. He was unsure where he had landed and relieved when the soldiers who appeared were British. Bishop had to wait until the following day before he could fly his aircraft back to Filescamp Farm where he discovered that the action, his first victory, had been confirmed by a number of witnesses and this had saved him from being posted back to England.

His second victory was on 31 March, at 7.30 a.m., flying Nieuport A6769 with two other aircraft, on escort duty for six FE2bs of No. 11 Squadron which was on an important photographic reconnaissance well inside enemy-held territory. Bishop later described the event when the Nieuports were flying about 1,000ft above the FE2bs and six Albatros scouts were spotted climbing up to attack the reconnaissance machines, and a further two diving down to attack the British scouts. The three Nieuports dived down and Bishop 'managed to frighten off two of the Boches' and then spotted a British machine being attacked by one of the Albatros: 'Forgetting everything else, I turned back to his assistance.' Bishop attacked this Albatros and opened fire twice at 50yd range striking the enemy machine in the centre section. Immediately it fell out of control into a spin behind enemy lines. He then 'rejoined the photography machines, which unfortunately in the meantime had lost one of their number'.

Although his normal flying technique was still 'ham-fisted', once Bishop went into attack he had adapted his flying tactics to gain the upper hand over the enemy through height, surprise and by attacking out of the sun. Furthermore, his excellent shooting abilities, combined with a very keen sense of situational awareness, made him a formidable fighter pilot.

Bishop, in addition to leading his flight on patrols, was increasingly flying solo sorties. These lone patrols hunting enemy machines were much in the manner of Albert Ball who had earlier flown with No. 60 Squadron and was then the top British 'ace'. Bishop was intent on bettering this victory total and, like Ball, he was never completely happy with having the responsibility of other pilots' lives and preferred a role in combat with only himself to consider.

The following month, known as 'Bloody April' by the RFC pilots due to the ascendancy of the German Fokker aircraft and the subsequent crippling casualties to both RFC crew and aircraft, was a situation in which Bishop was in his element. He regarded the increased number of enemy aircraft as more targets for his guns, but his squadron was less fortunate and had a high loss rate for the month: thirteen of the original eighteen pilots were shot down, along with seven of their replacements. However, the squadron did have thirty-five confirmed victories during April, of which a third were Bishop's.

In the first week of April, all-out efforts were made to attack enemy observation balloons in readiness for the forthcoming British offensive, and Bishop was credited with the destruction of one kite balloon, together with its attendant scout, on 7 April. For this action he was awarded a Military Cross (gazetted on 26 May) and on the following day, Easter Sunday, the day before the start of the Battle of Arras, he claimed his fifth victim, but returned to base sobered by a near miss when a bullet had pierced the aircraft's windscreen, narrowly missing him. He celebrated his new status of 'ace' by having the nose of his aircraft painted blue.

On 25 April Bishop was promoted to captain and made flight commander of C Flight, and by the end of the month he had been credited with twelve victories and the destruction of an observation balloon. During the first week of May Bishop increased his number of victories by four, including two on the 2nd, before he returned to England for two weeks' leave on 7 May.

In London, Bishop, the latest protégé of Lady St Helier, was introduced to all her society friends who included members of the royal family, many senior politicians, and personages such as Max Aitken, the influential Canadian newspaper magnate. Bishop much enjoyed his new-found celebrity status during this period of leave.

He returned to France on 22 May and within two weeks had taken part in the action for which he was awarded the VC. On 18 June the supplement to the *London Gazette* No. 30235 published the citation for the award of his DSO, for destroying two enemy aircraft in the action on 2 May. Consequently at his VC investiture he was also presented with his DSO and MC awards.

By the end of 1918 Bishop had been demobilised and had returned to Canada where he had been offered the opportunity of a year-long lecture tour in the USA.

This tour, which was well paid, did not meet with approval in all quarters and Bishop was compared to Piper Lindlater, a nineteenth-century recipient of the VC who had appeared in music halls wearing his full uniform, much to the outrage of many senior military figures. During December 1918 David Henderson, one of the founding fathers of the RFC, then based at the British Embassy in Washington DC, was contacted on this matter and this letter in Bishop's file has the handwritten annotation, 'Spoke to Col. Henderson. H.E. does not mind'.

Bishop left the USA lecture tour after a few months and in July 1919, together with another Canadian VC recipient, William Barker, set up an aviation business, BBAL, a charter airline. Unfortunately the business struggled with financial difficulties and the partnership was later dissolved. The difficulties both men suffered in their attempts to acclimatise themselves to civilian life, and their 'hell-raising' lifestyles, did little to aid their airline business.

The year 1920 was not a good one for the Bishop family. Not only did William suffer serious head injuries and blurred vision in an aircraft crash and the subsequent loss of his pilot's licence, but his wife gave birth to a daughter who tragically only survived for a few weeks.

In late 1921 Bishop and his wife came to live in England where, using his many contacts including Lady St Helier, he was very successful in particular with sales of a new type of pipe patented by a French company. The couple's first child to survive was born at 139 Wigmore Street, London on 13 June 1923 and was named Arthur Christian William Avery Bishop. His godparents were Prince Arthur of Connaught and Princess Louise. Bishop's occupation on the birth certificate was given as 'Lieut. Colonel Canadian General Staff (Reserve) V.C. – Company Director of Stanmore'. The family was then living at Brockley Hill House, Stanmore, Middlesex. A daughter, Margaret Marise, was born at 27 Welbeck Street, London on 15 February 1926. On this occasion Bishop's occupation was described as 'Financier of St Pancras' and the family address was 18 Chester Terrace, St Pancras, London.

The Wall Street Crash of 1929 hit Bishop's finances hard and he and his family later returned to Canada, but he was still living in London in March 1930 when his good friend William Barker VC was tragically killed in a flying accident. British newspapers reported Bishop's great distress on hearing this news.

Bishop was appointed vice-president of the McColl-Frontenac Oil Company, but from 1931 his work and connections were increasingly with the RCAF in which he was promoted to air vice-marshal in 1936. Also in this year he became an honorary, and the only non-German, member of the German Aces Association and he was photographed in Berlin, seated between Goering and Udet.

In 1938 he was appointed air marshal, head of the Air Advisory Committee, and was made director of recruiting two years later in January 1940. The RCAF used Bishop's status as Canada's premier ace of the First World War to encourage recruits. He was a tireless campaigner and so successful that some applicants were turned away. He was so enthusiastic in his efforts selling war bonds and conducting numerous inspection tours that the pace, together with his increasing intemperance, led to his exhaustion and at his own request he was relieved of his official duties in 1944.

In recognition of his military service in two world wars Bishop was awarded the Commander of the Order of the Bath in the King's Birthday Honours list on 1 June 1944 and in the same year he received the Canadian Efficiency Decoration.

Bishop worked part-time as an executive for the oil industry from 1945 until his retirement to Montreal, Quebec, in 1952 where he and his wife Margaret led a very active social life. He attempted to enlist in the RCAF at the outbreak of the Korean War, but his request was turned down.

Four years later, on 11 September 1956 and at only 62 years of age, William Bishop died at his winter home in Palm Beach, Florida. He was cremated at St James's Crematorium, Toronto (Ref 56199). His ashes were buried in Greenwood Cemetery, Owen Sound, Ontario.

Bishop's only son, Arthur William Bishop, enlisted in the RAF as a fighter pilot and survived the Second World War. He was a journalist and author of a number of books on Canadian military history including *Courage of the Early Morning*, a biography of his father, published in 1965.

Bishop's life had always been eventful and he was not shy, on occasion, about embroidering the truth. He had always had his detractors, but the greatest controversies began after his death. In 1978 a stage musical of his life and career, *Billy Bishop Goes to War*, was first produced in Vancouver. Based on Arthur's biography, it was subsequently staged in over fifty cities in Canada, the USA and Great Britain, where it was presented in August 1980. Two years later the Canadian National Film Board released a drama-documentary, *The Kid Who Couldn't Miss*, which cast doubt, not only on the veracity of Bishop's winning VC action, but also on the validity of many of his other victories.

This production was not well received and was even described as second-rate by one of Bishop's detractors. The findings of a subsequent Canadian Senate investigation regarding this film were not conclusive, but did question various points in connection with the German airfield raid near Cambrai.

Thousands of words have since been written about Bishop's 'victories', but his detractors have not been completely successful in proving their case. It is a fact that in his autobiography and in many subsequent articles published in the 1920s and '30s, the description of Bishop's exploits was comparable to such writers as W.E. Johns, the creator of Biggles, the Boys' Own fictional flying ace. Even Bishop in later life referred to these stories, saying, 'It is so terrible that I cannot read it today ... It was headline stuff ... Yet the public loved it.'

The citation of his VC gained in June 1917 was only based on details Bishop related and these were not witnessed. This lack of evidence is one of the major bones of contention. Details of recommended awards were supposed to be kept confidential, but in No. 60 Squadron, at least, these rules had been relaxed, as shown by details in a letter of 1 June 1917 to Margaret. Bishop wrote he had just learned that 'when I got my DSO, I was recommended for the VC'. Existing documents confirm that he was recommended for the DSO on 7 May, but no papers exist to prove that Scott had originally asked for a VC. After Major Scott's recommendation for the VC on 2 June, as was the usual practice, corroboration of the action was then sought, but no reliable witnesses could be found.

However rumours had begun as early as 19 June regarding 'a young British pilot' who had smashed four machines on an enemy airfield, and by the beginning of August stories circulated that an unnamed 'colonial' airman had been recommended for a VC. One plausible theory is that the awards process had developed its own momentum and to arrest its progress at this late stage with the possibility of unfavourable newspaper reports would have been problematic, particularly as the final major Allied advance of the war had just begun.

Bishop is commemorated in Canada in many ways: in Ontario there is the Owen Sound Billy Bishop Regional Airport, and also at Owen Sound the Billy Bishop Home and Museum, and the 167 Air Marshal Bishop Squadron, Royal Canadian Air Cadets. Toronto has Billy Bishop Way near Downsview Airport and also Billy Bishop Toronto City Airport. Pearson International Airport was originally named Bishop Field Toronto Airport, Malton. In Hamilton the Memorial School has a Billy Bishop entrance. In 2009 the name of Air Vice-Marshal William Avery 'Billy' Bishop was added to the wall of honour at the Royal

Military College at Kingston. A hazardous materials training school is named CFB Borden Billy Bishop Centre and at the Brampton Flying Club there is the Billy Bishop Hangar. Ottawa Airport has the 'Billy Bishop Room' for VIPs and a roadway on private land here is named Billy Bishop Private.

In Winnipeg, Manitoba, the Bishop Building is to be found at the 1st Canadian Air Division and the Canadian NORAD Region Headquarters. On the Alberta–British Columbia border, Mount Bishop (Canada) is a 9,350ft high mountain. Vancouver has the Billy Bishop Legion Branch 176. One of the prestige awards for aviation in the Air Force Association of Canada is the Air Marshal W. A. Bishop Memorial Trophy.

In Greenwood Cemetery at Owen Sound, Bishop is commemorated not only on his own stone, but his name is also engraved on his grandparents' headstone. Two other VC winners are also buried in this cemetery, Thomas Holmes and David Vivian Currie.

Bishop's medal entitlement was: VC, CB, DSO and Bar, MC, DFC, BWM, VM (MiD), 1939–45 War Medal, Canadian Efficiency Medal, Silver Jubilee Medal 1935, Coronation Medals 1937 & 1953, GVI Efficiency Decoration, Croix de Guerre avec 2 Palmes, Legion d'Honneur First Class and the Aero Club of America Medal of Merit. (Although he was awarded the 1914–15 Star, Bishop did not go to France until January 1916. And Air Ministry, London, document in his file dated 16 July 1923 regarding the distribution of campaign medals has this meda deleted.) His medals are held at the Canadian War Museum, Ottawa. Bishop's name, together with the other VC recipients of the RAF, appears on the roll of honour left of the altar in St Clement Danes Church, the Strand, London.

J.T.B. McCUDDEN

France, 23 December 1917
to 2 February 1918

On 9 November 1917, Captain James McCudden MC and Bar, MM, Croix de Guerre, returned from leave in England to No. 56 Squadron where he was in command of B Flight. The squadron had recently been equipped with the new SE5A fighter aircraft and, since its arrival on the Western Front seven months earlier, it had acquired the reputation of being an elite unit with many experienced pilots, none more so than McCudden, who had eighteen victories to his credit.

The squadron moved from Liettres to Laviéville, 4 miles west of Albert, on the afternoon of 12 November. For some time after their arrival, the weather was misty and flights were not possible until the 18th when McCudden led a patrol south of Havrincourt and attacked a DFW CV, which crashed at Bellicourt. Two days later, on 20 November, the Battle of Cambrai commenced at 5.30 a.m. when over 400 British tanks advanced against the heavily fortified Hindenberg Line with the assistance of aircraft carrying out low-level bombing and strafing of enemy strongpoints. No. 56 Squadron initially made use of an advanced landing ground near Bapaume, but the weather deteriorated, low cloud prevented flying from late morning onwards, and it was not until three days later that air patrols recommenced.

On 23 November, McCudden flew with his patrol towards Cambrai, crossed the front lines south of Bourlon Wood and, due to the low cloud level, most aircraft were below 3,000ft in an area around Bourlon Wood. After an inconclusive attack on a DFW over Cantaing,

McCudden and another of his patrol went to the assistance of a Bristol Fighter which was being attacked by two enemy aircraft over Marcoing. McCudden manoeuvred into position and fired a short burst at one of the enemy machines from behind; an Albatros DV went into a vertical dive and crashed a mile east of Noyelles.

It was not until 29 November that McCudden claimed another victim, a DFW CV two-seater, which he shot to pieces south of Bellicourt whilst on an early morning patrol with his flight. He also shot down a similar enemy aircraft during the afternoon when his patrol engaged three two-seaters, and later, confirmation was received of two victories for the flight, including the machine destroyed by McCudden that crashed south-east of Havrincourt. On the last day of the month, McCudden again led his patrol over the lines near Bourlon Wood where 'the enemy were absolutely raining gas shells' and there they became involved in an inconclusive fight with several Albatros aircraft. A formation of seven two-seaters were then spotted, flying west over Cantaing, which the British aircraft attacked and McCudden forced his opponent down inside British lines near Havrincourt. His own aircraft suffered a holed radiator in the encounter and he was forced to land alongside the LVG CV where the mortally wounded pilot was receiving treatment. McCudden telephoned his squadron for a breakdown party to repair his aircraft and to remove the brand new German machine. He made his way back to Lavieville by foot, rail and RFC tender, arriving in the early evening. During this journey he was frustrated at not being in the air, 'as there were dozens of Huns up, and our pilots ... had their hands full'.

Two days later, McCudden was allocated a new aircraft, SE5A B4891, which had been fitted with modified elevators and a strengthened undercarriage, and by 4 December he had his 'special gadgets fitted on' and the 'guns and Constantinesco gear working'. The first victory in this machine was on the following day when he shot down a Rumpler near Hermies; but it was in his previous aircraft, SE5A B35, that McCudden accounted for another Rumpler near Holnon Wood on 6 December. Later that same day, again flying B4891 and leading a patrol of six aircraft, McCudden shot down an Albatros DV over Fontaine, and he attacked a new type of enemy two-seater machine, a Hannover, over Bourlon Wood and drove it down in a damaged condition. Despite regular patrols and considerable contact with enemy aircraft, he had no further confirmed victories until 15 December when, on a lone morning patrol, he attacked a Rumpler and caused it to crash east of the Bois de Vaucelles. Also on this day McCudden was awarded the DSO, the citation later appeared in the supplement to the *London Gazette* no. 30780 of 5 July 1918:

2nd Lt. (T./Capt.) James Byford McCudden, M.C., M.M., Gen.List and R.F.C.

For conspicuous gallantry and devotion to duty. He attacked and brought down an enemy two-seater machine inside our lines, both the occupants being taken prisoner. On another occasion he encountered an enemy two-seater machine at 2,000 feet. He continued the fight down to a height of 100 feet in very bad weather conditions and destroyed the enemy machine. He came down to within a few feet of the ground on the enemy's side of the lines, and finally crossed the lines at a very low altitude. He has recently destroyed seven enemy machines, two of which fell within our lines, and has set a splendid example of pluck and determination to his squadron.

It was another week before McCudden added to his number of victories when he engaged two DFW two-seaters and forced one down to crash south-west of St Quentin. Over the next seven days he achieved nine aerial victories: four two-seaters on 23 December, three more on the 28th (accounted for in about thirty minutes) and another pair of LVG machines on the following day. The weekly RFC communiqué, when reporting this event, recorded that this was the first time that four enemy machines had been destroyed in a day by one pilot. His total of confirmed victories for the month of December was fourteen, nine of these on high-flying solo patrols. McCudden later wrote that one of his big advantages over enemy aircraft was that:

It was an exception to the rule to see an S.E. Above 17,000 feet ... with its war load My machine had so many little things done to it that I could always go up to 20,000 feet whenever I liked ... [and] by getting high I had many more fights ... than most people, because they could not get up to the Rumpler's height.

On New Year's Day, the very cold conditions at 19,000ft thwarted McCudden's attempt to increase the squadron's victory total to 250 when, after stalking a Rumpler for over thirty minutes, his Lewis gun froze and the belt on the Vickers machine gun broke as he attacked. Two days later he was awarded a Bar to his DSO (gazetted on 18 July 1918), the citation of which included the confirmation that he had brought down thirty-one enemy machines.

In December 1917 Viscount Northcliffe, the newspaper magnate, was put in charge of the Ministry of Information. With notable exceptions such as Albert Ball, the British Government had previously not followed the German and French in identifying individual airman for propaganda purposes and Northcliffe believed that this should change. Consequently, on 3 January an article was published in the *Daily Mail* focusing on McCudden and entitled 'Our Unknown Air Heroes'.

It was not for over a week, despite several engagements with enemy aircraft, that he shot down an LVG near Graincourt on 9 January 1918, bringing B Flight's total to 100 out of the 250 credited to No. 56 Squadron. His flight was the first in the RFC to reach this figure and McCudden received a message of congratulations from the newly appointed commanding opfficer of the RFC, General J.M. Salmond.

At this time the bright red spinner, acquired from the LVG forced down on 30 November, was fitted to B4891 as McCudden reckoned that the use of this would give him extra speed. On 13 January he flew this upgraded aircraft for the first time and achieved a hat-trick of victories over enemy two-seater machines. After leaving his airfield at 9.30 a.m. he attacked the first of these, an LVG, ten minutes later and, after approaching unseen from the rear with the sun behind him, fired a burst from both guns at about 100yd range and the machine crashed north of Lehancourt. McCudden later wrote: 'I hate to shoot a Hun down without him seeing me, for although this method is in accordance with my doctrine, it is against what little sporting instincts I have left.'

Within twenty minutes he had shot down two more aircraft, a DFW and an LVG, the latter after one burst of fire at a range of 400yd. Later that day McCudden was ordered to No. 1 Squadron at Bailleul, 'giving particulars to all the pilots concerning my methods of fighting' and he did not return to No. 56 Squadron until 18 January where, flying his earlier SE5A, B35, he had victories over two-seater enemy aircraft on both 20 and 24 January. Of the latter victim, a DFW, which was his 43rd confirmed victory, McCudden was quite dismissive of its crew, 'because they had no notion whatever of how to defend themselves' and in his opinion, 'during their training they must have been slack, and lazy'.

McCudden had observed that, during the preceding days, Rumpler aircraft were out-climbing him when flying at heights over 16,000ft and discovered that more powerful Maybach engines had been fitted. Consequently he arranged that his own Hispano-Suiza engine should be fitted with high-compression pistons. After a successful test flight on 28 January, McCudden considered that his machine 'was now a good deal superior to anything the enemy had in the air'. Two days later he reinforced this when he shot down, in rapid succession, an Albatros DV and a Pfalz D III at Anneux, and on 2 February he fired a burst into an LVG which crashed near Vélu Wood.

Poor weather conditions hampered patrols and it was not until over two weeks later, on 16 February, that McCudden destroyed two Rumplers and a DFW in less than thirty minutes in the late morning.

After landing at Lavieville he took off in another BE5A whilst repairs were carried out to his own aircraft, caught up with a Rumpler and, after he had fired a burst from both guns, the enemy machine went down, losing all four wings as it fell. On the following day he shot down a further Rumpler, and on 18 February he added another Albatros Scout to his list of victims.

Three days later McCudden claimed another Rumpler shot down in flames near Méricourt. On 25 February, he was in bed with a bad cold and was sent home with no further flights. On the following day McCudden persuaded his superiors to allow him to fly once more and, before 10 a.m. he was flying a lone patrol. After combat with an LVG near Masnières, which he damaged, and an inconclusive engagement with two Hannover aircraft, he shot down a Rumpler with a short burst of fire, which crashed in flames east of Oppy. A few minutes later, McCudden claimed his fifty-seventh victory when he fired 300 rounds into another Hannover which fell apart and crashed near Chérisy.

His younger brother, Jack, was a pilot in No. 84 Squadron with eight victories and the MC to his credit; however, James McCudden worried about his brother's reckless flying. Jack tried to live up to his older brother's reputation, but not with the same degree of care and expertise, despite very good advice from his commanding officer, Major William Sholto Douglas. The brothers met from time to time and, when he visited No. 84 Squadron in late February, James again 'proffered words of caution'.

On 1 March McCudden had his final solo flight and returned after an indecisive encounter with two enemy aircraft.

The squadron organised a large dinner in Amiens in his honour and representatives from all squadrons in the brigade were present, in addition to the French Commandant of Amiens. In the days that followed, he was also given dinner by General Higgins at Brigade HQ and invited to tea with the Third Army Commander, General Sir Julian Byng. All ranks of his squadron subscribed towards a silver model of an SE5 with which he was presented at a farewell concert on 4 March; by the following afternoon he was in London.

McCudden's record with No. 56 Squadron was impressive: he had destroyed a minimum of fifty-two enemy aircraft out of the seventy-seven recorded by his flight when under his command. During this same period his flight had lost only four pilots: a real tribute to his leadership and attested to the success of his tactics.

McCudden spent part of his home leave with his brother before Jack left to rejoin No. 84 Squadron on 17 March. Sadly his brother was reported missing in action the following day and it was later established that he was shot down over Busigny, near le Cateau, in a dogfight with aircraft from *Jasta 1*. (Second Lieutenant John Anthony McCudden, MC, aged 20, No.84 Squadron, RFC, is buried in St Souplet British Cemetery, 4 miles south of le Cateau, ref. III.D.4.)

On 29 March the award of his VC was announced and the supplement to the *London Gazette* of 2 April carried the citation:

2ND LT. (T./CAPT.) JAMES BYFORD MCCUDDEN, D.S.O., M.C., M.M., GEN.LIST AND R.F.C.

For most conspicuous bravery, exceptional perseverance, keenness, and very high devotion to duty.

Captain McCudden has at the present time accounted for 54 enemy aeroplanes. Of these 42 have been definitely destroyed, 19 of them on our side of the lines. Only 12 out of the 54 have been driven out of control.

On two occasions, he has totally destroyed four two-seater enemy aeroplanes on the same day, and on the last occasion all four machines were destroyed in the space of 1 hour and 30 minutes.

While in his present squadron he has participated in 78 offensive patrols, and in nearly every case has been the leader. On at least 30 other occasions, whilst with the same squadron, he has crossed the lines alone, either in pursuit or in quest of enemy aeroplanes.

The following incidents are examples of the work he has done recently:

On the 23rd December, 1917, when leading his patrol, eight enemy aeroplanes were attacked between 2.30 p.m. and 3.50 p.m. Of these two were shot down by Captain McCudden in our lines. On the morning of the same day he left the ground at 10.50 a.m. and encountered four enemy aeroplanes; of these he shot two down.

On 30th January, 1918, he, single-handed, attacked five enemy scouts, as a result of which two were destroyed. On this occasion he only returned home when the enemy scouts had been driven far east; his Lewis gun ammunition was all finished and the belt of his Vickers gun had broken.

As a patrol leader he has at all times shown the utmost gallantry and skill, not only in the manner in which he has attacked and destroyed the enemy, but in the way he has during several aerial flights protected the newer members of his flight, thus keeping down their casualties to a minimum.

This officer is considered, by the record he has made, by his fearlessness, and by the great service which he has rendered to his country, deserving of the very highest honour.

On 6 April, at Buckingham Palace, McCudden was invested with a Bar to his MC, the DSO and Bar and the VC; he later wrote, 'there was not a prouder man living'. He was the first member of the RAF to be awarded this honour, the RNAS and RFC having merged on 1 April to form the RAF. He had not told his family of the investiture and, afterwards, he celebrated in London with his good friend Edward Mannock.

Less than a week later, on 10 April he was posted to No. 1 School of Aerial Fighting at Ayr, Scotland under the command of Lieutenant Colonel Lionel Rees VC, and it was while McCudden was here, 'training the young', that a friend suggested he write about his RFC experiences. Consequently, on 7 July he delivered the handwritten manuscript – in pencil on the pages of several service notebooks – to C.G. Grey, editor of the weekly magazine *The Aeroplane*. It was published shortly after McCudden's death under the title *Five Years in the Royal Flying Corps* and republished in 1930 with the less appropriate title of *Flying Fury*.

Meanwhile, No. 1 School moved to Turnberry on 11 May and, on 25 June, he was notified of a new appointment as commanding officer of No. 91 Squadron, which was forming up at Tangmere. However, after learning that it would be some months before this squadron was employed on operational duties, McCudden made strong requests for an overseas posting. He had reportedly been turned down for command of No. 85 Squadron and one of this squadron's pilots recorded that, when McCudden was suggested to them as the new commander, the pilots did not want him as: 'He gets Huns all by himself but he doesn't give anybody else a chance at them. We asked for Mickey Mannock'. (Major Edward Mannock was later appointed to command of No. 85 Squadron.)

There were those that contested McCudden's reputation as a flight commander and that he restricted his pilots when in action, but in reality he allowed the more experienced fliers freedom in their fighting methods and only exerted more control over the less adept members of his flight to improve their chances of survival. It should be remembered that Major William Bishop had been in command of No. 85 Squadron and was not known to be the strictest of squadron leaders.

On 9 July he visited his sister, Mary, in the War Office annexe in the National Liberal Club Building where she worked before leaving to take up the command of No. 60 Squadron at Boffles, 4 miles north-east of Auxi-le-Château. 'I'm going off to France again,' he told her, 'I've come to hand you over my medals.'

He took off from Hounslow just after 1 p.m. in a new SE5A, C1126, en route for Boffles and, after a brief stop at RAF HQ, Hesdin, he landed at Auxi-le-Château airfield, shortly before 6 p.m.

An anonymous eyewitness account recorded that the SE5 made a 'wonderful landing' and, after the pilot had asked for directions to Boffles, took off again and 'could not have been higher than 70ft when it became obvious that he was in trouble … and flew straight into the small wood on the far side'. (It has since been established thatproblems with the air intake on the factory-fitted carburettor probably caused his SE5A to stall. A number of accounts reported that McCudden turned back towards the airfield when the aircraft stalled, but those who knew him thought it highly unlikely he would make such an elementary flying mistake.)

McCudden was found unconscious in the wreckage, with serious injuries including a fractured skull, and was immediately taken to No. 21 Casualty Clearing Station at Wavans, where he died three hours later.

McCudden was buried the following day in a ceremony attended by General Salmond, virtually all of the pilots from Nos 56 and 60 squadrons, together with many other RAF personnel. The service did not please many of those who attended and comments such as 'all in Latin and mumbled … nothing human in it at all' and 'poorly arranged and rushed through' were later made by pilots; one pilot also wrote that von Richthofen had a far better funeral. McCudden's headstone in the tiny Wavans British Cemetery, 2 miles from Auxi-le-Château, is situated at B.10 and bears the following inscription beneath the incised VC:

> Fly on dear boy
> From this dark world of strife
> On to the Promised Land
> Of eternal life

❖ ❖ ❖

James Thomas Byford McCudden was the third of six children born to William T.H. McCudden and his wife, Amelia Emma (née Byford). William, although born in County Carlow, was of Northern Irish descent, with a French mother, while Amelia's grandmother came from Hanover, and she also had Scottish origins. The couple's first child, William, was born in 1891; Mary Amelia (Cis) the following year; James on 28 March 1895; followed by John Anthony (Jack) three years later; Kathleen in 1900; and finally, Maurice in 1901. All the children were born in the Female Hospital at Brompton Barracks, Kent. William senior had risen to the rank of sergeant major in the Royal Engineers before his retirement in 1907 when the family moved from the married quarters of Brompton Barracks to Chatham. Afterwards they went to 22 Belmont Road, Gillingham, later living for a time in Sheerness.

The newly established airfield at Eastchurch, on the Isle of Sheppey was only a short distance from Sheerness and naturally proved a fascinating place for the young McCudden brothers to visit. It is unsurprising that all four brothers were to eventually join the Royal Flying Corps at various times.

James was educated at the garrison schools at Brompton and, on 26 April 1910, after brief employment as a Post Office messenger, he joined the Royal Engineers as a boy soldier. Six months later he was graded as a bugler and sailed for Gibraltar on 24 February the following year. He returned to England in September 1912 and was attached to No. 6 Company, RE, stationed at Weymouth, and it was here that he applied for a transfer to the Royal Flying Corps.

His application was successful and, on 28 April 1913, McCudden became No. 892 Air Mechanic second class. He was posted to Farnborough on 9 May as an engine fitter and his new RFC career was jeopardised almost immediately when he omitted to check ignition switches when practising propeller swinging on a Caudron aircraft. This machine rolled across the hangar and caused damage to another aircraft, in addition to hitting the commanding officer's motor car. This incident resulted in five days' detention in the guardroom, before being released on open arrest, and it was then that he had his first flight as a passenger in a BE2A. He was later awarded seven days' detention and fourteen days' loss of pay for the Caudron incident.

On 15 June he was posted to No. 3 Squadron at Larkhill and moved with the unit to Netheravon the following day; it was here that he had further flights, in Henry Farman and Blériot machines, and by December had increased his personal flying hours to thirty. On 1 April, McCudden was delighted when he was promoted to air mechanic first class, as his wage doubled, and in the period immediately following he was able to make a number of flights with his brother, William, now a sergeant, who had transferred from the RE to the RFC a year earlier than James in May 1912.

War against Germany was declared on 4 August 1914 and No. 3 Squadron, under the command of Major J.M. Salmond, was preparing to fly to France with the other RFC squadrons. McCudden had been hoping to fly with Flight Lieutenant E. Conran in Blériot 389, the aircraft for which he was then responsible, but the day before departure it was decided that Lieutenant Conran would fly a single-seater Parasol Blériot.

In the early morning of 12 August, the three flights of heavily laden aircraft of No. 3 Squadron commenced taking off, their first stop being Swingate Downs, Dover, before the crossing to France. A and B flights took off without serious mishap, but the last aircraft of C Flight, Blériot XI-2 260, piloted by Second Lieutenant Robert Skene and flying with Air Mechanic R.K. (Keith) Barlow returned to the airfield for adjustments. On the second attempt the aircraft crashed shortly after take-off in a small wood ½ mile from Netheravon and, after running to the scene, McCudden found both the pilot and his friend Keith Barlow dead in the wreckage. These two airmen were amongst the earliest wartime flying casualties incurred by the RFC.

McCudden and the squadron transport sailed early that evening from Southampton on a small tramp steamer, the *Dee*. He disembarked at Boulogne the following afternoon, where he met his brother, William, who was in charge of squadron transport.

The squadron arrived at Amiens the next day where, together with the other aircraft of the RFC, they were based until 17 August when orders were received to fly to Maubeuge. Unfortunately, another flying accident claimed the lives of 2nd Lieutenant Copeland Perry and Air Mechanic Parfitt when their BE8 625 stalled and crashed in flames soon after take-off. McCudden travelled by car in a convoy with the squadron transport and arrived at Maubeuge in the evening.

Following the Battle of Mons on 23 August, the BEF retreated before superior numbers of German troops, so No. 3 Squadron also moved back to landing strips and airfields at le Cateau, St Quentin and la Fère, and had reached Compiègne by the end of August. Their airfield (the local racecourse) was bombed on 28 August by a large enemy biplane, which in turn was challenged by Lieutenant Norman Spratt who, in a series of feint attacks in his unarmed Sopwith Tabloid, forced it to land.

The main role of the aircraft was reconnaissance and their very ineffective armament was limited to rifles, pistols, steel darts, hand grenades and, on occasion, full cans of petrol for primitive bombing. The ground crews had to work long hours, often through the night, to keep the machines airworthy, as replacement aircraft were difficult to obtain.

On 6 September, the tide turned in favour of the Allied forces when French forces counter-attacked the Germans at the Battle of the Marne. This counter-attack was made possible due in no small part to the valuable reconnaissance reports of the RFC. No. 3 Squadron was at a landing ground near Melun, south-east of Paris, and were ordered to advance north-east. When McCudden, with the transport, arrived at Pezarches, 20 miles south of Meaux, reports came in that one of the squadron pilots was missing. (Lieutenant Victor Lindop, flying BE8 479 was hit by enemy artillery fire and crashed on 7 September. He had the dubious privilege of being the first member of the RFC to be made a prisoner of war.)

The squadron was based at Fère-en-Tardenois for a time and used an advanced landing ground near Serches for their work on bombing raids and spotting for the artillery. At the end of September, No. 3

Squadron commenced their move northwards via Amiens, Abbeville and Moyenville, and arrived at St Omer on 12 October. The squadron aircraft were much employed in artillery co-operation work and, over the next few weeks, McCudden had opportunities to fly as gunner/ observer – armed solely with a rifle.

On 20 November, McCudden was promoted to corporal and, four days later, the squadron moved to Gonnehem, north of Choques; when the weather conditions permitted, the aircraft flew artillery spotting missions over the la Bassée Canal. The squadron was being re-equipped with Morane Saulnier Parasol machines and, as these aircraft were fitted with the French Le Rhône engines, it was decided in late January to send squadron mechanics to the Paris works for a week's course on this engine. McCudden and three others had a very instructive and enjoyable time in the French capital.

McCudden continued to fly as observer/gunner – the first Lewis guns arrived with the squadron during January – when possible and he observed that the majority of enemy aircraft were able to achieve greater flying heights than the RFC aircraft.

The problems associated with early bombing attempts were tragically illustrated on 12 March when a Morane of A Flight was being loaded with six 10lb Mèlinite 'bombs' – converted French artillery shells – when two exploded, killing eight men, including the pilot, Captain Reginald Cholmondley, and injuring others of the ground crew. (The eight dead airmen are buried in Choques Military Cemetery.) Less than a week later, on 18 March, the commander of C Flight, Captain Eric Conran, was seriously wounded by shrapnel during a bombing raid near la Bassée and his machine, Morane-Parasol 1872, was badly damaged. Captain H.D. Harvey-Kelly DSO took over as flight commander and, on the first day of April, McCudden was promoted to sergeant and was now in charge of all engines in C Flight.

During April, William McCudden returned to England and was posted to Fort Grange Military Aerodrome, near Gosport, as a pilot-instructor. Two weeks later, James was devastated when he received the sad news that his brother William had been fatally injured on 1 May when a Blériot XI-2, in which he was giving instruction, crashed at Gosport. The crash was probably caused by a flooded carburettor.

In early May, Morane Parasol 1972, which had been damaged in March, was returned, fit for service and McCudden, in a flight with Captain D. Corbett-Wilson (a pioneer aviator who was the first pilot to fly from Wales to Ireland in 1912), noted the machine's much improved climbing ability. On 10 May Captain Corbett-Wilson and his 18-year-old observer, Second Lieutenant I.N. Woodiwiss, failed to return from a reconnaissance flight. A German aviator later dropped a message stating that the Morane had been shot down by anti-aircraft fire near Fournes and the bodies of the British airman buried near the village. After the armisitice their remains were moved to Cabaret-Rouge British Cemetery, Souchez.

McCudden received further sad news when he heard of the death of his brother-in-law, Arthur Spears, married to his sister, Mary, who was killed on 27 May when the minelayer HMS *Princess Irene* exploded just off Sheerness when being loaded with mines. Spear was a dockyard worker and one of the 352 fatal casualties.

The squadron moved to Auchel, 12 miles east of Béthune, on 1 June and McCudden commenced regular flights a week later, gaining experience as an observer. At the end of the month, his name was put forward for pilot training, but he could not be spared from his engineering duties. However, McCudden did achieve some 'private' flying instruction from Flight Sergeant J. Watts.

The squadron was involved in observation work during the Battle of Loos in late September. As the year progressed, more aircraft from both sides were involved in patrols over the lines and No. 3 Squadron suffered further casualties. McCudden had his first aerial combat on 19 December when he exchanged fire with a Fokker monoplane scout when on a long-range reconnaissance sortie over Valenciennes. Further contact with enemy aircraft continued into the New Year and, on 21 January, McCudden was informed that he had been awarded the Croix de Guerre and that afternoon, in a field investiture at Lillers, he was presented with his medal by General Joseph Joffre.

Two days later, McCudden was promoted to flight sergeant as his application for pilot training had been finally approved, and at the end of the month he left No. 3 Squadron. His flying instruction commenced on 22 February in a Henry Farman F20, followed by further training with No. 41 Squadron at Shoreham and, on 16 April 1918, McCudden qualified for his Royal Aero Club Certificate No. 2745 in a 'Longhorn' Maurice Farman. Two weeks later he was posted to the Central Flying School at Upavon and, on 7 May, gained his Second Class Pilot's Certificate and was made an assistant instructor. By the end of the month he had qualified for his First Class Certificate and his RFC wings.

A little over a month later, on 5 July, McCudden flew from Farnborough to St Omer in a BE2d, and two days later he joined his new unit, No. 20 Squadron, who were equipped with FE2b and FE2d two-seater bombers. The squadron was based at Clairmarais, north-east of St Omer, and their patrolling sector was fairly quiet as the majority of enemy aircraft were in action further south where the Battle of the

Somme had commenced on 1 July. Although McCudden flew operational patrols from 10 July, he had no combat with enemy aircraft in his short stay with the squadron and was posted to No. 29 Squadron on 7 August.

This squadron, which flew DH2 Scouts, was based at Abeele on the French–Belgian border between Steenvorde and Poperinge. McCudden was posted to C Flight and allotted machine No. 5985, commencing flying operational sorties the following morning. Routine escort and bombing patrols followed for the next four weeks before he was credited with his first victory on 6 September when he fired two drums of ammunition at a white Albatros two-seater which McCudden last saw diving steeply downwards. Confirmation was later received that a German machine had crashed at Gheluve, so McCudden was awarded the victory despite his combat report containing no claim.

Over the next few weeks McCudden had a number of inconclusive combats with enemy aircraft and two attempts at destroying German observation balloons, which culminated in the award of a Military Medal on 1 October (gazetted on 8 December).

McCudden returned to England for a week's leave on 5 October and, less than three weeks after his return to France, the squadron moved to Izel-lès-Hameau, a few miles west of Arras, where regular patrols soon commenced covering an area from north of Arras to Gommécourt. On 1 November he applied to be considered for a commission.

A few days later, on 9 November, a six-aircraft patrol took off with the intention of flying to Bapaume via Albert and from there to Arras, the route taking them deep inside enemy-held territory. Bapaume was reached without any encounter with enemy scouts, but three of the formation of DH2 aircraft had returned to base with engine trouble. Over Achiet-le-Grand, McCudden spotted a number of enemy aircraft and the British machines were soon involved in a dogfight that they were fortunate to survive; the three aircraft all suffered considerable damage. The squadron CO congratulated the pilots on their return, having heard a glowing report from a British anti-aircraft battery that had witnessed the action. It was later confirmed that the five German aircraft were Albatros DII machines of *Jasta 2*.

McCudden flew on patrols for the remainder of the year, but with no further confirmed victories, and on the first day of 1917 he was granted his commission as second lieutenant and given 'kitting' leave in England.

Shortly after rejoining his squadron on 23 January, McCudden was part of an early morning patrol over Monchy-le-Preux when, in pursuit of an Albatros Scout, he was attacked by a Fokker biplane and his aircraft's propeller was broken; he was forced to land 'in a field just behind Arras' where a new propeller was later fitted. (Manfred von Richthofen was credited with shooting down McCudden, although the damage to the propeller was caused by empty cartridge cases from his own gun.) Three days later, McCudden attacked an enemy two-seater and, later, confirmation was received that this aircraft had gone down out of control. On 2 February he was also jointly credited with shooting down another two-seater with his CO, Major A.W. Grattan-Bellew.

Within two weeks, McCudden had increased his total of confirmed victories to five when he shot down a Roland Scout at Monchy on 15 February. On the following day, after returning from a patrol, he was awarded the Military Cross (gazetted 12 March), the citation read:

2nd Lt., James Thomas Byford McCudden, Gen. List, and R.F.C.

For conspicuous gallantry in action. He followed a hostile machine down to a height of 300 feet, and drove it to the ground. He has shown marked skill on many previous occasions, and has destroyed two hostile machines and driven down another one out of control.

A week after his award, McCudden was posted to England on instructional duties. On 23 February he was granted ten days' leave, which he mostly spent in London, where, on one visit, he met Captain Albert Ball and the two airmen joked about their three medal ribbons apiece.

McCudden often visited the theatre with his sister, Mary, and on occasion would buy the music, which she would later play for him on the piaNo. He found that, with his officer's uniform and medal ribbons, he enjoyed more instant popularity than when an NCO. He named one of his aircraft after a dancer, 'Teddie', and he and Edward Mannock competed for her affections. Mary later recalled her brother introducing her to Ivor Novello, composer of the very popular wartime song *Keep the Home Fires Burning*, who was serving in the RNAS.

After his leave was over, McCudden spent a few days each at Hythe, Turnberry and Orfordness, giving talks on aerial fighting before being posted as fighting instructor to the 6th Training Wing and based at Joyce Green airfield, near Dartford. Here he taught the novice pilots aerial combat techniques and indoctrinated them with his precept that 'the correct way to wage war is to down as many as possible of the enemy at the least risk, expense and casualties to one's own side'. One of the men under training was Mannock, who had cause to thank McCudden when, after getting his machine into a spin, he fortunately remembered the advice recently imparted to him and was able to correct the problem.

McCudden remained at Joyce Green until the middle of April when he embarked on a tour of various training airfields in East Anglia giving demonstrations and lecturing, followed by a week at the Central Flying School on a Fighter Instructor's Course at the end of May. It was at this time that McCudden, after 450 hours' flying, had his first crash, when a Bristol Scout he was delivering to Joyce Green developed engine failure and was badly damaged in a crash-landing near Maidstone.

On 1 June McCudden was promoted to captain and took his 19-year-old brother Jack up on training flights at Joyce Green; he later wrote that, although very keen, his younger brother was an over-confident flier. Also on this day, when McCudden landed at Croydon airfield in his unarmed Sopwith Pup, he was told that a formation of German bombers had crossed the south coast and were heading for London. He quickly returned to Joyce Green and, while his Lewis gun was being fitted, the enemy aircraft could plainly be heard above the clouds. He took off again and soon saw the formation of two-engine Gotha bombers flying south-east. However, he was over 20 miles east of the Essex coast before he got close to the rearmost aircraft and expended all three drums of ammunition with no apparent effect on the bomber. He then returned to Joyce Green 'very dispirited, cold and bad-tempered'.

McCudden spent the next few weeks on instructional visits and was much impressed with the aggressive spirit of the pilots in No. 56 Squadron whom he met at the end of June. Another large formation of Gotha aircraft attacked targets in the London area and, again, McCudden was unsuccessful in his attack on these bombers.

He was sent on a refresher course on 12 July and joined No. 66 Squadron at Estrée-Blanche where he flew Sopwith Pups on mostly uneventful operations for three weeks; after a short leave he returned to Joyce Green. On 12 August he was advised that he was to be posted to No. 56 Squadron as commander of B Flight and arrived at Estrée-Blanche three days later.

The Allied offensive later to be known as 'Third Ypres' had commenced in late July and the airmen could see the shell-pocked muddy terrain below, which McCudden compared to a large farmyard covered with muddy hoof prints.

McCudden quickly had his machine, SE5A B519, fitted to his exacting requirements and began to impose his precise engineering and maintenance standards on the flight's ground staff in addition to instilling in his pilots the need for team performance. He admitted that he was a 'stickler for detail in every respect' and he spent hours testing and aligning his guns. After he had 'fired the best part of a thousand rounds from each gun ... there was certain amount of booing from his fellow officers' when he entered the mess, as his actions were considered 'a bit of a show off'. When questioned on this incident several months later, one of the pilots concerned said, 'I'm afraid at that time we just didn't understand Mac's worth'.

His first victory came on 18 August when he shot down an Albatros DV east of Houthem, after problems with his guns had forced him to break off an earlier attack on an enemy two-seater machine. McCudden and his flight were then outnumbered by a formation of German scouts, but with their superior speed returned to their base airfield, as he was never afraid to break off a conflict when he considered it was not advantageous to continue.

A further victory for McCudden on 19 August was followed by two more enemy aircraft shot down over Polygon Wood the next day, all being Albatros DV machines. Other pilots of B Flight were also claiming victories, but in common with the other pilots, McCudden experienced repeated problems with his guns, which failed at crucial moments and this, in his opinion, had denied him at least six victories. Eventually, by dint of many hours working on his guns, the problems were mostly overcome. In an evening patrol on 14 September, his flight engaged seven Albatros DV machines of *Jasta 10* over Roulers and McCudden, flying SE5A 4865, quickly shot down one of the enemy aircraft with a short burst from his Lewis gun. Five days later, on a lone patrol, he shot down a DFW near Radiunghem, and on 21 September a two-seater near Gheluve.

On the evening of 23 September, due to low cloud, large numbers of aircraft of both sides were visible below 9,000ft and McCudden led B and C flights across the lines where he shot down a DFW near Houthem. The British formation then went to the aid of an SE that was being attacked by a 'silvery blue German triplane' over Poelcappelle. The triplane was initially engaged by McCudden and Second Lieutenant Arthur Rhys-Davids, but very quickly all of the SE5s were circling the Fokker DR I which forced down two of the British machines with damage to engines and put bullets through all his opponent's aircraft before crashing north of Frezenberg. The actual crash was witnessed by McCudden and the victory credited to Rhys-Davids. McCudden later described the pilot as 'the bravest German airman whom it has been my privilege to see fight'. The pilot was Leutnant Werner Voss, a leading German pilot with forty-eight victories.

McCudden added to his list of victories an LVG and an Albatros Scout on consecutive days in late September, followed by two further enemy aircraft on 1 October. Two days later awards were announced, including a DSO for Rhys-Davids, a second MC Bar for Barlow and a Bar to McCudden's MC (gazetted 18 March 1918).

It was two weeks before McCudden claimed another victim, an LVG CV, which he followed with a Rumpler four days later before returning to England on 23 October for two weeks' leave, leaving Rhys-Davids in command of the flight in his absence. A few days after arriving in London, McCudden heard that Rhys-Davids was missing in action and further bad news followed when a fellow RFC officer told him that his favourite aircraft, SE5A B4863, which 'left nothing to be desired' had been crashed on take-off by another pilot. (Lieutenant Arthur P.F. Rhys-Davids DSO MC and Bar is commemorated on the Arras Flying Services memorial.) Despite this gloomy news McCudden managed to see 'nearly every show in town' during his leave before rejoining No. 56 Squadron on 9 November.

❖ ❖ ❖

After her son's death, his mother, Amelia, was much in demand and attended a Buckingham Palace Garden Party and was selected to lay a wreath on the tomb of the Unknown Warrior in Washington in 1921. Sadly she was widowed in July 1920 when her husband fell from a train.

McCudden memorabilia in the form of a belt, together with the control column from his SE5A, are held by No. 56 Squadron, while the Imperial War Museum holds a number of items, including oil paintings by William Orpen and E. Newling, the windscreen from his crashed aircraft, a pocket compass and items of uniform such as a flying helmet, gloves and jacket.

McCudden's medals (VC, DSO, MC and Bar, MM, Croix de Guerre, 1914 Star, BWM, Victory Medal) together with those of his father and his brothers, William and Jack, are held by the Royal Engineers Museum, Chatham. The museum also holds the engraved brass plaque from his original grave marker.

The name of James McCudden, together with that of his brothers, William and Jack, appears on the Brompton Civic War Memorial in Gillingham and the Sheerness War Memorial on the Isle of Sheppey.

The three brothers are also inscribed on Carlow Great War Memorial, Leighlinbridge Memorial Garden, Co. Carlow, Ireland, which notes that their father was born in Carlow.

A memorial in the McCudden family plot (Section CC, Grave 959) at Maidstone Road Cemetery, Chatham, records the name of William Senior, his four sons – William, James, John and Maurice – together with their brother-in-law, Arthur Spears. A plaque in St Henry and Elizabeth Roman Catholic Church in Sheerness is inscribed with the names of brothers James, William and John McCudden, along with that of Arthur Spears.

James McCudden's name appears with the other VC winners of the RFC, RNAS and RAF on the panel in St Clement Danes Church, the

Strand, London. When areas of Brompton were redeveloped in the 1950s it was decided that several of the new streets would be named after VC winners with a local connection, and one such is McCudden Row.

At the opening of the RAF Museum, 15 November 1972, among the guests was Squadron Leader Arthur Spears Junior, who had known Douglas Bader when with No. 3 Squadron at Kenley, and who now accompanied his mother, Mary (née McCudden). Bader described the incident:

> Plucking up courage, Mary approached the Group Captain and introduced herself as Jimmy's 'Cis'. 'Good gracious me,' Sir Douglas replied, 'I couldn't have done what I have without your brother. It was because of your brother that I did what I did!'

In the late 1970s, Sappers Walk, off Gillingham High Street was so named in honour of the Royal Engineers and James McCudden VC features on one of the bronze panels.

The name of James McCudden VC was inscribed on a VC 10 aircraft serial number XV104, and after this aircraft was taken out of service the scroll bearing his name was finally transferred to machine number ZA147 – alongside the name of his great friend Edward Mannock VC – in April 2013. This VC 10 made its final flight on 26 September 2013 and is scheduled to be broken up.

In March 2009, James McCudden VC and Edward Mannock VC were the subjects of the BBC *Timewatch* episode 'WWI Aces Falling'.

In later years, McCudden's fellow RFC and RAF contemporaries shared their memories of him. Air Vice-Marshal Arthur Gould Lee considered 'he was a complete soldier, thought like a soldier, even walked like a soldier', while Major Ludlow-Hewitt recorded that McCudden 'was far from being the glamorous fire-eating hero of fiction [and] was a gentleman in the true and real meaning of the word'.

The final word on this pilot, considered by many to be the greatest, rests with Major General Sir Hugh Montague Trenchard, KCB, DSO who wrote in the Prefatory Notes to *Five Years in the Royal Flying Corps*:

> His skill and daring speak for themselves. Only the finest courage and unsurpassed mastery in the art of flying and fighting in the air could account for such a record of unflagging work and incessant victory ... His determination and nerve were tremendous, and there was no finer example of the British pilot.

A.A. McLEOD

Over Albert, Somme, France,
27 March 1918

As the war entered what was to be its last year it was long known that the enemy was planning a major attack on the Western Front, and it was also expected that they would attack the Allied lines at their weakest points. The role of the RFC was outlined by its commander Major General Hugh Trenchard: his squadrons were to carry out extensive bombing attacks on enemy-held road and rail networks, their artillery positions and reserves.

No. 2 Squadron RFC, based at Hesdigneul-Lès-Béthune on the outskirts of Béthune, and equipped with Armstrong Whitworth FK8 aircraft, had undertaken numerous reconnaissance and bombing missions since their deployment to this airfield on 30 June 1915. After a short but intense artillery bombardment, the long expected German offensive began on 21 March on a 50-mile front from south of Arras to the River Oise below St Quentin. Many British infantry battalions were overwhelmed with the ferocity of the enemy attack and were forced to fall back rapidly in the face of superior numbers. As a consequence the workload on No. 2 Squadron soon increased and many crews flew up to three sorties a day when the weather allowed. As enemy ground troops moved forward, so their aircraft units did likewise and occupied airfields from which the RFC had departed when enemy artillery had moved within range.

Six days after the great offensive began, the enemy was still making forward progress and despite stubborn resistance, British troops were still falling back. In the Amiens sector, concentrations of enemy troops had been reported south of Albert, the ruins of which had been abandoned by the British during the night, and new defensive positions taken up on higher ground to the west of the town. The weather was overcast and misty and despite this aircraft from No. 2 Squadron were ordered to find and attack the enemy troop concentrations reported to be in the Bray-sur-Somme area. Six aircraft, each with a full bomb load, were detailed for this morning sortie and included pilot Second Lieutenant Alan McLeod and Lieutenant Arthur Hammond, his observer, who were flying in FK8 No. B5773.

The six aircraft took off at 9.40 a.m. as a group, but McLeod soon became separated in the thick cloud and after nearly two hours' flying and unable to locate his objectives, McLeod now needed to refuel. Eventually he found the landing ground of No. 43 Squadron at Avesnes-le-Comte, 10 miles east of Arras, and badly damaged his machine's tail skid when he landed the heavily loaded aircraft. It was not until 1 p.m. that McLeod took off again, in the direction of Albert, after the FK8 had been fuelled and repaired.

After a further two hours' flying the weather did improve, but there was still no sign of the reported troop concentrations and so McLeod decided to return to base. However an observation balloon was then spotted beneath them. McLeod immediately began a shallow dive in its direction, but before the balloon was in range of either guns or bombs, Hammond pointed upwards to a Fokker flying at 3,000ft, probably part of the customary protection for the balloon. McLeod immediately changed direction and began a very steep climb towards the enemy aircraft, and when close enough he manoeuvred in such a way that enabled Hammond to fire a burst from his Lewis gun at the enemy triplane which was not expecting to be attacked by the British two-seater. The enemy aircraft fell into a spin and crashed on German-held ground near Albert.

Unfortunately for McLeod, this attack had been seen by a further eight Fokker triplanes which emerged from cloud and dived down in line to attack the AW FK8. The first enemy machine attacked with its guns firing, but Hammond waited until it was within his range and with a long burst set it on fire and it fell away. The next attacker, Leutnant Hans Kirschstein, flew under McLeod's aircraft and raked the big aircraft from nose to tail which wounded Hammond in two places. At the same time another Fokker attacked from a different direction and Hammond was again wounded, as was McLeod, in his leg. Despite his nauseating pain Hammond fired at the closest enemy machine, which quickly burst into flames and exploded. Kirschstein then came in for another attack and on this occasion some of his bullets hit McLeod's fuel tank in front of the cockpit, which then caught fire. The flames, fanned by the wind, quickly burned away the cockpit floor. McLeod's boots and leather flying coat were on fire and parts of the aircraft controls were smouldering. Kirschstein, convinced that McLeod's aircraft was doomed, broke off the engagement and went off in search of other victims. He later recorded the time of the attack as 3.20 p.m. and the position just under 2 miles south-west of Albert.

Meanwhile Hammond, with no floor to support him, had climbed out to sit on the fuselage and held on to the Scarff ring Lewis gun mounting with his feet 'on the bracing wires at the side of the fuselage'. McLeod had swung one leg out of the cockpit on to the lower left wing. With one foot on the rudder pedal and a hand on the control column he attempted to fly the machine crab-like to keep the flames from Hammond. Another of the enemy aircraft flew in for a final look at the burning machine but came too close, and Hammond, despite his injuries and precarious position, fired a burst from the Lewis gun and the Fokker heeled over and fell to the ground.

McLeod did not release his bomb load as he was unsure of his whereabouts and did not know if he was above Allied positions. Amazingly he managed to control his aircraft well enough to crash-land, and although he was then under enemy fire from ground troops, the crash site was not far from friendly positions. McLeod was thrown clear when the aircraft hit the ground, but Hammond was trapped in the burning wreck. Under hostile machine-gun and shell fire he dragged Hammond from the burning aircraft and attempted to carry him away, but in his wounded state he was unable to do so. Consequently he half rolled and half dragged Hammond towards a shell hole and while doing this, his aircraft's bombs exploded and McLeod was wounded by shrapnel. Once the two men had reached shelter McLeod collapsed from exhaustion and loss of blood. During the whole event Hammond had been wounded six times and McLeod five.

It was some time before the nearest friendly troops, men of the South African Scottish regiment, rescued the flyers and carried them to their trenches where their wounds were dressed. McLeod and Hammond spent several hours there under enemy bombardment until, under cover of darkness, stretcher-bearers carried them more than a mile to a dressing station. One of the airmen's rescuers later said that 'the observer was too bad to talk; both smelt terribly of burnt flesh'.

The two airmen were taken by ambulance to a CCS at Amiens for further treatment, and the following morning by hospital train to Étaples. On 31 March McLeod was then sent via Boulogne to the Prince of Wales Hospital in London.

Initially McLeod and Hammond had been reported missing, and in a letter to Dr McLeod, Major Snow, the commanding officer of

No. 2 Squadron, wrote, 'I have to advise you that your son, Lieut. A.A. McLeod has been missing since yesterday morning ... Without exaggeration he was the most gallant and fearless officer I have ever met in the flying corps ...'

Meanwhile it was not long before McLeod attempted to reassure his father that he was not badly hurt, and in a letter written before the end of March he wrote that his wounds were not causing him pain and there was no need for his father to worry. Major Snow was soon to write again with the much better news that, 'he is on our side of the lines and not ... a prisoner of war ...' and finished by writing that he hoped McLeod's action would be rewarded as it deserved.

Despite McLeod's subsequent protestations in the days that followed that he was 'as fit as a fiddle', his wounds were more serious than he knew, or was told, and his father travelled to England to be with him and helped in his convalescence. McLeod's mother and sisters were kept informed of his progress by frequent telegrams.

As Major Snow had hinted in correspondence to McLeod's father, the two airmen were rewarded for the action of 27 March, McLeod with a VC in particular for his heroics in saving his observer's life and Hammond with a Bar to his MC.

The supplement to the *London Gazette* No. 30663 dated 1 May 1918 published the citation for the award of the VC:

2ND LIEUTENANT ALAN ARNETT MCLEOD, ROYAL AIR FORCE.

While flying with his observer (Lt A.W. Hammond, M.C.), attacking hostile formations by bombs and machine gun fire, he was assailed at a height of 5,000 feet by eight enemy triplanes, which dived at him from all directions, firing their front guns. By skilful manoeuvring, he enabled his observer to fire bursts at each machine in turn, shooting three of them down out of control. By this time, Lt McLeod had received five wounds, and while continuing the engagement, a bullet penetrated the petrol tank and set the machine on fire.

He then climbed out onto the left bottom plane, controlling his machine from the side of the fuselage, and by side-slipping steeply kept the flames to one side, thus enabling the observer to continue firing until the ground was reached. The observer had been wounded six times when the machine crashed in 'No Man's Land', and 2nd Lt. McLeod, notwithstanding his own wounds, dragged him away from the burning wreckage at great personal risk from heavy machine gun fire from the enemy's lines. This very gallant pilot was again wounded by a bomb while engaged in the act of rescue, but he persevered until he had placed Lt. Hammond in comparative safety, before falling himself from exhaustion and loss of blood.

The citation for the award of a Bar to his Military Cross to T/Lieutenant Arthur William Hammond, one of whose legs had been amputated after their rescue, was gazetted on 26 July 1918.

It was not for over five months that McLeod was sufficiently recovered to receive his award, and on 4 September, using two sticks and accompanied by his father, he was invested with his VC by the King at Buckingham Palace. Later that month McLeod and his father returned to Canada.

❖ ❖ ❖

Alan Arnett McLeod was born on 20 April 1899 to Alexander Neil McLeod and his wife Margaret Lilian (née Arnett) at 292 Main Street, Stonewall, 25 miles north of Winnipeg, Manitoba. Alexander was a previous mayor of Stonewall where he had a medical practice. Alan had two younger sisters, Margaret Helen and Frances Marion.

At the age of 14, Alan joined a summer training camp of the 34th Fort Garry Horse at Fort Sewell in June 1913 where 'mostly he groomed horses, shovelled manure and the like. But he was thrilled, they even let him wear a uniform.'

On the outbreak of war in the following year, McLeod attempted to join the cadet wing of the Royal Flying Corps, but he had to wait until after his eighteenth birthday before the RFC would accept him. His training began on 23 April 1917 at the University of Toronto where he satisfactorily completed the course by early June and was then sent to Long Branch, just west of Toronto. He had his initiation flight on 4 June in a Curtis JN4 and after a little over two hours of instruction, made his first solo flight five days later. By 16 June he had been posted to Camp Borden for advanced training. McLeod's first impressions of the camp were not favourable, as he wrote home shortly after he arrived: 'It's an awful hole here … just a mass of sand and tents … I just hate this place.' Despite these initial misgivings he qualified as a pilot at Camp Borden by the end of July.

Further training at the School of Aerial Gunnery followed and his letters written at that time showed his eagerness to go overseas as rumours concerning such a move circulated in the camp. On 9 August he wrote that he would be 'going over in the next draft, whenever that is'.

Following home leave, Second Lieutenant Alan McLeod travelled to Montreal and on 20 August embarked on board the SS *Metagama* for

England. This was exactly four months after he had left school and after he had five hours solo flying in his logbook. The sea journey took longer than anticipated due to a U-boat threat; the ship was forced to put into port in Ireland for safety, but it eventually docked on 1 September.

After ten days' leave in London, during which he wrote that there had been a bombing raid every night, he was sent to Hursley Park, Winchester, where he received further training including the Wireless and Observers' Course before a posting to No. 82 Squadron at Waddington, Lincolnshire. This squadron was equipped with Armstrong Whitworth FK8 (AWFK8) two-seater aircraft, which McLeod described as 'having the aerodynamics of a cow'. No. 82 Squadron was soon to be sent to France, but McLeod, as he was not yet 19, had been transferred to No. 51 (Home Defence) Squadron which flew FE2b two-seater biplanes and was based at Marham, Norfolk. He served with this unit for two months and frequently flew on night patrols.

Possibly due to the shortage of trained pilots McLeod was posted overseas before his nineteenth birthday, and in late November he arrived at the RFC Pilot's Pool at St Omer. On the 29th he was assigned to No. 2 Squadron RFC based at Hesdigneul-Lès-Béthune, on the south-west outskirts of Béthune. He was assigned to B Flight of this squadron which flew AWFK8s on army co-operation work in addition to day and night bombing sorties. He wrote home reassuring his parents, 'Just to let you know how safe I am … the Squadron I'm in has only had 1 man killed in the last 6 months … the casualties in the RFC in France are a great deal less than they are in England & in Canada … at Borden 6 were killed in one week.'

After two weeks McLeod began flying artillery spotting missions and on 19 December, in FK8 B5782 with Lieutenant Comber as observer/gunner, he attacked a formation of eight yellow and green Albatros scouts. Comber shot one down out of control with his Lewis gun.

In the new year, on 14 January, with Lieutenant R. Key as observer, McLeod took off, ordered to attack a kite balloon at Bauvin, 10 miles south-west of Lille. Enemy observation balloons were well protected, with experienced anti-aircraft gunners and fighter aircraft often in attendance. Consequently it was not an easy target. McLeod climbed above the balloon under considerable anti-aircraft fire and began to dive towards it when three enemy Albatros were spotted diving in his direction. He continued the dive down to the balloon, which was at 3,000ft, and when level he pulled up, which enabled Key to rake it with fire from his Lewis gun and set it aflame. McLeod banked to avoid the burning debris and as an Albatros attempted to manoeuvre under the British aircraft, Key fired and shattered part of the enemy aircraft's upper wing and the machine broke up. After some exchanges of fire with the two remaining enemy aircraft, McLeod returned to base.

Two days later, on another artillery co-operation flight near la Bassée, again with Lieutenant Key, McLeod came under accurate fire from an anti-aircraft battery and also small-arms fire from nearby buildings. He dived on the battery, raked it with machine-gun fire and followed this attack with bombs. He then strafed a column of troops before a return to his work with the artillery.

On 14 January his commanding officer, Major W.R. Snow, sent details of McLeod's actions at Bauvin and la Bassée to OC No. 1 Wing who in turn submitted McLeod's name for the award of a Military Cross. This award was not confirmed, but McLeod was Mentioned in Despatches.

On 27 January McLeod began two weeks' leave in England and stayed at the Savoy Hotel on the Strand. On the night of 28 January Gotha aircraft bombed London and over 100 people were killed and injured in an air-raid shelter at nearby Long Acre when Odhams Printing Works was hit by a large bomb.

McLeod returned to France from his leave and in the following weeks, with the other airmen of his squadron, was kept busy in patrols and sorties over a wide area of the front.

After winning a VC when flying in operations over Albert, and a subsequent six months in hospital, he returned to Canada with his father. Alan McLeod received an official welcome home when he arrived with his father at Winnipeg railway station on 30 September, which was later followed by a public reception in Stonewall. He told the crowds that he was only home on leave and would be rejoining the RAF in January. By now the RNAS and RFC had combined to form the RAF on 1 April.

Tragically, just four weeks later McLeod contracted a very virulent strain of Spanish influenza and died in Winnipeg General Hospital on 6 November 1918. His funeral was three days later and large crowds paid their respects as the cortège, where a gun carriage carried his flag-draped coffin, made its way to the Old Kildonan Presbyterian Cemetery where he was buried in Grave 238 with full military honours.

At the Highlanders' Memorial Church, Glasgow, a memorial tablet to McLeod was unveiled on 27 January 1924 by Colonel Sir John Lorne McLeod, ex-Lord Provost of Edinburgh. It was reported that 'all the McLeods of the Highland Light Infantry and the Argyll and Sutherland Highlanders' were present at this ceremony.

Alan McLeod is commemorated in Stonewall by a plaque in his former home at 292 Main Street and also a bust at Stonewall Collegiate in the high school library. Alan McLeod VC Avenue in the town was named in his honour.

In 1940 the RCAF authorised a booklet, *Canada's Air Heritage*, which was distributed throughout the service. The book profiled only four men, Bishop, Barker, Collishaw and McLeod, and in addition the RCAF commissioned oil paintings of these men, copies of which were sent to schools and air bases across Canada.

Alan McLeod was inducted into the Canadian Aviation Hall of Fame in 1973. An acrylic painting by George Tanner was commissioned by the Heritage Department of Air Command in 1994 to become part of the visual display of the McLeod display held in the Air Command Museum. The aircraft are depicted to be from *Jasta 11* of *JG 1*, being all red, but in fact Hans Kirschstein flew with *Jasta 6* so it is likely they attacked McLeod and Hammond. This *Jasta* had their aircraft striped like zebras, and were not red at all.

On 3 April 2004, the 80th anniversary of the RCAF, Hangar 11, a First World War building at Canadian Forces Base Borden Museum and now the Air Force Annex, was dedicated to the memory of McLeod.

In St Clement Danes Church, the Strand, London, his name appears with those other VC recipients of the flying services on the wall left of the altar. McLeod's medal entitlement was: VC, BWM, Victory Medal and MiD oak leaf. In 1967 McLeod's medals and personal letters were donated to the Canadian War Museum in Ottawa by his sister Mrs Helen Arnett, but at the time of writing the medals are on loan and displayed in the Bishop Building, Headquarters of Canadian Air Division, Winnipeg.

A. JERRARD

Near Mansue, Italy, 30 March 1918

No. 66 Squadron, which had been transferred from France, arrived equipped with Sopwith Camels in Milan, Italy on 22 November 1917. They were part of British military forces sent to help Italian troops in their fight to fend off an Austrian invasion. (Austria was part of the Austro-Hungarian Empire which had firm financial support from Germany.) Lieutenant Alan Jerrard joined the squadron at Treorso, north-west of Venice, on 22 February 1918. He quickly made his mark with this new squadron when five days later, flying a Sopwith Camel, he shot down out of control a Berg scout, and a week later on 7 March he attacked and set fire to an enemy observation balloon. The squadron moved to San Pietro-in-Gu, north-east of Vicenza, on 10 March and, flying from there the next day, he claimed two more Berg scouts, one of which crashed and the other was driven down damaged. Another enemy scout, this time an Albatros, was shot down by him ten days later.

The weather worsened towards the end of the month and on 30 March it was so cloudy with poor visibility that no early morning patrol was attempted. Later, however, the clouds thinned and an offensive patrol of three aircraft was ordered to take off. The pilots, all flying Sopwith Camels, were Captain P. Carpenter in B7387, Lieutenant H.R. Eycott-Martin in B7283 and Lieutenant A. Jerrard in B5648 'E'. Carpenter was the most experienced of the three with seven victories to his credit and also the award of Military Cross. Jerrard, who had slept in late, did not bother to dress properly and merely put on his heavy flying overalls over his pyjamas.

The three aircraft took off and flew east towards the front lines. As they climbed at about 11.35 a.m. five enemy aeroplanes were spotted flying at 14,000ft, which was about 2,000ft above them. The enemy comprised one Rumpler reconnaissance machine escorted by four Albatros D III Scouts, heading back towards their base.

Up to this point both British and Austrian versions of the action are similar, but accounts of later events vary considerably. The indisputable fact is that the three British pilots attacked enemy aircraft and that after the combat Jerrard crash-landed in enemy territory and was made a prisoner of war. The other two British pilots returned to their base where they were debriefed by their squadron commander Major Tudor Whittaker.

The Austrian version of events is chiefly based on the account of Oberleutnant Benno Fiala von Fernbrugg, commander of *Flik 51J*, the Albatros unit involved. According to him he was the leader of four Albatros Scouts which escorted one of their own reconnaissance aircraft to land safely at its home airfield of Mansue, and the escorts then turned north towards their own airfield. Three Camels dived out of the sun from a 'great height' and the first British aircraft (Jerrard) was soon involved in a dogfight with an Albatros. Von Fernbrugg was attacked by another Camel, but he was able to fire into its underside. This British aircraft was then attacked by the Hungarian Feldwebel Fejes who forced it to turn south. Von Fernbrugg attacked Jerrard's Camel again, which caused the Camel's engine to stop, and Jerrard crash-landed his aircraft about 2 miles south of Mansue airfield. The left wings were ripped off and the tail was detached in the crash. A very bruised and shocked Jerrard was extricated from the wrecked aircraft by Austrian soldiers and he was pictured sitting amongst the wreckage in a very dazed condition.

Von Fernbrugg landed at his base airfield about 2 miles away, drove a car to the crash site and then took Jerrard to Oderzo for debriefing. Later examination of the crashed Camel revealed a total of 163 bullet holes, including several in the fuel tank, which latter damage almost certainly prevented the aircraft catching fire. Austrian records show that only one of the four Albatros pilots was injured. Fejes, whose aircraft had forty-six bullet holes, had a slight foot wound. One other aircraft landed with an overheated engine due to a bullet-fractured pipe. The records also show that three of the four Albatroses were sent to *Flienstappenpark* for repairs. Apart from von Fernbrugg, whose claim of victory over Jerrard was officially recognised, Fejes claimed a Camel shot down in Italian lines.

The British version of events was initially given verbally to the squadron commander, Major Tudor Whittaker, by the two Camel pilots, Carpenter and Eycott-Martin at their debriefing. The pilots' written reports were made shortly after and Whittaker signed a typed combat report of the action. The details in Whittaker's combat report, which differed little from Carpenter's handwritten version were:

Owing to bad visibility and other instructions from the Squadron Commander, the W.O.P [Western Operational Patrol] went on patrol and then went on to the old Eastern Patrol. At 11-35 a.m. a formation of four Albatross D.III's and one Rumpler 2-seater were observed about 14,000 feet over Fontane (38.U.9690) crossing our lines. Patrol immediately attacked them from about 13,000 feet but were unable to get within range so held off in the sun. Patrol observed that EA [Enemy Aircraft] were obviously making for their own aerodrome and Capt Carpenter shot down and crashed one D.III at about three miles south of MANSUE. Lt Jerrard attacked another D.III and followed it down to about 100 feet from the ground, where it burst into flames. Lt Martin confirms Capt Carpenter's crash and Lt Martin and Capt Carpenter confirm Lt Jerrard's. Capt Carpenter and Lt Martin, who were now at about 6,000 feet saw Lt Jerrard attacking the other machines. The leader on looking round saw Lt Jerrard at about 50 feet over the aerodrome shooting it up and attacking machines one after another who were trying to take off. At this time there were about 19 EA in the air. Lt Jerrard was attacking six D.III's. Lt Martin went to Lt Jerrard's assistance and crashed a D.III which was on Lt Jerrard's tail, in a field next to the aerodrome. This was confirmed by Capt Carpenter. Just after Lt Jerrard crashed his second EA into the same field and this is confirmed by Capt Carpenter, Lt Jerrard continued to shoot up the aerodrome and at this moment all the machines, with the exception of those shot down, were in the air. Capt. Carpenter, who was attacking 3 D.III's lost sight of the other two Camels for the moment. A D.III climbed on to Lt Martin's tail and was shot and crashed by Lt Jerrard two fields north of the aerodrome confirmed by Capt Carpenter and Lt Martin. Meanwhile Lt Martin attacked another D.III and drove it into the ground without firing a shot. The machine was seen to crash by Capt. Carpenter and Lt Martin. At this moment Lt Jerrard was attacking vigourously [sic] six D.III's. Capt. Carpenter and Lt Martin went to his assistance but were driven off by other EA. Capt Carpenter and Lt Martin drew away to break off the fight owing to superior numbers but Lt Jerrard remained attacking with great vigour every EA who came within range of him. Lt Jerrard then joined the formation but was flying very weakly as though wounded. 10 D.III's were following Lt Jerrard. Capt Carpenter and Lt Martin were unable to go to his assistance owing to other EA and observed Lt Jerrard, who although apparently wounded, repeatedly attack these EA until he crashed four miles West of MANSUE Aerodrome.

Based on the British combat report six enemy aeroplanes were destroyed in combat, one by Carpenter, two by Eycott-Martin and three by Jerrard, and also a minimum of nineteen enemy aircraft were airborne during the action.

Meanwhile Jerrard was questioned by his Austrian captors and in the official report of Jerrard's interrogation was his statement:

> On March 30 I was flying in formation with two other Camel fighters near the Front when we met an Austrian fighter squadron near Mansue. I attacked an Albatros fighter successfully, then having lost height during the dogfight my engine started to misfire and run rough. I was pursued by other Austrian fighters and eventually shot down.

The records of Austrian aviation units in the region near Mansue showed no attack on any airfield and the only Albatros fighters involved with British Camels was *Flik 51J* commanded by von Fernbrugg. The unit based at Mansue airfield on 30 March was *Flik 32D*.

On the basis of the available information it would seem feasible that the action on 30 March more resembled the Austrian version rather than the version sent off by Major Whittaker, and as all concerned parties are no longer living, further accurate investigation is difficult.

Meanwhile Lieutenant Jerrard was more concerned about his circumstances as he had no clothing except for his flying overalls over his pyjamas. His Austrian captors displayed a degree of chivalry by dropping a note near to No. 66 Squadron's airfield, requesting that listed items be dropped for Jerrard. This was achieved and two bundles of clothing, cigarettes and other requested items were dropped on an Austrian airfield addressed to Jerrard, who after his routine questioning was completed, was sent to a POW camp at Salzburg.

The *London Gazette* No. 30663, dated 30 April 1918, published the citation for the award of the Victoria Cross to Lieutenant Alan Jerrard. This citation was a short version of the No. 66 Squadron combat report.

Jerrard managed to escape from his prisoner of war camp at the end of the war and reach Allied lines. He was repatriated and on 5 April 1919 he was invested with the Victoria Cross at Buckingham Palace by King George V.

❖❖❖

Alan Jerrard was born at 13 Vicar's Hill, Ladywell, in the Borough of Lewisham, south-east London on 3 December 1897, the son of Herbert

Jerrard and his wife Jane Remington (née Hobbs). The family moved to Sutton Coldfield in 1902 where Herbert became headmaster at Bishop Vesey's Grammar School. Alan was educated at his father's school, followed by Oundle Scool in Cambridgeshire and from there went on to Birmingham University in 1915.

Jerrard left university at the end of 1915 and volunteered for military service. He received a commission as second lieutenant in the 5th Battalion South Staffordshire Regiment, TF, on 2 January 1916.

A few months after his appointment Jerrard applied for a transfer to the Royal Flying Corps and was accepted for ground instruction at the School of Military Aeronautics, Oxford, on 16 August. This was followed on 23 September by a posting to No. 25 (Reserve) Squadron at Thetford, Norfolk, for initial flying instruction. Less than two months later, on 20 November, he was posted to No. 9 (R) Squadron at Mousehold Heath, Norwich, and on 5 December moved to No. 59 Squadron at Narborough also in Norfolk, where the squadron was being formed for duties in France. He did not join this unit due to illness but stayed at this airfield with No. 50 (Reserve) Squadron at Narborough until he was fit for duty.

After his recovery, Jerrard was ordered to the Central Flying School (CFS) at Upavon, Wiltshire, for final pilot training, from which he qualified as an RFC pilot on 14 June 1917. He was then briefly posted to No. 40 (Training) Squadron at Beddington, Croydon, before moving to Spitalgate, Lincolnshire to gain further experience in flying two-seater RE8s with No. 20 (Training) Squadron. Again this was a short stay for on 4 July, two days after his promotion to lieutenant, London Colney was his destination for training as a single-seat scout pilot. This lasted less than two weeks as Jerrard was posted to Liettres, a few miles south of St Omer, France, on 24 July where he joined No. 19 Squadron equipped with Spad S VII Scouts.

Jerrard flew his first operational patrol on 29 July but became separated from his formation and eventually landed at St Omer. On his second patrol, less than a week later, he was one (A8830) of six Spads on an evening sortie searching for enemy aircraft. Again, in the misty conditions, he lost contact with the other members of the patrol and, still unfamiliar with the terrain, flew very low in an attempt to find his bearings. He spotted a long convoy of enemy transport and immediately strafed the column with his Vickers machine guns and set fire to some of the vehicles before climbing through the mist and low clouds to about 10,000ft where the engine of his aircraft cut out. He tried to restart the engine without success so, with his visibility very limited, he glided down to attempt a landing, but crashed into a railway embankment near St Marie Cappel, north of Hazebrouck, where he was literally dug out of the wreckage by nearby troops. Jerrard suffered several fractures to his nose and jaw and was taken for medical treatment and eventually to hospital in England where he spent several months recovering from his injuries.

After a short flying refresher course early in 1918 he was again posted for operational duties, this time in Italy which had been neutral at the start of the war but had come in on the side of the Allies in summer 1915.

❖ ❖ ❖

After the Armistice of November 1918, Alan Jerrard remained in the RAF and was a member of Syren Force posted to Murmansk on the Barents Sea in north-west Russia in July 1919, when British military units were sent to assist the White Russian forces after the Bolshevik Revolution of November 1917. The operation was a failure and British forces were withdrawn from Russia by early October 1919.

A supplement to the *London Gazette* dated 12 July 1920 did carry the name of Flying Officer Alan Jerrard VC, 14th Wing, Royal Air Force, (Italy) in the list of those Mentioned in Despatches with the note that this entry had been 'Omitted from Gazette dated 1st January, 1919'.

In the years that followed, he served in various capacities at RAF Henlow, Sealand, Grantham and Halton, finally retiring from the service due to poor health with the rank of flight lieutenant in 1933. In his later years he went to live with his cousin, Brigadier Charles Jerrard, at Uplyme, Dorset.

On 14 May 1968 Alan Jerrard died in Buckfield Nursing Home, Lyme Regis and after a funeral service with full military honours three days later, he was cremated at Exeter and Devon Crematorium (ref. 8310). His ashes were interred on 31 May in the grave of his wife, Eliza Maria Kathleen, who died on 10 February 1961, at Hillingdon and Uxbridge Cemetery (ref. JU5, Uxbridge section). The inscription under his name on the headstone is 'Ever Brave Loyal and Generous'.

Jerrard's VC was loaned by him to the centenary exhibition of the award in 1956, and his other contributions were a photograph of himself with his captors, which was displayed beside a portrait photograph loaned by the Air Ministry and what the catalogue described as a 'copy of the original "combat report"', loaned by No. 66 Squadron.

The family still hold letters received by Alan Jerrard's parents from his flight commander and commanding officer which 'describe his action and bravery for which he was awarded the VC'.

His decorations were, for many years, on long-term loan to the Royal Air Force Museum at Hendon, but in 2011 these were acquired by the Michael Ashcroft Trust and are now on display in the Lord Ashcroft Gallery at the Imperial War Museum, Lambeth, London. The medal entitlement of Flight Lieutenant Alan Jerrard is VC, BWM (1914–20), Victory Medal (1914–19) and MiD oak leaf, King George VI Coronation Medal (1937), Queen Elizabeth II Coronation Medal (1953), Knight, Order of St Anne (Russia), Medal of Military Valour (Italy).

Jerrard's name is inscribed on the RAF VC Memorial inside St Clement Dane's Church, the Strand, London and there is a memorial plaque bearing his name at Lewisham Civic Centre in south-east London. He was one of eight VC holders with links to the borough and the plaque was unveiled on 9 May 1995.

At a Salisbury auction on 18 July 2012 a large silver-gilt Monteith bowl, engraved with a Victoria Cross and inscribed to Lieutenant Alan Jerrard VC, was sold at a lower auction estimate of £8,000. The buyer was a Clive Richards. This bowl, which had been passed down through his family, had been presented to Jerrard by the Staffordshire Territorial Force Association. As a postscript to this sale a presentation was later made of this bowl to the Bishop Vesey's Grammar School by retiring chairman of governors, Clive Richards OBE. It is to be presented at Speech Day 'as the occasion befits' for outstanding contribution to the school. Memorial plaques are also erected and dedicated to the school's two First World War VC winners, Lieutenant Alan Jerrard RAF and Lieutenant Charles Bonner DSC who won his VC in 1917.

Only one of the many pilots flying Sopwith Camels during the First World War was awarded the Victoria Cross. This was Lieutenant Alan Jerrard, of No. 66 Squadron, No. 14 Wing BEF, RFC.

E. MANNOCK

France, 17 June to 22 July 1918

Major Edward Mannock had returned to England from France on 18 June 1918 with more than fifty victories over enemy aircraft to his credit and had already been awarded the DSO and MC with a Bar to each. On the day prior to his arrival in England Brigadier-General T. Webb-Bowen, commander of 2nd Brigade RAF, had approved the recommendation for Mannock to be awarded a second Bar to his DSO. The rapidity with which he had been recommended for the three DSO awards – in less than a six-week period – emphasised the impressive talents of this airman who at over 30 years of age was much older than many of his contemporaries. His reputation as a first-class patrol leader was well known within the RAF although, as with the great majority of pilots of the time, he was almost unknown to the public.

Before he commenced his new posting as squadron commander of No. 85 Squadron (he was assigned this command after pilots of this Squadron had allegedly objected to the appointment of Major James McCudden) based at St Omer he first visited the airfield at Clairmarais South on 3 July where No. 74 Squadron, his previous unit, was based. Some of his friends here later commented that he was in an emotional state and it would appear likely that he was suffering from what would now be classified as battle fatigue.

Under their previous commander, Major William Bishop VC, No. 85 Squadron, equipped with SE5A Scout aircraft and comprised of talented pilots from a number of countries, had not performed as a cohesive unit. The flight commanders had virtually run the squadron as they saw fit, while Bishop flew on his numerous solo patrols. Mannock quickly imparted his own individual methods of fighting to his squadron pilots, with the emphasis on working as a team.

On 7 July, in his first action as commander, he led the squadron on a offensive patrol in the Doulieu area where a formation of Fokker D VII machines was located and in the ensuing action No. 85 Squadron pilots claimed seven enemy aircraft either destroyed, out of control or driven down, of which two were credited to Mannock.

Two days later Major James McCudden, a very good friend of Mannock's, was killed in a flying accident at Auxi-le-Château airfield. The death of McCudden greatly depressed Mannock, who became more vengeful toward the Germans and often took greater personal risks in subsequent attacks. On one occasion he badly damaged a German two-seater, which he then followed to the ground until it crashed. He then strafed the wreckage, killing all of the crew. Within a week he shot down four more enemy scouts, followed by an Albatros C XII two-seater on 19 July and a day later another two-seater and two Fokker D VII scouts, both near Steenwerck. Mannock added a Fokker DR I triplane to his total on 22 July, which he shot down near Armentières.

Lieutenant Donald Inglis, a New Zealander, had been with the squadron in France for almost two months but had no confirmed victory On 25 July, Mannock suggested that the he and Inglis should attempt to find enemy aircraft – he had been unofficially advised by friends in a British front line unit that two enemy machines were strafing Allied trenches on regular low flying patrols. This sortie was first attempted that afternoon but Inglis had a problem with his SE5A, E1294, which the ground crew could not quickly remedy and the planned patrol was postponed.

On the following morning shortly after 5 a.m. the two prepared for take off from St Omer airfield and Mannock, who was flying his usual aircraft, E1295, confirmed to Inglis that he should 'sit close to my tail'. They flew very low, rarely exceeding 50ft over the front lines, and suddenly Mannock turned west, climbed rapidly before diving to attack a DFW two-seater. It is probable that the Mannock killed or injured the rear gunner when he opened fire, as Inglis later recalled that the German observer was not shooting when he followed Mannock in his own attack and sent the enemy machine down to crash in flames near Lestrem.

A few days earlier Mannock had berated a friend in No. 40 Squadron, Captain George McElroy, for reportedly flying low to confirm his victories, telling him, 'don't go down on the deck ... you'll get shot down from the ground.' Yet in contradiction of his own mantra, on this occasion Mannock circled low over the crashed DFW before he headed for home still at a low height. Very heavy rifle and machine-gun fire from enemy trenches opened up and Inglis, who was following Mannock, observed that 'a flame came out of the right hand side of his machine, after which he apparently went out of control. I went into a spiral down to 50 feet and saw his machine go straight into the ground and burn.' Inglis climbed, and shortly after his own aircraft was hit by ground-fire and the petrol tank holed when he was at a height of about 150ft. However, he made a forced landing just yards behind the British front line near St Floris. Inglis was rescued from his aircraft by men of the 24th Welsh Regiment and taken to a dugout where, soaked with petrol and in a very shocked condition, at first all he could say was, 'the bloody bastards have shot down my major in flames'. At 8.30 a.m. No. 85 Squadron received the following message from 24th Welsh Regiment:

> Major Mannock down by machine gun fire between Colonne and Lestrem after bringing E.A. [Enemy Aircraft] two-seater down in flames at Lestrem. Lt Inglis shot through petrol tank. Landed on front line at St Floris. Machine O.K. Pilot O.K. Machine likely to be shelled. Salvage tonight if possible. More later. Machine at Sheet 36a S.E. Or 36 N.W., K.31.D.14.

Among the witnesses to the action was Private Edward Naulls, D. Coy, 2nd Essex Regiment, stationed between Mont Bernanchon and Pacaut Wood, who, when interviewed some years later by Wing Commander Keith Caldwell, a wartime friend and colleague of Mannock, recalled:

> Just after 5 am, a Gerry [sic] low-wing monoplane ... appeared at Pacaut Wood and cruised to and fro over no man's land. Shortly before 5.30 am, two British fighter aircraft, one flown by Major Mannock and the other by Lt Donald Inglis, a New Zealander, arrived on the scene from the St Omer direction and engaged the Gerry in combat. A few bursts from their guns set it crashing in flames at Lestrem behind Pacaut wood. Mannock then dived to about 40 feet. The remaining trees in Pacaut Wood were of varying heights, the tallest about 30 feet. Mannock's aircraft cleared them by a few feet. Inglis circled at about 100 feet.
>
> Suddenly there was a lot of rifle fire from the Gerry trenches, and then a machine-gun near Robecq opened up using tracers. I saw these strike Mannock's engine on the port side. A blueish-white flame appeared and spread rapidly, smoke and flames enveloped the engine and cockpit. His aircraft, the prop still spinning and making smoke rings, made a right-hand turn and came towards our line but, just short of the line, it turned left towards Pacaut Wood and went down in a long glide over the trees and beyond, gradually losing height until it hit the ground in the direction

of Merville. A column of black smoke shot up. Inglis started to climb away but his engine stopped. I distinctly heard it splutter twice before it stopped and he made a forced landing just behind the front lines held by a company of the Welsh Regiment near St Floris.

That evening the pilots of No. 85 Squadron were joined in their mess by friends of Mannock from other units who had come to 'cheer the lads up' and although more drinks were consumed than usual the attempts to liven up the dinner resulted in rather forced jollity. Mannock's friend and fellow pilot from No. 74 Squadron, Ira Jones recorded in his diary of that day, 'Mick is dead. Everyone stunned. No one can believe it. I can write no more today. It is too terrible.'

Many of Mannock's RAF colleagues and his friends were of the opinion that he should have been awarded the Victoria Cross and also that his total number of official victories was higher than that quoted; in the citation to the award of the second Bar to his DSO it had stated, 'This officer has now accounted for 48 enemy machines'.

The lobbying on Mannock's behalf continued after the Armistice, in particular by Ira Jones, who compiled what he considered to be an accurate list of victories for Mannock which totalled seventy-three – 'coincidentally' one more than William Bishop, the highest-scoring Commonwealth airman. During early May, newspaper reports stated that 'the Ministry for the Air Service has decided that the late Major Mannock was the champion British "ace". He brought down 73 enemy machines' and some suggested he should be awarded a posthumous VC.

Meanwhile, the Minister for Air, Winston Churchill, ordered an investigation into the claims for the posthumous award and the Air Ministry requested full details of Mannock's service from the RAF with particular reference to his aerial combats after 16 June 1918. At the beginning of July a further request was made by the Air Ministry for confirmation of the total number of machines for which Mannock had accounted be checked, especially the eleven victories credited to him after 16 June.

A quick decision was then made as the *London Gazette* of 18 July 1919 published the citation for the award of the Victoria Cross to Mannock. This citation, in addition to describing his victories achieved between 17 June and 22 July also specified that he was receiving the award for 'bravery of the first order in Aerial Combat' and that this, 'highly distinguished officer, during the whole of his career in the Royal Air Force, was an outstanding example of fearless courage, remarkable skill, devotion, to duty and self-sacrifice, which has never been surpassed'. In the final paragraph of the citation it was noted that 'the total number of machines definitely accounted for ... is fifty' and that the total of forty-eight specified previously quoted should have read forty-one. It is not known how this total figure was decided upon, but more importantly the posthumous award had been announced.

❖ ❖ ❖

Edward Corringham Mannock was born on 24 May 1887 to Edward Mannock, a corporal in the 2nd Dragoons, Royal Scots Greys, and his wife, Julia (née O'Sullivan), at Brighton according to the 1891 Census. No documentation has yet been located to confirm this birth and it is possible that Julia Mannock returned to her home at Ballincollig, east of Cork, and that Edward was born there. (Various birthdates and places have been quoted, but Edward's birth at Ballincollig on the above date appears to be likely.)Army postings necessitated a number of moves for the family. When Corporal Mannock completed his term of service the family were then living near Belfast. Civilian live appeared not to suit him, and he rejoined the army. Within a few months the family had moved to Meerut, India, where they were to remain for nearly six years. Here that the young Edward had problems with one eye, possibly an amoebic infestation, which caused temporary blindness, but the condition improved over time so that his vision returned to something near normal. Edward received his early education at the Army School in India, and although he enjoyed both cricket and football he was more often to be found reading books

Edward's father left for active service in the South African War and upon returning to India his second period of military service was drawing to a close. The family returned to England and civilian life, living in Military Road, Canterbury. This situation did not last long; the hard-drinking ex-corporal was soon to take the family's savings and abandoned his wife and children, not making contact or giving any support. Edward was 12 years old and the family was now living in very straitened circumstances. He continued his education at St Thomas School, Canterbury until he was 13, when he took up employment as an errand boy and barber's assistant. He later joined his brother Patrick working as a clerk at the National Telephone Company. He found this work boring and applied for a job as linesman, but as the vacancy was in Wellingborough, Northamptonshire, he had to leave home. Fortunately, Mannock met a local man, Jim Eyles, who offered him accommodation.

Jim Eyles and his wife, May, became like a new family to Mannock and he settled in with them very well. In Wellingborough in addition to playing cricket for the Wesleyan Club he took an interest in politics and became secretary of the local Independent Labour Party. He also joined the Home Counties (Territorial) RAMC and at the annual summer camp became known as something of an orator.

Mannock still sought more excitement and after borrowing money from his brother Patrick and Jim Eyles, he obtained his passport early in January 1914 and a month later travelled to Constantinople, Turkey. There he obtained a job working for the English Telephone Company in charge of a wire- and cable-laying gang, and was employed as a district inspector when war was declared between Great Britain and Germany in August. Turkey dithered but eventually, after pressure from Germany, threw in her lot with the Central Powers in November.

Edward Mannock was interned, as were many foreign workers, in primitive conditions with poor rations. Due to a number of escape attempts, and his patriotic and rebellious attitude, Mannock was subjected to severe beatings and spells of solitary confinement, and his health suffered badly. In England Jim Eyles was worried when letters from Mannock had stopped arriving and he contacted the American Embassy in Turkey for information. After much diplomatic activity, and with the help of The Swiss Red Cross, Mannock was finally released and repatriated to England in March 1915. Jim Eyles and his wife were shocked by his appearance. He was suffering from fever, had lost a lot of weight and had been categorised as 'unfit for military service'. It would seem likely he had made much of his 'poor eyesight' to his captors.

Mannock had developed an obsessive dislike of the Germans and their allies after his treatment in Turkey. In May he enlisted in the 3/2nd Home Services Field Ambulance Company of the RAMC as a sergeant in the transport section. Mannock found this appointment not to his liking as many of his fellow soldiers seemed to be looking for a 'safe billet'. Consequently he sought a more combative role and in April 1916 obtained a transfer to the Royal Engineers. He was posted to the RE Depot at Fenny Stratford near Bletchley, Buckinghamshire, as a cadet for officer training, where the idea of being a tunnelling officer appealed to his him as he would be able to 'blow the bastards up!'

After completing his training Mannock was commissioned, but he was still chafing to get to the front. He had given a lot of thought to the air war and his application for a transfer was finally approved in June. Mannock was posted to No. 1 School of Aeronautics at Reading in August, and during the following month he progressed to No. 9 Reserve Squadron at the Central Flying School, Hendon, for flying lessons.

Mannock's next move was to No. 10 Reserve Squadron at Joyce Green, Dartford, where he first met James McCudden, who was an instructor there at that time. The two men had a mutual liking and respect for each other, and under the tutelage of McCudden and the other instructors Mannock achieved his Aero Club Certificate No. 3895 and was awarded his RFC wings on 28 November 1916 (on the certificate his birthplace is given as Cork). Further training followed before Mannock was assessed as proficient and selected to become a single-seat aircraft pilot in March 1917. He was posted to the No. 1 Aircraft Depot, Clairmarais, St Omer. He arrived on 2 April, and on 6 April he was posted to No. 40 Squadron, based at Treizennes, between St Omer and Béthune. The squadron had recently been re-equipped with Nieuport 17 Scouts, which, although not a match for the latest Albatros Scouts they opposed, were the best that the RFC could supply at that time. The squadron commander, Major Leonard Tilney, assigned Mannock to C Flight to replace a Canadian pilot shot down that morning in an attack on a German balloon line.

Mannock's first few weeks on active service were not at all auspicious as he was slow to settle in to his new surroundings and although flying on contact patrols, he achieved no victories. His social background was so different from many of his public-school-educated contemporaries, and his rather insular and outspoken attitude did not initially enable him to make many friends. Various mechanical problems dogged his flying and he was often to return early from patrols with jammed guns or engine problems, so much so that rumours began to spread that he was not up to the task. It should also be remembered that during this month, 'Bloody April' as it was christened, the RFC suffered its worst casualties of the war. The need for reconnaissance patrols was high as the Battle of Arras progressed and the slow and outdated FE2 and BE2 spotter aircraft were shot down at a rate of ten to every one German machine. The RFC and RNAS recorded losses in excess of 350 in this month alone. Thus it was very important that all aircrew were seen to 'pull their weight'.

Mannock did have cause for apprehension; as well as some initial crash-landings, he had been forced to land an aircraft after one of the wings had fallen off in-flight and on another occasion his aircraft windscreen had been shattered by enemy fire, covering him with glass fragments and oil. He privately admitted to 'feeling nervy and ill ... afraid I am breaking up'.

The criticisms of Mannock reached Major Tilney, who called him to his office and was considering sending him back to England. In his own defence, Mannock told his commanding officer that he had been scared but knew that he could beat this inner fear. Tilney was impressed by this forthright manner and decided to keep him with the squadron. If Mannock had been completely truthful he might also have admitted that he had also spent this period adjusting his flying and gunnery techniques to compensate for the less than perfect vision of his left eye.

During April the squadron moved airfields, first a brief stay at Auchel, a little west of Béthune, and on 25 April to Bruay, nearly 20 miles north-west of Arras, but it was not until 7 May that Mannock claimed his first victory when, flying in a patrol of five other Nieuports, he shot down a barrage balloon in flames. The low-flying raid was very successful and although one squadron pilot was killed the remaining five all claimed balloons as victims. After inspecting the many bullet holes in his aircraft, some very close to his head, Mannock noted in his diary, 'I don't want to go through such an experience again.'

Mannock drove down enemy two-seater aircraft on both 25 May and 1 June but claimed for neither as they went down on the German side of the line. It was nearly a week later that he recorded his first victory. He was, with other squadron aircraft, escorting a formation of FE2b bombers over Lille early in the morning of 7 June when he spotted and attacked an Albatros DIII. He fired thirty rounds into it from a range of about 10yd and sent it spinning down out of control.

Two days later Mannock was again part of a formation of Nieuports in an evening action near Douai, after he recorded in his diary that although he scored hits on two enemy machines with his Lewis gun 'nothing definite as regards their absolute destruction could be vouchsafed'.

Mannock had now developed close friendships with Lieutenant William Maclanachan, a Scot who had joined the squadron in May, and an Irishman, Lieutenant George McElroy. He referred to these two as McScotch and McIrish respectively and was instrumental in tutoring them both into becoming very good fighter pilots.

On 12 June Mannock was briefly blinded by a small fragment of metal in his right eye. Although he made a safe landing he was carried from the aircraft and admitted to hospital, where a speck of metal was removed. He needed to wear a bandage over his right eye, and although taking part in no operational flights he did fly to nearby airfields to meet friends before he was given leave in England on 17 June. This incident would appear to confirm that the vision in his left eye was adequate for flying.

After an unhappy spell in London, where his mother was now an alcoholic and demanding that he send her more money, he journeyed to Wellingborough and stayed with Jim Eyles and his family. When his leave was over he returned to No. 40 Squadron and on 12 July emptied a drum from his Lewis gun into a DFW CV two-seater over Avion. Victory was confirmed when this machine crash-landed upside-down in Allied territory. Mannock and others quickly visited the crash site and he wrote in his diary that they found a black and tan terrier dead in the observer's seat: 'I felt exactly like a murderer. The journey to the trenches was rather nauseating – dead men's legs sticking through the sides ... This sort of thing, together with the strong graveyard stench and the dead and mangled body of the pilot … combined to upset me for a few days.' The next day he shot down a DFW near Billy-Montigny.

The notification of his award of a Military Cross (gazetted 17 September 1917) was telephoned to the airfield on 19 July while Mannock was out on patrol – the recommendation for this award, dated 14 July, itemised the four actions from 4 May onwards in which Mannock had achieved victories. When Maclanachan heard the news he arranged for the MC ribbon to be sewn on to Mannock's spare uniform jacket, which was then left hanging on the door of his hut to await his return.

The citation to this MC award specified that Mannock was 'showing a very fine offensive spirit and great fearlessness', emphasising that he was now confirming the faith shown in him by Major Tilney in not sending him home and was starting to silence his previous critics. However, Mannock had witnessed an aircraft going down in flames on 21 July (Second Lieutenant F.W. Hook) which did unnerve him reatly, and he later began carrying a revolver, telling Mclanachan that he would shoot himself if ever his aircraft caught fire. (RFC pilots were not issued with parachutes.)

Mannock was promoted from second lieutenant to acting captain and made flight commander on 22 July, and on 5 August he claimed another victory over an Albatros, shot down out of control and confirmed by two of his fellow pilots.

Now that he was in command of a flight Mannock started to put some of his ideas into practice. He considered that the day of the solo fighter was over and that coordinated formations could inflict the maximum damage on the enemy with the least number of casualties to the RFC and RNAS pilots. It was about this time when Major Keith Caldwell, visiting a friend at No. 40 Squadron, first met Mannock and he later recorded, 'I had quite a talk then with "Mick" Mannock. It was the first time I'd met him and I was very impressed with his dedicated keenness.'

An advanced landing ground had been set up by No. 40 Squadron at Petit Sains, about 12 miles south of Béthune, where some of the pilots would be based during the day and would be able to respond quickly to the approach of any enemy aircraft over the front lines, less than 2 miles away. In mid-afternoon on 12 August an enemy aircraft was spotted from this field and Mannock immediately took off. In a low-level action of less than five minutes he wounded the pilot who crash-landed his Albatros DIII Scout behind Allied lines near Petit-Vimy. This was Mannock's sixth official victory and the pilot was later identified as Leutnant Joachim von Bertab, who had at least five victories to his credit.

Further success for Mannock followed three days later when he was officially credited with two of the squadron's six claims and on 17 August he shot down a DFW two-seater, which crashed near Sallaumines.

Later in the month the Nieuport 23 Scouts began to arrive at the squadron. They were a little faster than the type 17 being used, but still the German Albatros Scout had the advantage with its superior armament of two machine guns and greater manoeuvrability. The final days of August were quiet for the squadron and it was not until 4 September that Mannock recorded further victories.

All three actions on this day were against DFW two-seater aircraft the first at about 10 a.m. when he used all three drums of Lewis gun ammunition in an attack on a DFW spotted high over Noux-les-Mines, in which he wounded the observer. This action was in full view of the advanced landing ground and caused much excitement as the enemy machine was finally seen to be diving down east of Lens. A further encounter at 11.30 a.m. was also with a DFW and although the result appeared inconclusive both Mannock and Sergeant Herbert, who was flying with him, were credited with this victory. The final combat of the day, in the late afternoon, resulted in Mannock shooting down yet another DFW which caught fire and broke up before crashing near Souchez. Mannock recorded in his diary that the flaming aircraft 'was a horrible sight and made me feel quite sick', although he was not doubt pleased on landing when 'the boys gave a me a great ovation'. As Caldwell was later to write, 'the great thing about Mannock was that many of his successes were won in front of his followers so that they could see how it was done.'

Two days later Mannock was involved in combat sorties and although it is quite probable that he sent an Albatros Scout down out of control he made no claim. Inclement weather greatly reduced flying and it was 11 September before another DFW was claimed by Mannock who, flying a Nieuport 23 in an engagement with three such machines, sent one down out of control near Oppy Wood which brought his official total of accredited victories to twelve. His thirteenth came on 20 September. Only three days elapsed before Mannock shot down a yellow and green two-seater over Oppy, and on 25 September, after he had fired a complete drum from his Lewis gun into a Rumpler, it crashed near Sallaumines. Although involved in numerous combat sorties, he claimed no further victories during the remainder of the year.

In early October Mannock returned to England on leave and on the 18th the award of a Bar to his MC was announced (gazetted 7 March 1918). The recommendation was dated 6 September and specified his actions from 5 August to 6 September. He was back at Bruay in late November, and the squadron was re-equipped with SE5A aircraft the following month. Although Mannock liked this new aircraft, problems with jamming guns did annoy him and he considered this denied the pilots a number of victories. One of the problems was that because a number of British factories were producing ammunition a degree of tolerance in bullet casing size was allowed, and the larger size casings were prone to causing jams. Mannock often advised pilots to load their own Lewis guns.

On 1 January 1918 Mannock scored his first victory in the new aircraft, attacking a Hannover CLIII which crashed near Fampoux. After months of continuous air fighting, Mannock was at times very tense and full of foreboding about his fate. Orders had been received for a home posting and that night a leaving party was held for Mannock with the squadron's infamous 'Lady Killer' cocktails and quantities of champagne much in evidence. He was on fine form and entertained all with 'one of his marvellous speeches'. In an after-dinner speech, the squadron commander, Major Leonard Tilney, was not stinting in his praise for Mannock. Tilney later wrote in the squadron diary, 'his leadership and general ability will never be forgotten by those who had the good fortune to serve under him'. Mannock sailed the following afternoon after an amazing send-off when 'the car was loudly cheered by the officers outside the Mess and we found the road lined with cheering mechanics'. Fellow pilot Captain Gwilym Lewis, wrote in a letter home: 'Our expert Captain Edward Mannock, has recently been sent home very much against his will. He has been out here about eight or ten months and has 18 Huns to his credit.'

Mannock stayed at the RFC Club in Bruton Street, London, during his leave. He was initially attached to the Wireless Experimental Station at Biggin Hill, where he made a nuisance of himself in his efforts to obtain another overseas posting. In mid-February his wish was granted when he was appointed as a flight commander to the new No. 74 Squadron. Major Keith Caldwell, a very experienced New Zealand pilot, was appointed CO and he later recorded that he was 'delighted to find that Mannock was the senior flight commander'.

Mannock wasted no time in imparting his ideas concerning teamwork and his own set of rules, which he considered would keep his pilots alive. One of his fundamental points, later recalled by many of these fliers, was 'gentleman, always above; seldom on the same level; never underneath' – his diktat when attacking enemy scouts – and this he had painted on the walls on the walls of classrooms and hangars.

During his time at London Colney, Mannock made two visits to Wellingborough and a local newspaper published details of the flying display by 'Paddy' and another airman, Second Lieutenant Henry Dolan, put on in front of large crowds on the first of these visits in February. It was also reported that Mannock had '17 enemy machines to his credit' and would soon be returning to the front.

On the last day of the month the squadron flew to St Omer. The following day, 1 April, when the RFC and RNAS merged and the RAF was formed, No. 74 Squadron moved to Teteghem airfield near Dunkirk for gunnery practice. After a week they moved to la Lovie near Poperinge before their base at Clairmarais, St Omer, was reached on 11 April, a little over a year since Mannock had first arrived at this airfield.

Meanwhile the major German offensive *Kaiserslacht*, which had commenced on 21 March south of Arras, finally ceased its advance short of Amiens, due mainly to the Germans lack of logistics support and was called off on 5 April. A new German attack, Operation Georgette, was launched on 9 April north of the la Bassée Canal, and three days later No. 74 Squadron was ordered to patrol near Merville, where advanced German troops were digging in. Mannock's flight took off with the final instruction to his pilots. 'Remember, to fight is not enough. You must kill.' A formation of Albatros Scouts was spotted east of Merville and after a short-range attack Mannock sent one Albatros D V down out of control. At least two more enemy machines crashed in this action, one of which Mannock credited to Dolan, to, in his own words 'buck the lad up'.

Later that day Mannock shot down another similar aircraft south of Lille, near Bois de Phalempin, and after a further offensive patrol in the early evening two further claims were made by B Flight, so the squadron ended its first day of combat with an impressive five victories.

Poor weather hampered flying operations for a number of days and it was not until 21 April that the squadron claimed three further victims. That same day news arrived that the highest scoring German airman, Manfred von Richthofen, credited with eighty victories, had been killed. At dinner that evening a toast was made to the squadron's first loss, followed by a toast to von Richthofen in which Mannock did not participate, reportedly saying, 'I hope the bastard burnt all the way down'.

Two days later Mannock attacked a Pfalz DIII east of Merville and this machine was seen to crash near Meurillon. Despite leading several patrols it was 29 April before Mannock claimed his twentieth victory when he fired forty rounds at an Albatros D VII, which went down in flames near Dickebusch Lake.

May was to be the most successful month for Mannock, beginning when he led an evening patrol on 3 May and all four SE5s involved were awarded a share of an LVG, which they attacked and shot down near Merville. Three days later he was in action against four enemy scouts over Dickebusch Lake, which culminated with the destruction of a Fokker DRI triplane near Gheluvelt. In a letter to a cousin on 8 May Mannock wrote that his 'bag [was] now 23 or 24'.

The squadron had a bad day on 8 May when three pilots were lost, two in an action against the triplanes of *Jasta* 26 over Gheluvelt and the third who crashed at Clairmarais airfield in flames after being in action in the same sortie.

Mannock was recommended for the award of a DSO (gazetted on 16 September) on 9 May and in addition to describing his victories from 22 April to 6 May the recommendation specified that, 'This officer has now accounted for 30 enemy machines, and is a wonderful asset to his squadron'. The actual DSO citation specified that in seven days he had destroyed seven enemy machines.

In an early evening two-aircraft patrol of 11 May, Mannock encountered a formation of eight enemy aircraft and he recorded the destruction of a silver and black Pfalz DIII which burst into flames north-east of Armentières. The following evening Mannock led the squadron in an attack on eight German aircraft, and in the ensuing combat near Wulverghem No. 74 Squadron pilots claimed six victories, three of these credited to Mannock. One SE5 was lost in the action, Lieutenant Henry Nolan MC, who had regularly flown as Mannock's wingman in recent weeks and whose death greatly upset the flight commander.

During the following days Mannock claimed victories over two further enemy aircraft on 17 May and another Albatros two-seater on the 18th. The recommendation for a Bar to his DSO was put forward by his Brigade Commander (gazetted 16 September 1916) and the final paragraph stated: 'In five days' fighting Captain Mannock has destroyed eight enemy machines, bringing his total up to thirty-eight. He sets a wonderful example in marksmanship and determination to get to close quarters: as a Patrol leader he is unequalled.'

It was on 21 May that he achieved his greatest daily total to date. Leading his flight on a morning patrol he attacked a green Hannover two-seater, which crashed into a tree near Couronne, and later that day, on an offensive sortie near Hollebeke, the squadron claimed six Pfalz Scouts, three of which were attributed to Mannock. He shot down yet another Pfalz D III, out of control, the following evening over Fromelles.

General Sir Herbert Plumer, 2nd Army Commander, had visited the squadron a few days before Mannock's hat-trick achievement and announced the award of his DSO.

In sorties during the remaining days of May Mannock achieved victories over five further enemy machines, two each on the 26th and 29th and a single Pfalz DIII two days later.

The constant patrolling and air fighting was taking its toll on Mannock's frayed nerves, and privately he admitted that he could see no end to the slaughter. (With hindsight it is easy to say that Mannock ought to have been retained in England for a longer period of rest, as not only was he battle weary, he was unfit; but No. 85 Squadron needed a top-class commander after Bishop's departure and there was none better qualified than Mannock.) He rarely showed these fears amongst his fellow pilots and would still burst into the mess after a successful action shouting, 'Flamerinos boys! Sizzle sizzle wonk', followed by a detailed account of his opponent's flaming demise. Such exhibitions of bravado were as much to hide his own fear of being shot down in flames as to instill a fighting spirit in the other pilots.

May had been a very successful month for No. 74 Squadron with twenty of the squadron's victories claimed by Mannock. June commenced with a trio of Pfalz D III aircraft shot down by him in an action over Estaires on the afternoon of the 1st, followed by another similar machine shot down near Kemmel the next day.

Poor visibility hampered flying for a few days and it was not until 6 June that Mannock claimed two further victories, both Fokker D VII aircraft, the second of which was shared with three other pilots of his flight. Three days later when he shot down a pair of Albatros two-seaters south of Kemmel, and a week later six of the squadron aircraft attacked a formation of eighteen Pfalz Scouts near Dickebusch Lake and Mannock claimed the only two victories. His final victory with No. 74 Squadron was on 17 June when he shot down a silver Hannover two-seater over Armentières.

Mannock departed for on leave on 18 June, and the following day Major Caldwell was informed that his A Flight Commander, in addition to being promoted major, was to take command of No. 85 squadron. Caldwell telegraphed this information to the RFC Club, London, to await Mannock's arrival. During this period of leave, Mannock met up with his friend McCudden, then stationed at Turnberry training fighter pilots, and was agitating for another overseas posting. He then visited his mother in Birmingham, before travelling to Wellingborough. Here, Jim Eyles noticed the change in his friend and at one point found him trembling and sobbing uncontrollably. The stress of the period of almost continuous fighting, and apprehension about taking over No. 85 Squadron in the footsteps of the famous 'Billy Bishop VC' was taking its toll on Mannock's nerves. Shortly afterwards Mannock left for his final tour of duty.

After the Armistice, despite the thorough battlefield searches carried out by the Imperial War Graves Commission, Mannock's remains were not identified, although a German 6th Army document, located in Berlin, stated that 'Flight Captain Mannock's body had been recovered and buried about 300m north-west of la-Pierre-au-Beurre near the road to Pacaut'. Jim Eyles tried to obtain information about his grave, but in

1924 the IWGC confirmed that no grave for Mannock could be identified. Consequently his name appears together with those of nearly 1,000 other airmen on the Flying Services Memorial to the Missing at Arras.

Mannock's brother Patrick later received his brother's tunic, revolver, identity discs and notebook – apparently removed by a German soldier prior to the burial. As none of these were fire damaged, a theory that he had burned to death when his aircraft crashed was dispelled.

Both Wellingborough and Canterbury claimed affiliation to Mannock, and his name appears on the Wellingborough War Memorial at Broad Street and also on the Canterbury War Memorial at Christchurch Gate. On 18 July 1925 a memorial plaque was unveiled in Canterbury Cathedral. Unfortunately it incorrectly gives 18 July as his date of death. For a number of years memorial services were held there by the RAFA, and when these ceased occasional services were held by the WFA but at the time of writing no service has been held since 2008. In 1937 a bed in the new Kent and Canterbury Hospital was endowed in his name.

The RAF Museum at Hendon houses a collection of papers relating to Mannock, including his 1914 passport and various letters.

King of Air Fighters by Ira Jones, a fellow pilot from No. 74 Squadron, was published in 1934. It brought the Mannock's exploits to a wide audience and attempted to qualify seventy-three victories for Mannock.

Shortly before the Second World War, a street on a new housing estate in Wellingborough was named Mannock Road. In 1939 a local news interview reported Jim Eyles as saying that something ought to have been done years earlier and that if Mannock had been in 'born higher in the world socially … he would have been honoured rather differently'. A colour portrait of Mannock had been hung in the Council Chamber some years earlier. In 1941 the Air Training Corps in Wellingborough was named 378 (Mannock) Squadron in his memory. Mannock is also remembered in Wellingborough by a plaque at 183 Mill Road (the earlier home of Jim Eyles), unveiled on the 100th anniversary of Mannock's birth, and in a memorial in Doddington Street Cemetery.

Mannock's name appears with other recipients of the VC on a plaque left of the altar in St Clement Danes Church, the Strand, London.

Canterbury later acquired another memorial, near where Mannock had lived. On 5 December 1957 a plaque on Mannock House, a block of new maisonettes at Military Road, Canterbury, was unveiled by Air Commodore Freddie West VC.

In Brighton, part of the Preston barracks was named Mannock Building, and at the time of writing there are discussions regarding the future redevelopment of this area. One of the OmniDekka buses operating in Brighton and Hove was briefly (September 2006–March 2008) named Mick Mannock.

The year 1987 marked the 70th anniversary of the founding of No. 85 Squadron and on 8 May a watercolour painting depicting Mannock and Lieutenant Dolan in action was on 12 April 1918 was presented to the squadron. The small presentation party included Tony Spagnoly, who, for many years, would insert a memorial notice to Mannock in the *Daily Telegraph* on the anniversary of his death.

In 1995 Mannock's name was inscribed on aircraft XV103. As the aircraft were replaced over time, the names were transferred and Mannock's name was transferred to ZA147 in April 2013, along with James McCudden's. This aircraft made its final flight five months later and is scheduled to be broken up.

Mannock's medal entitlement was VC, DSO and two Bars, MC and Bar, 1914–15 Star, BWM, Victory Medal and MiD oak leaf. His medals are now displayed in the Lord Ashcroft Collection at the Imperial War Museum, Lambeth, London, but as with many episodes connected to Mannock, their previous history is far from straightforward.

Mannock's father surfaced in south-east London and wrote to the Air Ministry in August 1919, first enquiring about his son's will and then, probably having learned that nothing was due to him, asking how he could claim Edward's VC. There are various versions of what happened next; either Edward Mannock senior was presented with the medals and sold them soon after for 5 shillings, or he kept the medals and they were later retrieved by Patrick Mannock. Another version is that Patrick received the medals initially and retained them. Whichever of the above is accurate, the facts are that the medals were at some point kept in a bank vault before being loaned to the RAF Museum, Hendon, in 1972, where they remained until, under instruction from the family, they were auctioned in June 1992. On 19 September, after much press publicity, a then record hammer price of £120,000 was recorded as the medals were sold to an unidentified buyer.

On the 90th anniversary of his death a plaque was unveiled at Sywell Aviation Museum near Wellingborough by the mayor, who had earlier attended a short service at the memorial to Mannock in Doddington Street Cemetery, Wellingborough.

In the years following his death much has been written about his life and military career, and more than once it has been suggested that Mannock is buried in Laventie Military Cemetery, La Gorgue. The remains of an unknown airman were recovered not far from Mannock's crash site soon after the war and interred in plot III.F.12. On a number of occasions information has been put before the

CWGC – and the IWGC before them – with the suggestion that this headstone should be replaced with one inscribed 'believed to be Major E Mannock'. The latest request was made in 2008 and this was later passed by the CWGC to the MOD, who since 2000 have undertaken the responsibility for naming unknown casualites. (This change occured after controversy arose regarding a headstone that had been inscibed with the name of Rudyard Kipling's son John.) The MOD responded that they were not prepared to accept the evidence and that no action should be taken in respect of marking the Laventie grave. Nevertheless, many believe this to be Mannock's final resting place, and Air Cadets from Wellingborough, whose unit bears his name, lay a wreath here on the anniversary of his death.

On 21 March 2009 A BBC *Timewatch* television programme entitled 'WWI Aces Falling' was shown, which covered the life and death of both Mannock and his friend James McCudden, and yet again military historians put forward a convincing case for Mannock's final resting place being in Laventie cemetery. In this same year one of the last photographs of Mannock was found in an old French photograph album.

Captain George McElroy MC and two Bars, DFC and Bar (McIrish) ignored the advice given him by his friend, and was shot down by ground fire five days after Mannock on 31 July 1918, when he followed down an enemy aircraft he had attacked. The 25-year-old pilot, who had amassed a total of forty-seven victories before his death, is buried in this cemetery, I.C.1.

Major Edward Mannock's legacy was the tactics he evolved and his 'rules of air fighting', many of which were incorporated into inter-war air training in the RAF. Many of the Second World War fighter pilots referred to him as their inspiration. Although some have said he hated his opponents, it could be more appropriate to say that he hated what they stood for. The precise number of his victories has been much discussed over the years, but many of those who knew him, and later others to whom he became a hero, would perhaps rather remember him for his fondness for the constant playing of 'Londonderry Air' on the squadron gramophone.

F.M.F. WEST

Near Roye, France, 8–10 August 1918

The German offensives, which had commenced in March of 1918, had ground to a halt and the Allies, now with the aid of the United States, were preparing for their own massive attacks in August. Utilising artillery, tanks and infantry, the preparations for the start of this offensive were very thorough and the relatively new unit of the armed forces, the Royal Air Force, was well utilised particularly, in the planning stages, in reconnaissance duties.

No. 8 Squadron, flying FK8 (Big Ack) two-seaters, based near Amiens, had, by early August, completed the aerial photography of their sector, at the cost of several aircraft and their crews. The photographs were mounted on large boards in the briefing marquee and studied in detail by the airmen in readiness for the forthcoming offensive. Major-General Sir John Salmond, head of the RAF in France (the Royal Flying Corps and the Royal Naval Air Service had amalgamated under the new name on 1 April) visited the squadron and talked to the airmen about their coming role in a few days' time. He explained that after the Allied dawn attack the Germans would counter-attack, throwing in reinforcements in certain sectors, and army HQ needed to know the positions of these reinforcements as quickly as possible.

On both the 8th and 9th Captain Freddie West, Commander of B Flight, together with his observer/gunner Flight Lieutenant John Haslam, went out on patrols when they used a technique of flying low over woods in deliberate attempts to draw enemy fire and so give away his position. This tactic led to damage to their aircraft, and on both days West had to crash-land at Vignacourt, which left him shaken and bruised. On 10 August they were flying at about 1,500ft above a layer of fog, attempting to find the group of Allied tanks with which they were to cooperate, advancing on Roye.

Suddenly, through a gap in the cloud, they spotted at the edge of a wood a very large enemy concentration of armoured cars, transport and troops who greeted their low-flying machine with concentrated fire from which West escaped into the clouds. Haslam replied with the single Lewis gun, but confirmation by West of what he saw was essential, so that he turned and made again for the gap in the clouds. Shortly after, he became aware of two aircraft behind, firing as they approached. He was soon wounded in his right foot as other enemy pilots fired at his aircraft. West then wheeled and dived into a funnel-shaped gap in the cloud and he recognised the shape of the wood from the aerial photographs he and the other airman had studied. He then turned for home, but two more enemy aircraft dived in to attack him, and when Haslam fired at them West was hit in his left leg and almost lost consciousness. He said later, 'the terrific pain was the only thing that seemed to keep me from going off entirely.' Needing to stem the flow of blood, West desperately twisted the seam of his shorts into a tourniquet.

In great pain, West attempted to make a landing, but even as he did so an enemy machine flew in low three times, its guns firing, trying to make sure of its victim. West recalled:

> When the Canadian soldiers rushed up to get me out, I asked them to get in touch with our Squadron, because I had some important information. To this they said 'All right, leave it to us', and within a matter of half an hour or so, an officer came and I gave him the details, '… masses of enemy infantry … at Ham and Hombleux … Many guns and tanks at Bussy …', and I always remember that the fellow concerned, Jock the station adjutant, forgetting that I was practically without a leg said 'Well done!' and gave me a cup of tea.

Recovering consciousness in the RAF Ward of a military hospital at Rouen, Freddie's first thought was that the pain in his leg had gone, replaced by violent pins and needles in his feet and toes, but when his mind cleared and he threw back the blankets, he was horrified to see that his left leg had been amputated. To make matters worse the enemy had begun bombing Rouen heavily and during September four adjacent wards were badly damaged. The temporary huts quickly collapsed whilst West and the other patients lay helpless on their beds hearing the planes coming and waiting for the falling bombs. West was amazed by the night nurse, 'this slip of a girl touring our large ward with a steady hand and a smiling face', who calmly carried on with her duties through the bombing raids.

After his stay in Rouen, West returned home and was transferred to the London Hospital in Whitechapel. Here, a few days before the Armistice, he was returned to his ward after an operation on his stump, still under the effects of the anaesthetic, and was greeted by the noise of his fellow patients rattling their spoons in metal mugs. It was not until he was fully conscious that he realised he had been awarded the Victoria Cross.

The seventh supplement to the *London Gazette* No. 30999 dated 5 November carried the citation:

LIEUT. (ACTG. CAPT.) FERDINAND MAURICE FELIX WEST, M.C.,ROYAL AIR FORCE

(Formerly of the Special Reserve, Royal Munster Fusiliers), in recognition of his outstanding bravery in aerial combat.

Captain West, while engaging hostile troops at a low altitude far over the enemy lines, was attacked by seven aircraft. Early in the engagement one of his legs was partially severed by an explosive bullet, and fell powerless into the controls, rendering the machine for the time unmanageable. Lifting his disabled leg, he regained control of the machine, and, although wounded in the other leg, he, with surpassing bravery and devotion to duty, manoeuvred his machine so skilfully that his observer was enabled to get several good bursts into the enemy machines, which drove them away. Captain West then, with rare courage and determination, desperately wounded as he was, brought his machine over our lines and landed safely. Exhausted by his exertions, he fainted, but on remaining conscious insisted on writing his report.

When the Armistice was announced, West and some other patients were allowed out for the evening and were 'picked up by an ambulance outside the "Monico" [Café Monico was in Shaftesbury Avenue and overlooked Piccadilly Circus] at six o'clock the next morning!' He was discharged from hospital in December and sent to Roehampton for the fitting of a conventional artificial leg, but he found this artificial limb clumsy. The Air Ministry paid West £250 for the loss of his leg, and after investing £200 in War Bonds he went 'off to Paris to spend the other £50'. While there, Freddie saw a shop selling wooden legs and invested £20 of his compensation in a new leg which, after a few fittings, was a big improvement on his 'Roehampton stump'.

West was now concerned for his future, in that he would soon be invalided out of the RAF with a pension of £100 per year, and so he once again thought of law. Based on his education, war record and age, Freddie was told he would be admitted to the Temple. It was at this time that West met Marcel Desoutter, a very early aviator who had lost his leg after a flying accident at Hendon in 1913. Initially fitted with a wooden leg, he, with his brother's help, had designed a new jointed metal alloy leg of half the weight. More importantly, it had enabled Desoutter to fly again. Freddie had a Desoutter leg fitted and made very good progress, enabling him to raise his own hopes about flying again. On a visit to the RAF Club, West made such an good impression on Maurice Baring with his new mobility (now needing only a walking stick to help him) that he was able to get an interview with Baring's chief, Air Vice-Marshal Sir Hugh Trenchard, in February 1919. Trenchard was so impressed by Freddie's recovery and eagerness to remain in the RAF that he put him forward for a temporary post as an RAF liaison officer at the Foreign Office, telling West, 'You will be our first Air Force diplomat.' A few days later, on the morning of 1 March 1919, he was presented with his Victoria Cross and Military Cross by King George V at a Buckingham Palace investiture.

❖ ❖ ❖

Ferdinand Maurice Felix West was born on 29 January 1896 to Lieutenant Francis Drake West (grandson of an admiral and a descendant of both William Pitt the Younger and Sir Francis Drake) of the East Lancashire Regiment and his wife, the former Comtesse Clémence de la Garde de Saignes. The family lived in Princes Square, London W2. Soon after his wedding, when his regiment was posted abroad, Lieutenant West resigned his commission to be with his young wife, but at the outbreak of the Boer War in October, three years after his only child was born, he rejoined the colours, only to be numbered among the British casualties sustained in 1902.

There had been some xenophobic disapproval from West's family when he married the French-born Clémence, and relations had worsened when he resigned his Army commission. His widow, still only 26 and ten years younger than her husband, was finally estranged by her husband's family after his death. Consequently she left England to be near her sister Marie, in Milan, a lady in holy orders.

Ferdinand and his mother moved from England to a fifth-floor flat in one of the tallest buildings in Milan. When visiting the convent where his aunt Marie was a nun he met the Chaplain, Monsignor Ratti. Ratti became a very good friend to Ferdinand, who had linguistic abilities resulting in him becoming trilingual – fluent in English, French and Italian – a skill that left him with the hint of a unique pronunciation for the remainder of his life.

Ferdinand's education was entrusted to a private school which, although it was in Milan, was run by a Swiss couple, Herr Heinz and his wife, assisted by both Italian and English staff. At the age of 9 he progressed to a big communal Milan school (*ginnasio*) where he had no difficulty in keeping up with the other students, who were in some cases as much as eighteen months his senior.

On 28 September 1910 Ferdinand had his first experience with early aviation together with its inherent risks when he travelled with a friend to the Piazza del Duomo in Milan to witness the progress of Peruvian-English Georges Chavez. Three weeks previously, Chavez had set up an altitude record of 8,487ft in a Henry Farman aircraft and was now about to attempt a crossing of the Alps from Brigue, Switzerland to Dommodossola, not far from Milan. His progress was signalled to the crowds on the Piazza by a series of flags flown there, each of different colours. The raising of a green flag alerted the watchers to the aviator being airborne and when a blue one was flown, the gathering went wild with excitement, shouting, 'Viva – viva Chavez!' for the colour indicated that his Blériot monoplane was well on its way.

Thirty minutes later a red banner appeared, indicating success. This had only just been hoisted when it was replaced by a black one, its appearance drawing from the gathering a lengthy moan, the sound of which struck the two youngsters as 'like the sea moaning and grinding on a pebbly beach'. There was no mistaking its message: Chavez had been involved in an accident.

What had in fact happened was that, having successfully negotiated the rigours of the flight, either he had been overcome by the extreme cold of the journey while attempting to land, or while doing so, the machine had stalled and crashed. The pilot was so severely injured that two days later he died in hospital, allegedly murmuring, '*Arriba, mas arriba*' – 'Higher, ever higher', words later to become the motto of the Peruvian Air Force.

In October West successfully passed his final matriculation and qualified to become a university student. Determined to read International Law, he selected Genoa and began his studies in 1912, and eventually passed the examinations with a thesis on Roman law before leaving for the summer vacation and temporary employment in a Swiss bank at the end of June 1914.

Shortly after the start of the war, West and a German colleague at the bank were involved in a brawl. Consequently West decided to leave the country for England and military service, his journey taking him via Italy to France where he learned to drive a motor car while waiting for a ship.

Arriving in Le Havre, West fell foul of the local Gendarmerie and was temporarily arrested, mainly due to his linguistic skills and his accent. But after a further twenty-four hours' captivity, he was released and put on a ship for England.

Once he arrived at Victoria Station, London, Freddie was approached by recruiting officers who 'helped' him to the nearest army recruiting office. He was passed fit and ordered to Waterloo Station to entrain for the RAMC Depot at Aldershot.

No. 39162 Private West's military career in the RAMC progressed well, and he rose to the rank of sergeant and applied for a commission. Appointed a second lieutenant in the Special Reserve of Officers in May 1915, he joined the Royal Munster Fusiliers, an Irish regiment that had already suffered severe losses in France. Second Lieutenant West arrived in France on 8 November and reported with a draft of men to the HQ of 2nd Munsters who were in reserve in the ruins of Mazingarbe. Within thirty-six hours of his arrival, the battalion was back occupying front-line trenches. By the end of the month this depleted battalion was withdrawn and from then until February 1916 used as a Pioneer battalion.

By early 1917, West was a company commander and acting captain, and had to visit Amiens, where on the expanse of the high plainland No. 3 Squadron RFC was based. In exchange for a loan of his horse, Lieutenant Edgar Golding promised him a flight. This single flight confirmed his desire to become an airman and he applied for transfer to the Royal Flying Corps, which was granted in April. His training programme included instruction in artillery spotting, including the heavy guns, and observing from the air the fall of their shot. The course held at Brooklands was quite brief and was quickly followed by a posting to No. 3 Squadron as an observer/gunner in one of the eighteen Morane-Saulnier Type 'P' two-seat monoplanes, commonly called Morane Parasols because of their high-wing configuration. West was to act as observer-under-training to Edgar Golding, who proved to be a pilot of as much as six months' experience, and it was not long before the two flew for the first time over the front line, where, from 2,000ft, West was able to identify many of the landmarks with which he had become familiar during his time in the trenches.

Fascinated by the sight of these, he began pointing them out to his pilot and had to be reminded that his duty was to keep a sharp lookout for enemy aircraft and have the twin Lewis guns kept ready. West occasionally flew as gunner to other pilots and it was while doing so with a Dick Brown that he encountered action for the first time.

During the summer of 1917, over the lines artillery spotting as usual, West identified an enemy aircraft which emerged from clouds firing at the Morane. West responded with a series of sharp bursts and suddenly the enemy swung away in the direction of his own lines.

Taking a last look round, West now went to tap Brown on the shoulder, immediately noting two round holes about 3in apart in the other's flying jacket, on the right side just below the shoulder strap, where the bullets had hit the pilot below the shoulder blade. This fact was confirmed when, leaning further forward, it was possible to see that Brown's right arm was useless and evidently numb since he was now attempting to fly the machine with the left alone. Even so, the journey back to Longavesne was completed without further incident.

Brown was sent to hospital and West was given a brief leave. Later he learned that Golding had been shot down and killed on 19 September. West had put in an application for pilot training which was accepted around this time, and he returned to Grantham, Lincolnshire for tuition.

The aircraft at this station were of the de Havilland DH6 type, and after five hours' instruction under Captain Readman, West was allowed to go solo on 15 November.

Freddie attempted a forbidden 'loop', in secret, some 5 miles from the airfield, with the result that he badly frightened himself and also made a very bad landing, having to walk back to base. He owned up to the squadron commander, Major Trafford Leigh-Mallory, who confined West's sentence to a reprimand. West was awarded his pilot's brevet just before Christmas 1917.

On 8 January 1918 he was posted to No. 8 Squadron, flying FK8 army co-operation two-seaters from Amiens, where his commander was Leigh-Mallory once again. Three days leave were granted before the new posting, which West and three fellow aviators spent at the Piccadilly Hotel in London dining and dancing. As he later recalled, 'My wings expanded on my chest. An RFC pilot, a man from the skies, was something new and exciting to the fair sex, something to arouse curiosity and admiration, something to talk about. I enjoyed myself while the going was good.'

At Amiens, Leigh-Mallory had called all the new arrivals together to explain that they were to be the eyes of the gunners and the tanks and also to warn about the dangers from von Richthofen's 'circus' of red-painted Fokkers who were active in this sector. When asked if any protection would be available, Leigh-Mallory said, 'They have Richthofen but we have McCudden, Captain James McCudden of 56 Squadron, behind us ... and there are other hunters out for German scalps – Captains Barker and Bishop and Beauchamp-Proctor; and Captain Ball ... you won't be playing a lone hand'. January and February 1918 were remarkable for the bitter weather they brought, so wintry, indeed, that little flying was possible over the snow-blanketed front and, the fuel ration not having been delivered to the base, all the earth-bound flyers shivered in the 'arctic' conditions.

By March it was clear that the enemy would soon take advantage of the improved weather, and on the Allied side steps were taken to repel the expected offensive. When the German push began on 21 March it led to a heavy workload for No. 8 Squadron, which was to occupy them into June. The duties consisted chiefly of reconnaissance and photography, the latter calling for a very high degree of courage, calling as it did for steady course-keeping in order to preserve the plates whatever the odds. West was delighted when he was finally alloted a personal observer, Lieutenant John Haslam, in whom he had every confidence.

On 21 April 1918, West, together with Lieutenant Richard Grice as observer, flew to Hamelet to inspect a machine which had force-landed. Finding the aircraft not suitable for flight but only for dismantling, West commenced a return to base. The final part of his flight followed the straight road from St Quentin to Amiens. About 2 miles from Amiens, Grice drew West's attention to three red Fokkers on their port side; these enemy aircraft were being fired at by anti-aircraft batteries as they pursued a lone English two-seater reconnaissance aircraft, an RE8, which was rapidly being overhauled by the lead Fokker. Expecting the slower RE8 to be shot down at any moment, West was surprised to see the German plane apparently out of control in a long parabolic dive, eventually crash-landing in a field not far from Corbie. Freddie flew down to investigate and managed to land on a flat field not far away. By the time he reached the crashed German machine it was surrounded by a crowd of Australian soldiers. On enquiring about the pilot, West was directed towards an elated artillery officer who announced, 'We've had a rare bit of luck! Guess who we've shot down?' West shook his head and the Australian said, 'Richthofen!' Seeing West's disbelief he held out a yellow leather wallet containing an envelope addressed to 'Rittmeister Freiherr von Richthofen'. West was shown the pilot's body and he later recalled, 'how unhappy I felt over the death of this man. He would have killed me without thinking twice if he had manoeuvred his machine anywhere near me, yet I was genuinely sorry he was dead.' West then telephoned the news through to Leigh-Mallory who was somewhat disbelieving, telling him, 'West, you're a responsible person and a promising pilot. Don't go and ruin your reputation by originating sensational rumours.' By the time

West and Grice had returned to their airfield, the story had been confirmed by Corps HQ and Leigh-Mallory's attitude had changed considerably.

On 19 June West was promoted to captain in the Royal Air Force and given charge of a flight. On the same day, together with Lieutenant Sharman as observer, he set off to bomb a suspected ammunition dump at Mericourt only to find, as they approached the target, a group of Fokker aircraft. West dived down rapidly to about 200ft so that Sharman could defend their aircraft from the German planes above, but they were at the mercy of ground fire. To make matters worse a balloon barrage protected the ammunition dump, the cables of which threatened seriously to damage West's machine. He later admitted that 'it would only be a matter of minutes before ground shrapnel broke up the machine or the Fokkers got us'. Just then about six British fighters arrived and engaged the German machines. Taking advantage of the ensuing dogfight, West climbed rapidly out of trouble and, seeing that the ground guns were distracted by the fight above, negotiated between the balloons and their cables. He dropped his bombs on the ammunition dump, the explosions from which caused his plane to rock dangerously, though it was not badly damaged. During this whole episode Haslam kept firing at balloons and any German plane which came within range. They returned to base with no further problems.

Some respite was afforded West in July when he was sent to enjoy a brief leave, and it was in this month that the *London Gazette* (supplement to No. 30813 dated 26 July) published the citations of both West and Haslam, both being awarded the Military Cross:

For conspicuous gallantry and devotion to duty. While on patrol he, with another officer, observed fifteen enemy motor lorries. As these could not be engaged by artillery by zone call, they flew 8,000 yards over the enemy lines at a height of 3,000 feet in the face of strong opposition from the ground, and dropped four bombs, obtaining direct hits on the lorries and doing considerable damage to their personnel. They then proceeded to attack them with machine-gun fire as they sought cover. A fortnight later they carried out, at a height of 150 feet, a reconnaissance of their corps front, on which an attack was expected. Despite the fact that the clouds were at 200 feet, and there was a thick mist, they obtained most valuable information. During this flight they directed and located the fire of our artillery on a concentration of enemy infantry. Throughout the operations their work in co-operation with our artillery was always of the greatest value, and their enterprise in attacking enemy troops and transports with bombs and machine-gun fire was splendid.

Both men were embarrassed when Leigh-Mallory sent for them after he had received General Rawlinson's congratulations for their awards as they considered that 'we've all been doing the same work', with Haslam saying, 'Well, I hope they'll give the medals in rotation, I'm going to look an awful B.F. around here wearing my ribbon'.

❖❖❖

In April 1919, West began work at the Foreign Office as an RAF liaison officer in a department staffed by a representative from each of the services, all three of whom were, to their great amusement, one-legged. The *London Gazette* of 1 August of that year showed the drastic cuts being made to the RAF when a bare 200 names were published for commissions. Fortunately for him, West's was one of the names, as were Haslam and Leigh-Mallory. On 26 June 1920, West attended the Buckingham Palace Garden Party given by King George V for all VC holders, and on 11 November was one of those forming the VC guard of honour for the Unknown Warrior at Westminster Abbey. He also represented the RAF in Brussels at a commemoration for Belgian pilots killed in the war. It was during this year, after being posted to Uxbridge, that West began flying again, although not 'officially'.

On 19 January 1921, after an eighteen-month engagement, Freddie West married Wynne Leslie at Westminster Cathedral. In 1923 West attended the RAF Staff College at Andover until the following year when he was posted flight commander at No. 17 Squadron at Hawkinge under the command of Air Commodore C.R. Samson. A posting to the Central Flying School at Upavon as adjutant between September 1926 and March 1928 was followed by a move, still as adjutant, to the RAF seaplane base at Calafrana, Malta. West enjoyed this particular posting for, as well as 'sufficient flying' there was 'plenty of sport, cheap living and a round of parties which never seemed to end before dawn'.

It was while stationed at Malta that West and his wife visited Rome to see a medical specialist about a possible spinal injury. No serious injury was detected and during his week's leave West was determined to visit his old friend from Milan, Monsignor Ratti. This was not easy as this gentleman was now His Holiness Pope Pius XI, but with his usual charm and perseverance Freddie achieved his aim. Following his short audience with the Pope, West recalled the telling comment, 'War is a great calamity, but the world does not have appear to have learnt its lesson.'

By 1932 West was back in England as a staff officer at the School of Army Co-operation before taking command of No. 4 Squadron RAF in October 1933. It was while with this squadron at Farnborough that

West, on one of his not infrequent visits to a racecourse, met the chief of air staff who told him that it was time he had a change, and very soon after, when summoned to the Air Ministry in early 1936, he was appointed as the first British air attaché to Finland, Latvia and Estonia.

West was able to acquire a chalet for himself and his wife on the small island of Degero some 12 miles distant from his office in Helsinki. He took delight, when travelling from his house to the mainland in his fast boat, in almost capsizing the swastika-bedecked craft used by the German military attaché on his journeys to Helsinki! There was much competition to sell aircraft and equipment to the Finns and, when the contract to supply two squadrons of Bristol Blenheims and ancillary equipment was won by the British, West was kept very busy.

West found that his fellow attachés from other countries – France, Poland, Latvia, Lithuania and Estonia – all believed war to be a certainty, so in May 1938 West sent this information to the Air Ministry with his own opinion that war was only a year away. He also requested that he be allowed to drive through Germany and visit Air Commodore John Vachell, his opposite number, in Berlin. West was informed that his prognosis was too gloomy, but that his German trip was sanctioned. After reaching Berlin he spent a few hours with Vachell and the naval attaché, both of whom agreed with him that war was coming soon, but who said that the ambassador, Sir Neville Henderson, was not of the same opinion. On visiting the ambassador that same evening, West was asked to give his reasoning on why he considered war to be imminent. His explanations were listened to politely and then Freddie was astounded when the main question levelled at him was whether RAF officers wore black suede shoes with a dinner jacket – as Vachell apparently did. West's opinion was that this subject of correct footwear was of more interest to Henderson than the current German situation!

In November 1938 West returned to the UK as officer commanding No. 50 Operations Wing at Odiham. This unit was sent to France soon after the announcement of war in September 1939. At Christmas Group Captain West was taken ill, brought back to England and diagnosed with a burst stomach ulcer. After treatment and recovery in Aldershot Military Hospital, and later passing the Medical Board, West, now an acting air commodore, was appointed air attaché in Rome where the climate was hoped to be an aid to his convalescence. This appointment was of short duration as he was ordered to leave Rome and go to Switzerland when Mussolini declared war on the Allies in June. An arduous train journey of several days followed before he and his wife were greeted by British legation staff at Berne.

West remained in Switzerland as air attaché during the Second World War and was much involved in intelligence gathering, assisting escaped British POWs and other activities which, quite early on, brought him under the watchful eyes of German agents, requiring the employment of an ex-Cossack by the name of Serge, who had no love for the Germans, as a chauffeur-cum-bodyguard. His reward for this very important work was announced when the supplement to the *London Gazette* – No. 36866 dated 29 December 1944 – published the name of Air Commodore Ferdinand Maurice Felix West VC, MC, Royal Air Force, amongst those to be additional commanders of the Military Division of the Most Excellent Order of the British Empire.

It was not until the autumn of 1944, when the Allied invasion of Europe had led to the opening up of the Swiss border, that West was able to leave Switzerland. He escorted an escaped German rocket scientist to Paris for onward travel to England, and whilst in Paris West took the opportunity of visiting his old friend, Sir Trafford Leigh-Mallory, who was then Commander-in-Chief Allied Expeditionary Air Force, but had just been appointed Commander-in-Chief in the Far East. West was asked if he wished to join his former commander but regretfully declined the invitation as his knowledge of that area was very limited.

In November West heard the disturbing news that the plane carrying Leigh-Mallory and his wife to his new posting was missing near the Alps. Many months later the burnt out wreckage was discovered a few miles south of Grenoble, and in the little communal cemetery of Allemont (Le Rivier) are buried Leigh-Mallory, his wife and the eight airmen from the plane.

During the autumn of 1945, while West was head of an Air Ministry department based in Belgrave Square, he was approached by Jimmy Rank, whom West had befriended during a visit to Switzerland. After ascertaining from West that another war would be unlikely in the next decade, Rank said, 'my brother Arthur intends to create a world organisation for the distribution of British films ... he believes that films can help towards a better understanding between peoples of the world and help toward a lasting peace. I believe you can play a useful role in my brother's scheme ...'

Soon West left the RAF and joined the Rank Organisation, in the following year becoming managing director of the associated Eagle-Lion Distributors and retiring as chairman in 1958.

West was present at the 1956 VC review in Hyde Park on 26 June, the Buckingham Palace garden party of 17 July 1962 and the VC & GC Association reunion dinner of 1981. At the age of 80, he was still active on behalf of the RAF Association and the Committee of the Victoria Cross and George Cross Association.

At the grand age of 92 Freddie West died in Princess Margaret Hospital, Windsor on 7 July 1988. He was the last survivor of the First World War air VC holders. His funeral was held on 20 July at St Edward the Confessor Catholic Church, Windsor, with the Central Band of the RAF playing outside the church both before and after the service. His medals and decorations were carried in the procession by his son Peter. The burial service was at Holy Trinity churchyard, Sunningdale, with the commanding officer and officers of No. 8 Squadron RAF providing a lining party. The cortège was led by a Guards piper and RAF trumpeters played the Last Post. Many representatives of the RAF attended the ceremonies. West's headstone bears the name of his mother, Clémence, who died in 1958, followed by the words 'and her only much loved son Air Commodore Ferdinand Maurice Felix West "*BEAU Chevalier sans peur et sans reproche*"'.

As with so many servicemen, the memories of life in the trenches remained with West for the rest of his life and shortly before his death he said:

> Life in the trenches ... was absolutely miserable ... what we suffered most was the lack of space. Live, work, fight within a few yards and all we could see between gaps was yards of wire and umpteen shell holes, so when ever we looked upwards and saw a man manoeuvring in the sky we were very envious.

West's VC was held by No. 8 Squadron RAF for a number of years before being returned to the family at their request. His awards and medals – VC, OBE, MC, 1914–15 Star, BWM, Victory Medal and MiD oak leaf, King George V Silver Jubilee Medal (1935), King George VI Coronation Medal (1937), Defence Medal (1939–45), War Medal (1939–45), Queen Elizabeth II Coronation Medal (1953), Queen Elizabeth Silver Jubilee Medal (1977), Knight, Order of the Crown of Italy, Knight, Legion of Honour (5th Class), Commander, Order of Orange Nassau (The Netherlands), Commander, Order of the Crown of Italy – were acquired by the Imperial War Museum with the assistance of a grant from the National Heritage Memorial Fund (Lot 271 in Sotheby's sale of 29 November 1994). These awards and medals are now displayed in the Lord Ashcroft Gallery at the Imperial War Museum, London. Along with the names of the other air VC winners, Ferdinand West appears on the wall of St Clement Danes Church, the Strand, London.

A.F.W. BEAUCHAMP PROCTOR

Flying Services, France,
8 August to 8 October 1918

The final major Allied offensive of the war was launched on 8 August 1918 by the British Fourth and French First Army. The main British all-arms attack was in the Amiens sector where, after a short, ferocious artillery barrage, the British, Canadian and Australian infantry divisions advanced on a front of over 10 miles, supported by twelve tank battalions and nearly 400 aircraft.

One RAF unit (the RFC and RNAS had amalgamated on 1 April 1918 to form the RAF) which had been much involved with the preparations for the attack was No. 84 Squadron, equipped with the very agile SE5a single-seater fighters. It had been based at Bertangles, 6 miles north of Amiens, since 4 April. The squadron commander was Major William Sholto Douglas and a South African, Captain Andrew Beauchamp Proctor MC, DFC, was the leader of C Flight. During the previous eight months the diminutive Proctor, who stood only a little over 5ft and needed modifications to his aircraft seating and controls in order to fly safely, had achieved thirty-two official victories over enemy aircraft and kite balloons and in the destruction of the latter he had become something of a specialist. His preferred attack method was to approach from below and fire at the basket beneath before attempting destruction of the actual balloon.

After returning to his squadron on 4 August from leave in England, Proctor was quickly back in action flying a new SE5a, D6856, and during the next two weeks he was credited with victories of a further kite balloon and six enemy aircraft including three of the new Fokker D VII Scouts. On 21 August he shot down an Albatros two-seater near Fay and the next morning, in an attack on enemy observation balloons, Proctor quickly destroyed two, at Assevillers and Hem, then attacked five others in succession. In every case the balloon observer was forced to escape by parachute. On the same date his official number of victories to date was confirmed as thirty-three aircraft and seven kite balloons and he was also recommended for a Bar to his MC (gazetted on 16 September), in particular for his work in leading offensive patrols, destruction of enemy aircraft and low-altitude ground attacks.

Two days later, Proctor shot down two Fokker DVII aircraft near Brie, followed on 25 August by victory over another similar machine which crashed south of Tempeux, and together with other pilots of No. 84 Squadron, he was credited with the capture of a Rumpler two-seater. His opportunistic tactics were well illustrated on 27 August when, on a morning patrol with his flight, he attacked and destroyed an observation balloon near Flaucort which was heavily guarded by anti-aircraft batteries and eight enemy fighters. Proctor was chased back to the front lines by these aircraft, but he eluded them by entering clouds and then flew back to the line of German balloons by compass bearing only. An hour after his first attack, he destroyed a second kite balloon at Mont St Quentin. Anti-aircraft fire damaged his engine and he was forced to return across the front lines at a very low altitude. A Fokker DVII was his final victim of the month when, on the evening of 29 August, he and Lieutenant Carl Falkenberg were jointly credited with its destruction near Brie.

As the Allied advance continued during September, the role of No. 84 Squadron became more focused on low-level attacks directed at a great variety of ground targets as well as the kite balloons vital for the enemy's observation. Often the squadron aircraft would take off from Bertangles at dawn and fly to advanced airfields from where the aircraft would operate during the day on orders from Wing HQ and return to their base airfield in the evening.

Flying was restricted by the unsettled weather during this month, particularly in the mornings, but Proctor was still able to destroy a further four balloons. On the first day of October the squadron attacked a line of observation balloons. One flight made the attack, with the other SE5s acting as protection, which soon proved necessary when a formation of Fokker DVII aircraft attacked. In the combat which followed, Proctor shot down two of the attacking aircraft. Two days later he was victorious over another enemy scout while kite balloons were his victims on both 2 and 3 October and on the latter date he also claimed victory over another Fokker DVII. Two days later, with another squadron pilot, Second Lieutenant A.E. Hill, Proctor shared in the destruction of yet another observation balloon west of Bohain.

On 8 October, in what was to be his last action flight, Proctor attacked a Rumpler two-seater which crashed near Maretz, but was himself attacked by eight enemy scouts as he began his return flight and in the ensuing dogfight he was badly wounded in the arm and only just managed to land his aircraft. He was quickly transported to hospital and after receiving treatment for his injuries, Proctor was invalided back to England on the hospital ship *St Denis* and eventually arrived at the Northumberland War Hospital, Newcastle-upon-Tyne, for further treatment, on 16 October 1918.

Prior to the action on 8 October he had been recommended for the award of a DSO (gazetted on 2 November), in particular for his attack of 22 August on observation balloons. Major Douglas later recommended Proctor for the VC, the citation of which was published in the supplement to the *London Gazette* No. 31042 of 30 November:

LIEUT. (A./CAPT.) ANDREW WEATHERBY BEAUCHAMP-PROCTOR, D.S.O., M.C., D.F.C., NO. 84 SQN., R.A. FORCE.

Between August 8th, 1918, and October 8th, 1918, this officer proved himself victor in twenty-six decisive combats, destroying twelve enemy kite balloons, ten enemy aircraft, and driving down four other enemy aircraft completely out of control.

Between October 1st, 1918, and October 5th, 1918, he destroyed two enemy scouts, burnt three enemy kite balloons, and drove down one enemy scout completely out of control.

On October 1st, 1918, in a general engagement with about twenty-eight machines, he crashed one Fokker biplane near Fontaine and a second near Ramicourt; on October 2nd he burnt a hostile balloon near Selvigny; on October 3rd he drove down, completely out of control, an enemy scout near Mont d'Origny, and burnt a hostile balloon; on October 5th, the third hostile balloon near Bohain.

On October 8th, 1918, while flying home at a low altitude, after destroying an enemy two-seater near Maretz, he was painfully wounded in the arm by machine-gun fire, but, continuing, he landed safely at his aerodrome, and after making his report was admitted to hospital.

In all he has proved himself conqueror over fifty-four foes, destroying twenty-two enemy machines, sixteen enemy kite balloons, and driving down sixteen enemy aircraft completely out of control.

Captain Beauchamp-Proctor's work in attacking enemy troops on the ground and in reconnaissance during the withdrawal following on the Battle of St. Quentin from March 21st, 1918, and during the victorious advance of our Armies commencing on August 8th, has been almost unsurpassed in its brilliancy, and as such has made an impression on those serving in his squadron and those around him that will not be easily forgotten.

It was not until 13 March that Proctor was discharged from hospital and while still convalescing there his name appeared in the New Year Honours List of 1919 listed as Mentioned in Despatches. Within two weeks of leaving hospital he embarked on a lecture tour of the United States with other RAF pilots, promoting the Liberty Loan. He also performed with other flyers in 'barn storming' exhibitions. Proctor returned to England at the end of July and was posted to the Seaplane School at Lee-on-Solent, Hampshire for a special flying course which he successfully completed a month later.

He was sent to the RAF College, Cranwell, at the end of August and on 1 November he was granted a permanent commission in the RAF with the rank of flight lieutenant. Less than three weeks later, on 27 November, Proctor attended a Buckingham Palace investiture where he was presented with his VC, DSO and DFC by the King. Shortly after this investiture he was briefly arrested in error by two police constables for 'wearing medals that he was not entitled to'!

In order that he might progress with his interrupted engineering studies and also visit his family, whom he had not seen since leaving South Africa in March 1917, Proctor was granted twelve months' leave from 4 February 1920 and he received a hero's welcome after disembarking from the *Armadale Castle* at Cape Town, South Africa, on 23 February.

He successfully completed his studies at the University of Cape Town and was awarded a BSc in Mechanical Engineering at the end of September. Proctor sailed back to England at the end of the year and was posted to No. 24 Squadron in February where he was recommended as a flying instructor and after completing a short refresher course his flying skills were recorded as 'superior'. He began an engineering course at Henlow before a posting to the Central Flying School, Upavon, on 15 March 1921.

Meanwhile Sir Hugh Trenchard had conceived the idea of an annual RAF Tournament (from 1921 to be known as Pageants). The first had already been held in 1920 and, among the select group of pilots to give exhibitions at the second such show, Proctor had been chosen as one. A demonstration of the destruction of a kite balloon was to be Proctor's part in the display and it was on 21 June, while rehearsing this manoeuvre for the exhibition due to take place at Hendon the following day, that Proctor's Sopwith Snipe E8220 began a loop at the top of which it fell away into an inverted spin. It crashed at Enford near Upavon and Proctor was killed. The cause of the accident was never satisfactorily explained, one theory being that there was insufficient time to completely modify the Snipe for Proctor's special requirements and that cushions used to add height on the seat may have become loose during the flight. At the time of his fatal accident he was inexperienced on the Snipe and it was also a possibility that his insufficient altitude and speed at the time indicated that he should have had more instruction on this aircraft.

In Proctor's death announcement published in *The Times* on 24 June it was stated, 'The hope is expressed that the Government may see their way to convey the body to South Africa for interment there'. In the event his funeral took place later that day at Upavon Parish Church in a service conducted by the Rev. G. Tonge. The Central Flying School band led the cortège where the coffin, draped with the RAF ensign, was taken to the adjoining cemetery for burial. There were many floral tributes and amongst the large number of mourners were representatives from the Dominion of South Africa and many RAF units.

In South Africa there were requests that the remains of the first South African to win the VC should be exhumed and brought back to South Africa. This was later arranged with the assistance and support of General Smuts and the prominent South African businessman and politician, Abe Bailey. Proctor's coffin arrived in South Africa aboard the *Balmoral Castle* on 8 August 1921 and, following a procession of the cortège through Cape Town, his remains were transported by rail via Kimberley to Mafeking where he was given a state funeral and burial in the town cemetery.

❖ ❖ ❖

Andrew Frederick Weatherby Proctor was born on 4 September 1894 (his baptism records confirm this date, although some RAF documents show a different date of birth) at the small port of Mossel Bay, Cape Province, South Africa, the son of South African John James Proctor and his Shropshire born wife Frances Wynne (née Weatherby). Andrew had an older brother, James Mildmay Faulkner who was two years his senior and a sister, Fedora Mary Louise, born in 1902. His father had served with distinction as a captain in the South African volunteer military forces and was OC of the Colonial Units at Queen Victoria's funeral in 1901. John Proctor was a teacher by profession and at the time of Andrew's birth he was employed at Beaconsfield, Mossel Bay and consequently progressed to become a house warden at Bishops Diocesan College, Cape Town and a headmaster at St George Grammar School at George, Cape Province. Andrew attended the schools where his father taught but stayed at Bishops as a boarder when the family moved over 700 miles north to Mafeking.

In 1911 Andrew enrolled at the South African College (now Cape Town University) and commenced studies on an engineering diploma course. The declaration of war in August 1914 interrupted his education and less than two months later on 1 October, he enlisted as signaller No. 6348 in the Duke of Edinburgh's Own Rifles; 'The Dukes' was a volunteer unit not unlike a British territorial regiment. (His earlier attempts at enlistment had been rejected due to his height of only 5ft 2in, but influence was exerted by the Mayor of Mafeking which facilitated his successful attempt.)

Initially employed on garrison duties in Cape Town, The Dukes served in the arduous conditions of the campaign in German South-West Africa (now Namibia) in a supporting role from February to July 1915. Proctor was transferred to the South African Field Telegraph and Postal Corps for three months before being demobilised in August 1915. He returned to college where he progressed well with studies on his engineering course and in the summer of 1916 passed his third-year examinations.

Meanwhile, increasing losses amongst members of the RFC led to the War Office organising a recruiting drive in South Africa led by an RFC captain, Allister M. Miller, a South African pilot with much experience on the Western Front who had previously been friends with Proctor at college. Tasked in October 1916 to find thirty volunteers, Miller enrolled 450 and in a further recruiting drive eight months later 2,000 were selected from four times that number of applicants. Proctor was amongst these volunteers and he enlisted in the RFC as an air mechanic, 3rd Class, on 12 March 1917. Around the time of his enlistment, at the instigation of his father, Andrew 'dropped' the name Frederick – thought to sound too Germanic – and added Beauchamp to his surname, as there was a link to an Anglo-Irish family of this name. Military documents usually hyphenated his surname, but Andrew signed his letters without a hyphen.

After arriving in England Proctor was posted to 6th Officer Cadet Battalion at Farnborough, Hampshire, on 26 March where his previous military service served him in good stead, and after only two weeks he was posted to the School of Military Aeronautics at Oxford for ground training. He was commissioned as a second lieutenant on 24 May and a week later was transferred to No. 5 (Reserve) Squadron at Castle Bromwich to begin flight instruction. Due to his small stature, modifications such as raising the pilot's seat and affixing blocks to the rudder bar needed to be made to any aircraft before he could fly it. Proctor had further flight instruction at Netheravon with No. 24 (Reserve) Squadron before an advanced course at the Central Flying School at Upavon, Wiltshire, in July after which he was awarded his wings and posted to 84 Squadron at Beaulieu, Hampshire on 29 July 1917. Proctor had extremely keen eyesight in addition to being a good shot and had the added advantage of being able to achieve more speed from his aircraft as he weighed about 25lb less than most of his contemporaries.

This squadron had been formed in January and, under the command of the experienced flier Major William Sholto Douglas, was forming up at Beaulieu for its first tour of duty on the Western Front. No. 84 Squadron flew the Avro 504, Sopwith Camel and Pup at Lilbourne from March 1917 until it was eventually fully equipped with the Royal Aircraft Factory SE5a Scout during August and flew overseas on 21 September 1917.

The squadron was based at Liettres, 15 miles south of St Omer, and for the first few weeks flew only routine flights near the front lines as the pilots became more acquainted with their aircraft and the close formation flying tactics which had been formulated by Captain James McCudden of which Douglas had become a strong advocate.

The formation principle as adapted by Douglas was that the best shot in each flight led the attack, while two pilots backed him up in a three-plane formation in which the two wingmen flew in echelon behind and to left and right of the leader. Each trio of SE5a machines flew a loose formation within clear sight of the leader, who was responsible for locating the enemy. Once action began the formation tightened as much as practical so that the aircraft of each flight fought as a unit. Douglas considered that it would be chaotic if his trio formations broke up, so he issued orders that any pilot who left the 'V' for any other reason than engine failure would be immediately transferred back to depot as 'unsatisfactory'. An added bonus was that, should one or both of the leader's guns fail to fire (not an uncommon occurrence at that time), one of the two wingmen was ready to fire instead. These tactics proved successful and No. 84 Squadron lost fewer men than any other fighter squadron on the Western Front.

On 12 November the squadron moved to Filescamp Farm, Izel-lès-Hameau, 13 miles north-west of Arras, and it was from here, ten days later, that Douglas led his unit's first offensive patrol in their hunt for enemy aircraft. Proctor, flying SE5a B597, participated in the destruction of a kite balloon which, with another pilot, he shot down in flames. A week later Proctor exchanged fire with an enemy two-seater, which dived away out of control, and a similar result was recorded for an aircraft fired at on 5 December, but since there were no witnesses neither of these were recorded as victories.

Towards the end of the year, on 29 December, No. 84 Squadron moved to Flez, on the outskirts of the ruined village of Guizancourt, 10 miles west of St Quentin. Less than a week later, on 3 January, Proctor was on a patrol in SE5a B539 when he spotted and attacked an enemy two-seater which he sent down to crash north-east of St Quentin. This was his first confirmed victory over an enemy aircraft and on the following day he despatched a second similarly, although its final fate was not witnessed.

The collection of 'probables' – enemy pilots likely to have been vanquished in combat, but unconfirmed – was to be a feature of Proctor's engagements with the enemy. This fact endorsed his superiors' opinion of his abilities, so that by the following month, despite his relatively low military rank of second lieutenant, Major Douglas detailed him as a patrol leader. He made his first flight in this new capacity on 15 February, when he attacked and forced down an enemy two-seater machine, and later in the same day his assault on an observation balloon forced the ground crew to winch it down. Two days later he attacked an Albatros DV Scout which went down out of control south-east of St Quentin. He also attacked an enemy two-seater which eventually escaped back across the lines.

South-east of la Fère, on 19 February, a victory over an Albatros DV Scout which crashed after it was riddled with bullets at close range by Proctor's guns was subsequently witnessed by Captain James McCudden. Later in the month a kite balloon was forced down and on the 28th he shot down a Pfalz DIII out of control, also near la Fère. The next month began with an enemy machine shot down out of control on 1 March followed by a kite balloon destroyed nine days later. The following day Proctor crashed his aircraft, SE5a B539, when a wheel hit an obstacle on landing and badly damaged the machine. Fortunately he was not badly hurt and was able to fly a new SE D259, on 12 March, when he shared a victory over an enemy two-seater with another squadron pilot, Captain Leask.

An unusual victory was achieved by Proctor on 15 March when he forced down an enemy aircraft, DFW CV, from *Flieger Abteilung* (A) 207, near Villeret behind British lines where this aircraft was then captured. Proctor's most successful action to date was two days later when he led a patrol to attack a formation of Pfalz D III Scouts near Busigny. He was credited with victory over three of these aircraft and was fortunate to avoid injury after his own aircraft was badly damaged by enemy fire.

A few days later, on 21 March, the German offensive, codenamed Operation Michael, commenced with an overwhelming attack by seventy-six German divisions against the British Third and Fifth Armies on a front from just south of Arras to 10 miles beyond the river Oise. General Gough's Fifth Army bore the brunt of the attack on its 42-mile front and the rapid enemy advance necessitated the RFC squadrons frequently moving airfields as the Germans advanced. Within a week No. 84 Squadron was based at Contenville-en-Ternois, over 20 miles north-west of Arras. On 1 April, the day when the RAF was formed, Proctor was promoted to lieutenant and a week later made captain and given command of C Flight. He was awarded the Military Cross (gazetted on 22 June), the citation of which concluded, 'He has at all times displayed the utmost dash and initiative, and is a patrol leader of great merit and resource.'

On 4 April the squadron moved to its new base at Bertangles, 6 miles north of Amiens, where it would remain for the next five months. Although his appointment as flight commander curtailed the relative freedom to patrol he had enjoyed previously, Proctor continued to fly using the tactics instilled in the pilots by Major Douglas. It was the squadron commander himself who later recorded that Proctor, 'revelled in the ideas that McCudden had put forward and which I was adopting ... The moral effect of his enthusiasm on the rest of the squadron was worth its weight in gold, and for that reason I very often let him lead the squadron, being content to go along as deputy leader.'

A little over a week after arriving at Bertangles, on 12 April, Proctor attacked and sent down out of control two enemy single-seater aircraft. On the 20th he drove down a two-seater machine behind enemy lines, and the following day, flying SE5a C1772, he shot down an Albatros Scout. C Flight, led by Proctor, attacked a formation of ten Fokker DRI aircraft on 23 April and in the action which followed he shot down the leading enemy triplane over Framerville.

During May 1918 German night bombing raids on Allied targets were a common occurrence and No. 84 Squadron participated in a number of unsuccessful attacks on these large aircraft. In the early hours of 15 May Proctor flew on a solo patrol, and after locating an enemy airfield used by the enemy bombers, waited a short distance away for the return of any such aircraft. A little before 4 a.m. he spotted a twin-engined AEG above him and attacked it and exchanged fire with the rear gunner whom Proctor claimed to have wounded. Ground defences had now been alerted and put up a barrage of fire, but he continued to follow and fire at the AEG for some distance beyond its airfield and Proctor last saw it damaged and diving before he returned to base.

By the end of the month Proctor's official total of victories, including kite balloons, had reached twenty-four. Five of these were recorded on 19 May when he sent a two-seater down out of control and destroyed an Albatros DV in a morning patrol, and in the early evening an encounter with five Albatros Scouts was described by Lieutenant Hector MacDonald:

My flight commander [Proctor] dove on the leader of the Hun formation. I dived immediately afterwards and got on the tail of a 'V' Strutter ... [this machine] waited for Captain Proctor to fly over him and then stalled underneath him. I immediately opened fire ... the Hun machine then fell over into a vertical sideslip.

Proctor was credited with the destruction of one Albatros as was MacDonald, and the flight pilots shared the victory over two more of the enemy scouts which collided after being attacked. During the last week of the month, Proctor claimed a further two observation balloons and four aircraft and on 28 May he was awarded a Military Cross 'In the Field' (gazetted on 22 June), the citation itemising his success over eight enemy aircraft and commenting that, 'He has at all times displayed the utmost dash and initiative, and is a patrol leader of great merit and resource.'

During the first two weeks of June, Proctor achieved victories over three enemy aircraft and five kite balloons and in the middle of the month he went on leave to England. On 24 June he was awarded the newly instigated Distinguished Flying Cross, DFC (gazetted 3 August 1918):

LT. (T./CAPT.) ANDREW WEATHERBY BEAUCHAMP-PROCTOR, MC

A brilliant and fearless leader of our offensive patrols. His formation has destroyed thirteen enemy machines and brought down thirteen more out of control in a period of a few months. On a recent morning his patrol of five aeroplanes attacked an enemy formation of thirty machines and was successful in destroying two of them. In the evening he again attacked an enemy formation with great dash, destroying one machine and forcing two others to collide, resulting in their destruction.

Proctor returned to France from England, for what was to be his final operational tour on 4 August.

In certain respects Andrew Beauchamp Proctor still remains something of an enigma and even his squadron commander, William Sholto Douglas, wrote in his memoirs, 'There was always a bit of a mystery about where he [Proctor] came from, and about his exact age.'

As far as this author is concerned, South African baptism records show that Proctor was born on 4 September 1894 at Mossel Bay in Cape Province but it is peculiar that both his 'headstone' in Upavon churchyard and the impressive memorial in Mahikeng (was Mafeking) cemetery – European Section 1050–1052 – show his age as 24 when he was killed which would assume a birth year of 1896. Some RAF documents held in The National Archives, Kew, also give his date of birth as 1896 and Commonwealth War Graves Commission records show his age as 23.

Although ecclesiastical records exist for his burial at Upavon no such documents have been located for his exhumation. The 'headstone' at Upavon is the non-World War (RAF) pattern as normally supplied by the MoD even though the date of his death falls before the CWGC recognised cut-off date of 31 August 1921 for First World War commemoration. Proctor's mother died in October 1918 whilst he was in hospital but his father had outlived him by almost twenty years when he died in Cape Town in January 1940.

Two years after his burial in Mafeking an impressive memorial, similar in design to the RAF memorial on the Embankment, London, was paid for by 'public subscription' and erected over his grave.

The Beauchamp-Proctor Flying Club, based at Mafeking Airport was established in 1971 and Proctor's gravestone in Mafeking cemetery is adorned with a brass spread eagle bearing the inscription 'on eagle wings I do thee bear', which is the insignia of the flying club.

Proctor's medal entitlement was VC, DSO, MC and Bar, DFC, 1914–15 Star, BWM, Victory Medal and MiD oak leaf. His medals and other memorabilia were in private hands a few years ago, but the author has been unable to confirm their present whereabouts. Captain Proctor's name appears with those of the other aviation VC winners on the wall left of the altar in St Clement Danes Church, the Strand, London. A portrait, in oils by Cowan Dobson, is held by the Imperial War Museum, Lambeth, London.

His commanding officer, Major William Sholto Douglas, summed up Proctor when he later wrote: 'He had … an extraordinary zest for attacking the enemy at any height and under any conditions … and he had always been most persistent in his wishes to remain with the squadron. For all his size that little man had the guts of a lion.'

W.G. BARKER

Forêt de Mormal, France,
27 October 1918

In October 1918 the Allied forces were advancing rapidly into France and Belgium, areas where the original BEF had seen action in August 1914 and, as then, it was a war of movement. In order to keep pace with the ever-changing situation the Allied airfields were also moved nearer to the retreating enemy.

No. 201 Squadron RAF was based at Beugnâtre airfield 2 miles from Bapaume and, the squadron's aircraft were Sopwith Camels. On 17 October Major William Barker joined the squadron on a ten-day roving commission. He had requested this particular posting as the commanding officer, Major Cyril Leaman, was a friend. Barker was flying the RAF's newest scout aircraft, a Sopwith Snipe E8102, powered by a Bentley engine and equipped with refinements such as oxygen for the pilot. Although evaluation of this machine in action was part of Barker's mission, his role did not always endear him to the squadron's other pilots when the Snipe outperformed the Camel, and he was able to fly much higher, 'waiting for targets'.

Cloudy and wet weather hindered operations against the retreating enemy and Barker was unable to fly patrols for four days; in the next three he took part in squadron sorties with other pilots but with no enemy contact. This frustrated Barker and when, on 26 October, he received orders to return the Snipe to the Aircraft Supply Depot and then go to London, he was annoyed he had not been able to attack any enemy aircraft.

The following morning there were few clouds when Barker took off in the Sopwith Snipe before 8 a.m. He quickly reached over 15,000ft and was still climbing. He was over the Forêt de Mormal, south of Mons, less than thirty minutes later when he spotted a white Rumpler two-seater aircraft above him at a height of over 21,000ft. Barker engaged the enemy machine and the two aircraft exchanged a few short bursts of fire while each manoeuvred for a favourable attacking position. At a range of over 100yd Barker again fired and either wounded or killed the German observer. He then closed in on the Rumpler and fired several short bursts into the aircraft and the Rumpler began to break up. One of the German airmen fell free of the aircraft and Barker became distracted as he watched the unusual sight of the man's white parachute open. He did not notice the approach of a Fokker DVII whose pilot had witnessed the fight and flown up towards the British aircraft. The first indication Barker had of this opponent was the sound of machine-gun fire and he was hit in his right thigh, which caused him to release the controls and the Snipe descended several hundred feet in a spin.

When he regained control of his aircraft Barker found himself amongst a formation of fifteen Fokker DVIIIs. He fired bursts at two and then from very short range fired at a third, which then burst into flames. The other Fokkers attacked him from all sides and he was hit again, in the other leg. This time he passed out and his plane went into another downward spiral and when he came to he had dropped to about 15,000ft and was in the midst of yet more enemy aircraft. Barker then attacked one Fokker from behind and set this aircraft on fire at the same time as another aircraft fired at him from behind. One bullet hit his left elbow and others damaged his aircraft. By now the fuel tank was holed, the ignition ruined and smoke was streaming from his engine. British aircraft crew did not carry parachutes at the time, so escape by this method was not possible. Barker then flew straight towards the nearest enemy aircraft with his guns firing and was fortunate to set this Fokker on fire and it dived out of his path. With both legs and his left arm now useless and faint from his injuries, he was unable to operate the throttle on his left and as this was still in the full-on position he had very little control of his Snipe as it spiralled downwards.

Barker then saw a British balloon and flew in its direction. He managed to crash-land close to it when the Snipe turned over after it was quickly stopped by barbed wire. Men of No. 29 Kite Balloon Section rushed to Barker's aid and extricated the semi-conscious pilot from the wreckage. It was obvious he was badly wounded and Lieutenant Frank Woolley Smith, serving with the balloon unit as an observer, had him driven to the nearest field dressing station while he applied pressure on an artery near Barker's groin to stem bleeding. After Barker's wounds were dressed he was taken by ambulance tender to No. 8 General

Hospital, Rouen where he was soon operated upon. Although his left arm had been virtually severed at the elbow the surgeons managed to save it. Barker remained in a critical condition for the next week but by 7 November he was able to write a letter to his friend at No. 201 Squadron, Major Leman, in which he admitted, 'By Jove I was a foolish boy but anyhow I taught them a lesson. The only thing that bucks me up is to look back & see them going down in flames.'

When this letter was written it was known throughout the hospital that Barker had been recommended for the award of a VC and a supplement to the *London Gazette* No. 31042 dated 30 November 1918 carried the citation for his award.

Barker's family was notified by telegram shortly after he was badly wounded but it was not until December that the Canadian Department of Militia informed the family of his condition or whereabouts.

Barker was transferred from No. 8 General Hospital, Rouen on 16 January and sailed to England on HM hospital ship *Grantully Castle*. Ten days earlier, Barker had been visited at the hospital by a Captain B. Johnston from Canadian GHQ who had been ordered to report on the pilot's condition. This report contained a description of the award winning action in which Barker admitted that 'he did not act with his usual care ...' Johnston also advised on the current state of Barker's recovery: 'The arm wound is healing very satisfactorily and Major Barker will have a certain amount of use of the arm ... The wound in the left hip ... will be rather a long time in healing.'

Later, on 4 February, he sent a letter home from the Anglo-Chilean Hospital, Grosvenor Square, London and wrote that soon he would be able to sit up but his 'left hip is still troublesome [and] my left elbow ... will take a long time yet'.

By late February Barker was able to walk short distances with the aid of a cane and on the morning of 1 March at a Buckingham Palace investiture he received his VC from the King. After receiving his award he was taken on a short tour of the palace by the Prince of Wales. According to his diary entry King George V presented 344 medals that day, including six VCs.

❖ ❖ ❖

William George Barker was born on 3 November 1894, the first of nine children of George Barker and his wife Jane Victoria (née Alguire), at their homestead at Dauphin, Manitoba. George was a farmer and blacksmith and in addition he ran a sawmill. In 1902 the family moved 50 miles west to a farm near Russell.

William was educated first at Londonderry School and then Russell High School and attained good marks despite frequent absences to help his father. He became an excellent shot as well as an experienced horseman and as his father was the first in the local area to use steam engines it followed that William became well acquainted with the workings of the combustion engine. During his teenage years he also attended farm exhibitions in Manitoba where pioneer aviators would appear, and the young man was enthralled by these early flyers.

William enlisted as a trooper in the militia, the 32nd Light Horse, in 1912 and the following year the Barker family moved back to Dauphin, a rapidly growing town where he attended classes at the Dauphin Collegiate Institute. On 1 December 1914 Barker enlisted in 1st Regiment, Canadian Mounted Rifles (CMR), and his attestation papers record that No. 106074 Private Barker, W.G. was 5ft 10in tall.

Barker's regiment trained in Manitoba and by March 1915 he had been assigned to operate one of the regiment's four Colt-Browning machine guns. The 1st CMR Brigade, of which his regiment was part, entrained for Montreal and on 12 June it sailed for England on board the SS *Megantic*. Barker disembarked at Devonport and entrained for Shorncliffe, Kent on 19 June where the regiment trained for three months. On 16 September Barker received his first-class machine-gunner's certificate, and four days later he embarked at Southampton for France. By the end of the month the 1st CMR was in trenches near Ploegsteert, Belgium and it was in this area and in the vicinity of the River Douve that the regiment, serving as dismounted troops, was to stay for the next few months. It was a relatively quiet section of the front and consequently the regiment suffered few casualties but trench conditions were pretty miserable.

Unhappy with life in the trenches, Barker had made an application to be transferred to the RFC, which was rejected, but on 1 December a second application was approved and he was posted to No. 9 Squadron at St Omer as a trainee observer with the rank of corporal. Later in the month the squadron flew its BE2c aircraft to Bertangles, 6 miles north of Amiens, from where Barker took part in many reconnaissance patrols as an observer. His aircraft claimed one Fokker shot down in March 1916.

Barker was commissioned into the RFC as a second lieutenant on 2 April and then posted to No. 4 Squadron at Baizieux, west of Albert. The Battle of the Somme started on 1 July and six days later he was posted to No. 15 Squadron then based at Marieux, north-west of Albert. On 21 July Barker's aircraft was credited with a Roland machine which was driven down out of control near Miraumont, and on 15 August with another similar enemy aircraft shot down which crashed in flames near Achiet-le-Grand. It was during this period that he was Mentioned in Despatches. Less than two weeks later, on 27 August, he qualified as an observer and was recommended for pilot training.

The British attempted one final attack before the winter and on 13 November the Battle of the Ancre began in thick mist, which hampered the artillery spotting of No. 15 Squadron, but on the following days Barker, whose pilot was Captain W.G. Pender, helped in the attempted contact of Scottish troops isolated in Frankfurt Trench near Redan Ridge following the British attack of 13 November. Unfortunately, despite brave rescue attempts and stubborn resistance by these men of 16th HLI they were eventually attacked and overwhelmed. In addition, again piloted by Captain Pender, over Y Ravine, Beaumont-Hamel, Barker 'engaged large numbers of infantry in trenches with Lewis gun fire, and reported their position to the artillery'.

Barker returned to England from France on 16 November and began his pilot training at Narborough, Norfolk. After spending his Christmas leave in London he completed his training at Netheravon, Wiltshire. He was promoted to captain and flight commander on 15 January and returned to France as a fully qualified pilot on 24 February 1917. He rejoined C Flight, No 15 Squadron, stationed at Clairfaye Farm, Lealvillers 4 miles south of Marieux.

The supplement to the *London Gazette* No. 29898 of 10 January carried the citation for the award of the Military Cross: 'For conspicuous gallantry in action. He flew at a height of 500 feet over the enemy's lines, and brought back most valuable information. On another occasion, after driving off two hostile machines, he carried out an excellent photographic reconnaissance.'

The aircraft of No. 15 Squadron were mostly employed in close co-operation with ground troops and flew numerous low-level sorties which invited attack from enemy fighter aircraft in addition to fire from ground troops. Barker flew on an almost daily basis and on 23 March he shot down a Fokker Scout which crashed near Cambrai. His name was frequently to appear in RFC communiques for reconnaissance work in co-operation with the 7th Infantry Division.

On 9 April Lieutenant Goodfellow and Barker, flying very low and under ground attack, directed accurate artillery fire on enemy troops in support trenches preparing to counter-attack Australian positions. During the following weeks, while the Battle of Arras was in progress, they also reported the positions of hostile artillery, machine-gun positions and concentrations of infantry in addition to attacking parties of enemy troops.

The supplement to the *London Gazette* No. 30188 of 18 July published the citation for the award of a Bar to Barker's Military Cross, 'For ... continuous good work in co-operation with the artillery ...' and he was again Mentioned in Despatches.

During May the squadron's BE2 aircraft were replaced by RE8s. Barker was injured by shrapnel, which narrowly missed his right eye while on a contact patrol on 7 August and after almost continuous flying for six months he was posted back to England as an instructor. This was RFC policy meant to give pilots a rest from operational duties. This appointment held no attraction for Barker and after being refused another posting in France he made 'a thorough nuisance of himself' by performing stunts in flying school aircraft and on one occasion a very low flight over London, very near the Air Ministry. Eventually he was offered the choice between a posting to No. 56 Squadron in France, flying SE5as, or No. 28 Squadron being formed at Yatesbury, Wiltshire, who were equipped with Sopwith Camels. He chose No. 28 Squadron and on 2 October was posted to this squadron in command of A Flight. Within a week this squadron flew to their new base at Droglandt near Poperinge, Belgium.

On the evening of his arrival in Belgium, 8 October, Barker led the three inexperienced flight commanders on a 'familiarisation' patrol along the trench lines and, against squadron orders, crossed into enemy-held territory. A formation of enemy aircraft was seen beneath them, later described by one of the pilots as 'a circus of 22 gaudily-painted machines'. Barker dived down towards these aircraft and fired a burst into the rear machine which caused it, an Albatros DV, to break up in mid-air and crash between Ypres and Dixmude. The British aircraft returned to base but Barker did not claim a victory or submit a combat report for this event, only recording that Camel B6313 was taken out for a test flight.

The squadron recorded its first official victories on 20 October when British bombers attacked Rumbeke aerodrome near Roulers with No. 28 Squadron Camels as part of the escort. A total of nine enemy aircraft were shot down which included two by Barker. He was in action the following day over Houthulst Forest and fired at another Albatros which glided down. During the following week he badly damaged a Gotha on 24 October and shot down two Albatros DV machines two days later between Roulers and Thielt. After this last encounter Barker admitted in his combat report that he had lost his bearings and had run out of petrol before he landed near Arras. Two days later, 28 Squadron was warned of a move to Italy as part of the Anglo-French support following the Italian defeat at Caporetto, and this transfer began on the following day.

The squadron arrived in Milan on 12 November, and after their aircraft had been reassembled, moved to Verona ten days later and after six days to their base at Grossa airfield near Padua. On the 29th patrols began and Barker led three other Camels in B6313 over Senegalia and at about 10,000ft they were attacked by five Albatros DV aircraft of *Jasta 1*. One enemy aircraft was driven down and another destroyed in the ensuing fight and Barker was credited with one of these victories. Less than a week later on 3 December, after completing escort duty for RE8s, Barker with two other pilots attacked an observation balloon north-east of Conegliano.

When a brightly painted Albatros of *Jasta 39* attempted to attack one of the Camels, Barker left the balloon and drove this enemy aircraft down to about 300ft when he was able 'to get a burst of fire into him'. The Albatros dived and crashed in flames, Barker returned to the balloon and at very close range fired again and it also caught fire and crashed. He then fired at the balloon ground crew and later attacked a staff car which overturned in a ditch; in addition he strafed and dispersed small parties of enemy troops. Barker's aggressive attitude was typified when he and another Camel pilot strafed an Austrian airfield at Motta on Christmas Day 1917.

Further successes for Barker followed with a balloon destroyed in flames on 29 December and three days later an Albatros of *Jasta 1* shot down over Vittorio followed on 24 January by another kite balloon at ConegliaNo. On 2 February four enemy aircraft were shot down in one encounter by the squadron, two each by Captain W.G. Barker and Lieutenant C. McEwen and three days later three more enemy machines were brought down, two by Barker and one by Second Lieutenant H.B. Hudson, all in the vicinity of Oderzo. A week passed before Barker and Hudson found and destroyed a group of five observation balloons near Fossamerlo, on 12 February. Barker had noticed that the thick ground mist made conditions ideal for attacking the balloons which were at a height of 1,000ft.

Barker went on leave from 13 February to 7 March and although he logged almost twelve hours' flying time from then until 16 March he did not achieve another victory until two days later. On the 18th Barker, flying B6313 with three other Camels, spotted seven Albatroses at 17,000ft and climbed to attack. The enemy aircraft dived; Barker followed one down and at 3,000ft and about 40yd range he fired a long burst with both guns. This aircraft crashed in a field near Villanova while the remainder avoided combat. The next day Barker, again with Lieutenants Cooper and Forder, spotted a group of enemy aircraft at 17,000ft and attacked them. Barker forced two Albatroses to spin down and fired at another which went down to 800ft when he closed in and fired 200 rounds at close range causing this DIII to crash north of Cismon. Captain Barker had further operational flights with No. 28 Squadron and his last patrol with this squadron was on 8 April when the squadron was then part of the RAF, formed when the RFC had amalgamated with the RNAS on 1 April.

Due to his tendency to fly unofficial patrols and not always to follow orders properly, Barker was not given the command of No. 28 Squadron when it became vacant. Consequently he requested a transfer and on 10 April he joined No. 66 Squadron at Liettres. He still retained his 'personal' Camel B6313 which was continually customised. In addition to paintwork and engine modifications he had fitted sights of his own design to the twin machine guns, which improved his aim. Other squadron pilots commented that Barker's enemy target would often be seen breaking up before they considered it even to be within range. Barker also kept a running tally of his victories with small flashes of white painted on the struts.

Barker claimed a further sixteen victories while with No. 66 Squadron. The first was Oberleutnant Gassner-Norden of *Flik 42J* in an Albatros DIII on 17 April and, less than three months later, on 13 July he shot down a Berg Scout and another DIII near Godega. While with this squadron, on 19 May, he was presented with the Croix de Guerre (gazetted on 20 September) and again Mentioned in Despatches.

On 14 July Barker, with promotion to major, took command of No. 139 Squadron at Villaverla. This squadron's aircraft was the Bristol Fighter, but Barker was permitted to take his Sopwith Camel B6313 with him and he continued flying patrols. He claimed his first victim four days later on 18 July when his patrol attacked five enemy aircraft over Asiago. Barker was credited with one LVG shot down and another victory shared with Lieutenant G. May.

Two more Albatros scouts were destroyed by Barker on 20 July and he shared victory over a third with two other pilots three days later. On 21 July the supplement to the *London Gazette* No. 30801 announced the award of the DSO for Barker, the citation confirming that he had 'on five different occasions brought down and destroyed five enemy aeroplanes and two balloons'.

No victories were recorded for Barker during August as he was much involved in preparations to put an Italian agent into enemy-held territory. It was Barker's task to fly a modified Savoia-Pomilio SP.4 bomber at night using radio and searchlight signals, drop off the agent and return to base. He was assisted in this mission by Lieutenant William Wedgwood Benn RAF who as well as navigating was responsible for the safe exit of the agent, Lieutenant Alessandro Tandura. Sixty officers and men were involved in the experiments and planning of this operation and as the use of parachutes was in its infancy, the method developed was for the agent to be positioned over a trap door in the aircraft where he was attached by a long rope to a parachute slung beneath the undercarriage. At the appropriate moment Barker shut down the engines and Wedgwood Benn, from the observer's seat, pulled a rope connected to the release bolts on the trap door. Amazingly this plan worked and on the night of 8 August Tandura was dropped near his hometown of Vittorio Veneto and was able to provide much valuable information. Barker's service records showed that forty hours' flying time were logged as 'Spy Dropping. Italy'. The *London Gazette* No. 30895 of 12 September announced the award of the Italian Silver Medal of Military Valour for this episode.

The award of a second Bar to his Military Cross was published in the supplement to the *London Gazette* of 16 September and the citation included: 'on one occasion [Barker] attacked eight hostile machines, himself shooting down two ... In two months he himself destroyed four enemy machines and drove down one and burned two balloons.' On this date when the Prince of Wales visited the squadron at Villaverla, Barker took him on a forty-five-minute flight in Bristol Fighter 7972 and probably flew over enemy territory. The prince was taken up on other flights as one of a fifteen-minute duration was recorded with another pilot later in the month.

Barker claimed three more Albatros scouts shot down on 18 September while on patrol near Feltre. These were his last victories in Italy and he flew his last patrol with No.139 Squadron on 29 September in Camel 6313. Orders were issued that this aircraft was to be sent to 7th Aircraft Park and dismantled but that, 'Major Barker will be allowed to take off any souvenirs'. Despite this official authorisation Barker was asked to return the timepiece from this Camel.

Having flown more than 1,400 operational hours since early 1916, Barker was posted to England at the end of September 1918 to command the fighter training school at Hounslow Heath Aerodrome. He took a short leave in London and persuaded his superiors at RAF HQ that he would best achieve results at the training school if he was allowed to visit the Western Front and update himself on combat techniques. Consequently the new Sopwith Snipe E8102 was allocated for his roving commission in early October 1918.

Whilst in hospital recovering from his injuries incurred in the Sopwith Snipe, the supplement to the *London Gazette* No. 30989 of 2 November had published the citation for the award of a Bar to his DSO:

CAPT. (T/MAJOR) WILLIAM GEORGE BARKER, D.S.O., M.C.

A highly distinguished patrol leader whose courage, resource and determination has set a fine example to those around him. Up to 20 July, 1918, he had destroyed thirty-three enemy aircraft – twenty-one of these since the date of the last award (second Bar to the Military Cross) was conferred on him. Major Barker has frequently led formations against greatly superior numbers of the enemy with conspicuous success.

Consequently at his VC investiture at Buckingham Palace, on 1 March 1919, Barker had received a total of six awards!

The following month Barker flew a Handley Page 0/400 over parts of London with a number of passengers including the Prince of Wales and in May he again took the prince on a flight, this time at Hounslow where the aircraft was the protype Sopwith Dove and the subsequent aerobatics were witnessed by Thomas Sopwith. This flight gave rise to such newspaper headlines as, 'Prince of Wales stunts with one-armed VC'.

On 29 April he was promoted to lieutenant colonel in the RAF but resigned this post and in May 1919 sailed for Canada on the *Mauretania*. With William Bishop, a fellow Canadian VC recipient, who had visited him in hospital, Barker formed Bishop-Barker Aeroplanes Limited (BBAL). Barker was still receiving treatment for his injuries sustained in 1918 and was admitted into an Ottawa Convalescent Hospital on 18 June 1919 and not discharged until a month later. He suffered from the gradual onset of arthritis in his limbs and, as with so many other returning troops, from neurasthenia and a difficulty in integrating again into civilian life. These factors led Barker to start drinking heavily and together with Bishop he gained a degree of notoriety for 'anti-social episodes'.

Not long after his return to Canada, Barker met and fell in love with Jean Kilbourne Smith who had been born at Owen Sound, Ontario, where she had grown up with her cousin, Billy Bishop. She was the daughter of Horace Smith, a self-made millionaire lawyer and shipowner who had nothing in common with his daughter's future husband and was not impressed by his war record.

There was a a vast difference between the two families: on one hand there were the Smiths, who lived an affluent lifestyle, and on the other were the Barkers, farmers who often struggled to make ends meet. Basically Smith considered that Barker was not good enough for his daughter and that he was a penniless opportunist. However, the marriage took place on 1 June 1921 at Grace Church-on-the-Hill, Toronto and the best man was Billy Bishop. The couple lived at 355 St Clair Avenue, West Toronto, and had one daughter, Jean Antoinette, born in 1923. Due in part to the vast social chasm between the families, Barker rarely visited his family in Manitoba.

By early 1922, BBAL, their aircraft business venture, had failed and the two men were forced to sell off their aircraft to pay the creditors. Barker joined the Canadian Air Force in the rank of wing commander in June, and was the commanding officer of the air station at Camp Borden until 15 January 1924. In 1923 Barker had been appointed aide-de-camp to King George V.

On 1 April 1924 he was made acting director of the newly formed Royal Canadian Air Force (RCAF). One of his important achievements with the RCAF was the introduction of parachutes. In June he was posted as RCAF liaison officer at the British Air Ministry in London. During May of the following year he began advanced studies at the Royal Air Force College, Andover, and graduated from there in March 1926.

When Barker and his family returned to Canada in June 1926 the director of the RCAF was then Group Captain James Scott, an officer for whom Barker had little respect. Consequently on 24 August Barker resigned from the RCAF. He attempted tobacco farming for a while in Norfolk County, Ontario, but a severe bout of pneumonia in early 1929 forced him to sell his share of the farms.

Later in this year, when he had recovered from pneumonia, he received a number of offers from aviation companies and in January 1930 became president of Fairchild Aviation Corporation based in Montreal. In that same month he was passed fit and received his commercial flying certificate. Fairfield was trying to sell aircraft to the Canadian Government and on 12 March a new two-seater biplane, the KR-21, was to be demonstrated to the RCAF at Rockliffe Ottawa Air Station.

Barker arrived at the airfield as the KR-21 took off on a flight by Fairfield's demonstration pilot who put the plane through its paces for about ten minutes before landing. It was not necessary for any further demonstration flights as the airfield staff had witnessed a number of flights that day, but Barker insisted on taking up the aircraft. He had promised a flight to friends but was persuaded to fly solo for the first flight. The plane took off at about 1 p.m. and after some steep turns, still at the relatively low height of 250–300ft, Barker climbed steeply for another manoeuvre and he stalled the aeroplane. The aircraft started to drop backwards then rolled over and dived headlong into the frozen Ottawa River. Barker was killed instantly.

The RCAF Court of Inquiry held two days later found that the aircraft was airworthy prior to flight and that the primary causes of the crash were 'an error of judgement on the part of the pilot' and 'loss of control due to too steep a climb without sufficient height to recover'.

Barker's wife's family did not want a church service and mourners were invited to Horace Smith's home in order to pay their respects to the dead flyer whose coffin was guarded by an RCAF RSM. At 3.30 p.m. on 15 March a short service of fifteen minutes took place prior to the cortége starting its 1¼-mile journey to Mount Pleasant Cemetery in Inglewood Drive. Led by the band of the Toronto Scottish Regiment and an honour guard of thirty-five RCAF airmen from Camp Borden, a gun carriage carried the flag-draped coffin followed by the RCAF Regimental Sergeant Major who held Barker's decorations on a purple cushion. Only the men of the Smith and Barker families walked in the procession to the cemetery. The coffin was escorted by senior military officers and the honorary pall-bearers included another winner of the VC. Five Canadian recipents of the VC carried a poppy wreath in the shape of the Victoria Cross. The procession also included over 3,000 military personnel, many in civilian dress, as well as senior national and local politicians. An estimated 50,000 people lined the streets and the area around Mount Pleasant Cemetery. Two three-plane 'V' formations circled and flew down over the long procession, a number of times dropping rose petals. The cortège stopped at the Smith family mausoleum in the cemetery, two buglers sounded the Last Post and the rifle party fired three volleys. Eight airmen pallbearers lifted the coffin and as they moved up the steps into the mausoleum the six light aircraft each flew very low and dropped the last of the rose petals. The coffin was taken inside and the Bishop of Toronto delivered a final eulogy before it was placed in Crypt Room B.

The large marble facing over the crypt was engraved with his rank as a lieutenant colonel and the pilot's wings engraved inside the crypt are those of the RFC, not the RCAF. This was the choice of his widow, Jean, who also commissioned a stained-glass window in the back wall of the crypt to her husband's memory.

Jean later remarried Gerald Greene who, amongst other interests, had a farm near Toronto. She always kept a portrait of William Barker in her living room together with a frame containing his medals which she refused to give to the nation during her lifetime.

On 6 June 1931 an airfield at Dufferin, Toronto, was named Barker Field, but after thousands of people had learned to fly there, the airfield was closed in 1953 and later sold for commercial development. The crash site beside the Ottawa River was, for a time, marked by a plaque, but this is not now to be found.

Ernest Hemingway wrote a short story, *The Snows of Kilimanjaro*, published in 1936, which fictionalised Barker's Christmas Day attack on an Austrian airfield in 1917. The story was later turned into a film in 1952 and again in 2011.

In 1940 the RCAF authorised a booklet, *Canada's Air Heritage*, which was distributed throughout the service. The book profiled only four men, Bishop, Barker, Collishaw and McLeod, and in addition the RCAF commissioned oil paintings of these men, copies of which were sent to schools and air bases across Canada.

During the Second World War, Jean Antoinette Barker was commissioned into the Royal Canadian Navy and was a plotter on North Atlantic convoys. Her mother Jean died in December 1983 and was the last to be entombed in the Smith family crypt.

In Dauphin, Manitoba, the Lt. Col. W.G. (Billy) Barker VC Airport bears his name and a plaque to commemorate him was placed here on 1 June 2000. Six years later a statue of Barker was unveiled on 26 July 2006 in the airport terminal. An elementary school was also named after him, as was the Dauphin Squadron of the Canadian Air Cadets. Manitoba Parkland Tourism has nominated 1 June as 'Billy Barker Day'.

Barker's only daughter, Jean Antoinette Mackenzie (née Barker), died in July 2007. On 22 September 2011, a memorial at Mount Pleasant Cemetery in Toronto was unveiled to mark William Barker as the 'most decorated war hero in the history of Canada, the British Empire, and the Commonwealth of Nations'. This memorial was paid for by his three grandsons who were present at the unveiling. Also present were two granddaughters, Elizabeth Ede and Janice Gruneberg, daughters of William Barker Ede who was born in Islington in the summer of 1919. Barker had met his mother while on leave in London during the war. The following year Southport Aerospace Centre named their new flight student accommodation building after Barker.

His name, along with the other air recipients of the VC, appears on the wall left of the altar in St Clement Danes Church, the Strand, London. Barker's medal entitlement was: VC, DSO & Bar, MC & 2 Bars, 1914–15 Star, BWM, Victory Medal and MiD oak leaf, Medal of Military Valour (Silver) and Bar (Italy), Croix de Guerre (France). His medals are held by the Canadian War Museum in Ottawa as is the fuselage of Sopwith Snipe E8102.

SOURCES

The sources used in the preparation of this book include the following:

The Victoria Cross files at the Imperial War Museum, London
Library and Archives Canada
The Royal Air Force Museum, Hendon, London
The National Archives, Kew, Surrey
The published researches of The Cross & Cockade Society,
    International
The London Gazette, 1914–20 (HMSO)

Newspapers and Journals include:

Aeromodeller
The Aeroplane
Air Pictorial
Air Stories
Cross & Cockade International Society Journal
Daily Mirror
Flight
Flying
Popular Flying
Scale Models
Stand To! The Journal of the Western Front Association
Sunday Pictorial
The Times
The Journal of The Victoria Cross Society
Cross & Cockade International recorded archives

W.B. Rhodes-Moorhouse

Butcher, P.E., *Skill and Devotion*, Radio Modeller Book Division, 1971
Clayton, A., *Chavasse – Double VC*, Leo Cooper, 1992
The Dictionary of National Biography, 1912–1921, OUP, 1922

Notes made at the Victoria Cross Centenary Exhibition, 1956
Various New Zealand newspapers

R.A. Warneford
Gibson, M., *Warneford V.C.*, FAA Museum, 1979
Rimmell, R.L., *Zeppelin*, Conway Maritime Press, 1984
Barbara Gilbert, Fleet Air Arm Museum
Robin Voice, Brooklands Museum Trust Ltd
The National Archives (NA) WO 158/635
VCS Journal, March 2011

L.G. Hawker
Hawker, T.M., *Hawker VC*, Mitre Press, 1965
IWM, *The Great War 1914–1918 (Air Services)*, 1938
Brown, E., *Knights of the Air*, Time-Life Books, 1980
Bruce, J.M., *Bristol Scouts*, Windsock Publications, 1994
Richthofen, An Autobiography, Robert M. McBride & Company,
    1920

J.A. Liddell
Daybell, P., *With a Smile and a Wave*, Pen & Sword Aviation, 2005
Powell, A.,*Women in the War Zone*, The History Press, 2009
NA WO 95/1365

G.S.M. Insall
Insall, A.J., *Observer. Memoirs of the R.F.C. 1915–1918*, William
    Kimber, 1970
Jones, Sqdn/Ldr I., *Air Fighter's Scrapbook*, Nicholson & Watson, 1938
Roe, F.G., *The Bronze Cross*, Gawthorn, 1945
Wing Commander (rtd) David H. Insall, late Royal Air Force of Oman
Mike Insall

R. Bell-Davies
Bell-Davies, Vice-Admiral R., *Sailor in the Air*, Peter Davies, 1967
Samson, Air Commodore C.R., *Fights and Flights*, Ernest Benn, 1930
Notes made in the FAA Museum, 1994
Records at St Catherine's House, London
navy-net.co.uk

L.W.B. Rees
Rawlings, John D.R., *Fighter Squadrons of the R.A.F.* MacDonald, 1969
Williams, W.A., *Against the Odds; The Life of Group Captain Lionel
    Rees VC*, Bridge Books, 1989

—, *Heart of a Dragon; The VCs of Wales and the Welsh Regiments*, 1914–82, Bridge Books, 2008
Notes made at interview with Lord Balfour of Inchrye
Western Daily Press, 18 December 1916
W. Alister Williams

W.L. Robinson
Rimell, R.L., *The Airship V.C.*, Aston, 1989
—, *Zeppelin*, Conway Maritime Press, 1984
Letters from Geoffrey W. Hopkins
Letter from General Sir Brian Horrocks
Letter from Mrs R.G. Libin
Dorset Library Service Local Studies
Recorded talk by Ronald Adam in Cross & Cockade International Archives
NA WO 158/935
NA WO 158/944

T. Mottershead
Cheshire County Council Library historical archives
Halton Borough Council archives

F.H. McNamara
Cobby, Capt. A.H., *High Adventure*, Kookaburra Publications, 1981
Cutlack, F.M., *The Australian Flying Corps*, Queensland University, 1984
Galdorisi, G. and Phillips, T., *Leave No Man Behind; The Saga of Combat Search and Rescue*, Zenith Press, 2009
Roberts, E.G., *Box Kites and Beyond*, Hawthorn Press, 1976
Schaedel, C., *The Australian Flying Corps*, Kookaburra Publications, 1972
Australian Dictionary of Biography
The Australian Society of WW1 Aero-Historians archives
Numerous Australian newspapers via trove.nla.gov.au/newspaper
www.awm.gov.au

A. Ball
Bowyer, C., *Albert Ball, VC*, William Kimber & Co. Ltd, 1977
Kiernan, R.H., *Captain Albert Ball*, John Hamilton, 1933
Lewis, C., *Sagittarius Rising*, Peter Davies Limited, 1936
Pengelly, C., *Albert Ball VC; The Fighter Pilot Hero of World War One*, Pen and Sword Aviation, 2010
RFC Communiques Nos 70–87, 1917

W.A. Bishop

McCaffery, D., *Billy Bishop. Canadian Hero*, James Lorimer &
    Company, Second Edition, 2002
Bishop, Lt Col W.A., *Winged Warfare*, Bailey Bros and Swinton, 1975
Canadian Military Journal, autumn, 2002
Notes in the author's files
www.billybishop.net
Library and Archives Canada: RG 150, Accession 1992–93/166, Box
    760 – 48

J.T.B. McCudden

McCudden, Maj. J.B., *Flying Fury*, John Hamilton, 1930
Chadwick, R.T., *McCudden VC*, Gillingham Public Libraries, 1971
Cole, C., *McCudden VC*, Kimber, 1967
Interview with Maj. W.F. Harvey
Interview with A V-M A.G. Lee
Interview with Prof. H. Barlow
Interview with and letters from Mrs. M. Cobley (née McCudden)
Talk by Mrs M. Cobley in *Cross & Cockade International* recorded
    archives

A.A. McLeod

Drew, G.A., *Canada's Fighting Airmen*, Maclean, 1930
Mason, T.B. *Scarlet & Khaki*, Cape, 1930
Raleigh, W. and Jones, H.A., *The War in the Air*, OUP, 1923–34
Canadian Aviation Historical Society Journal
www.legionmagazine.com

A. Jerrard

Saunders, H. St G. and Richards, D., *The Royal Air Force*, HMSO,
    1923–34

E. Mannock

Dudgeon, J., *Mick: The Story of Major Edward Mannock*, Hale, 1981
Franks, N. and Saunders A., *Mannock. The Life and Death of Major
    Edward Mannock VC, DSO, MC, RAF*, Grub Street, 2008
Jones, Sqdn/Ldr. I., *King of Air Fighters*, Nicholson & Watson, 1935
FlyPast Extra
The Post Office Engineering Union Magazine
W/C K. Caldwell interview. Air Historical Society New Zealand
    archive recordings
Canterbury Cathedral Archives

Canterbury City Council
David Cohen
Andrew Cormack FSA
Tony Freail
Edward Mannock VC file compiled by the late Tony Spagnoly
Andy Saunders
WFA East Kent Branch

F.M.F. West

Malinovska, A. and Joslyn, M.P., *Voices in Flight. Conversations with Air Veterans of the Great War*, Pen & Sword, 2006
Reid, P.R. *Winged Diplomat*, Chatto & Windus, 1962
Video tape in the archives of the Air Historical Society, New Zealand
Journal of the VCS, October 2013
www.8squadron.co.uk

A.F.W. Beauchamp Proctor

Uys, I., *For Valour. History of South Africa's VC Heroes*, Author, 1973
Wedgewood-Benn, W., *In the Sideshows*, Hodder & Stoughton, 1919
Whetton, D., *Proctor, Ace of the 84th Sqdn*, Ajay Enterprises, 1978
Kommando
The South African Military History Society Journal, Vol. 5 No. 5, June 1982
Joan Marsh
Ian Uys
John Wilmot

W.G. Barker

Bowyer, C., *Sopwith Camel: King of Combat*, Glasney Press, 1978
Cooksley, P.G., *Flight Royal*, Patrick Stephens, 1981
Ralph, W., *Barker VC: William Barker, Canada's most decorated War Hero*, Doubleday Canada Ltd, 1997
Winchester, C., *Wonders of World Aviation*, Amalgamated Press, 1938
Journal of the VCS, October 2013
Library and Archives Canada: RG 150, Accession 1992–93/166, Box 435–47

BIBLIOGRAPHY

Ashcroft, M., *Victoria Cross Heroes* (Headline, 2006)

Bailey, R., *Forgotten Voices Victoria Cross* (Ebury Press, 2011)

Barker, R., *The Royal Flying Corps in France* (Constable, 1994)

Baring, M., *Flying Corps Headquarters 1914–1918* (William Blackwood & Sons Ltd, 1968)

Barnett, G., *VCs of the Air* (Burrow, 1919)

Bowyer, C., *For Valour* (Grub Street Aviation Classics, 1992)

—, *Sopwith Camel: King of Combat* (Glasney Press, 1978)

Boyle, W.H. Dudley, *Gallant Deeds* (Jeeves, 1919)

Branch, N., *The Boys' Book of VC Heroes* (Publicity Products, 1953)

Brazier, K., *The Complete Victoria Cross* (Pen & Sword Books, 2010)

Bruce, J.M., *The Aeroplanes of the Royal Flying Corps (Military Wing)* (Putnam & Company Ltd, 1982)

Creagh, General Sir O'M., *The VC and DSO* (Standard Art Book Co., 1924)

Doherty, R. & Truesdale, D., *Irish Winners of the Victoria Cross* (Four Courts Press, 2000)

Douglas, W.S., *Years of Combat* (Collins, 1963)

Duguid, Col, A. F., *Official History of the Canadian Forces in the Great War 1914–1919, Vol. 1,* (Department of National Defence, Canada, 1938)

Fegan, T., *The 'Baby Killers': German Air Raids on Britain in the First World War* (Leo Cooper, 2002)

Gibson, Major E. and Ward, G. K., *Courage Remembered* (HMSO, 1989)

Gliddon, G., *When the Barrage Lifts* (Leo Cooper, 1990)

— (ed.), *VCs Handbook: The Western Front 1914–1918* (Sutton Publishing, 2005)

Guttman, J., *Sopwith Camel* (Osprey, 2012)

Hammerton, Sir John, *War in the Air* (Amalgamated Press, 1935)

Hare, P.H., *Mount of Aces. The Royal Aircraft Factory S.E.5a* (Fonthill Media, 2013)

Hart, P., *Bloody April: Slaughter in the Skies over Arras, 1917* (Weidenfeld & Nicholson, 2005)

—, *Somme Success: The Royal Flying Corps and the Battle of the Somme, 1916* (Leo Cooper, 2001)

Harvey, D., *Monuments to Courage*, 2 Vols (Kevin and Kay Patience, 1999)

Johns, W.E., *The Air VCs* (Hamilton, 1935)

—, *The Book of the VC* (Hamilton, 1935)

Johnson, S.C., *The Medals of our Flying Men* (Black, 1917)

Leask, G.A., *VC Heroes of the War* (Harrap, 1916)

Lee, A.G., *Open Cockpit A Pilot of the Royal Flying Corps* (Jarrolds Publishers, 1969)

Lewis, G.H., *Wings Over the Somme* (Bridge Books, 1994)

McKee, A., *The Friendless Sky: The Story of Air Combat in World War I* (Elmfield Press, 1973)

Merriam, F.W., *First Through the Clouds* (Batsford, 1954)

Percival, J., *For Valour. The Victoria Cross: Courage in Action* (Thames Methuen London Ltd, 1985)

Revell, A., *Brief Glory: The Life of Arthur Rhys Davids DSO MC and Bar* (Pen & Sword Books, 2010)

—, *High in the Empty Blue: The History of 56 Squadron RFC RAF 1916–1919* (Flying Machines Press, 1995)

Reynolds, Q., *They Fought for the Sky* (Cassell, 1958)

Richthofen, von M., *The Red Baron* (Pen & Sword, 2009)

Robinson, B. et al., *Air Aces of the 1914–1918 War* (Harborough, 1959)

Sheppard, R., *Extraordinary Heroes* (Osprey, 2010)

Skelton, T. and Gliddon, G., *Lutyens and the Great War* (Frances Lincoln Limited, 2008)

Smith, M.C., *Awarded for Valour: A History of the Victoria Cross and the Evolution of British Heroism* (Palgrave Macmillan, 2008)

Smithers, A.J., *Wonder Aces of the Air* (Gordon & Cremonesi, 1980)

Smyth, The Rt Hon. Sir John Bt, VC, *The Story of the Victoria Cross 1856–1963* (Frederick Muller Ltd, 1963)

Snelling, S., *VCs of the First World War: Gallipoli* (The History Press, 2010)

Stewart, Lt Col R., *The Book of the Victoria Cross* (Hutchinson, 1928)

Thompson, Sir R., *The Royal Flying Corps* (Hamish Hamilton, 1968)

Wise, S.F., *Canadian Airmen and the First World War; The Official History of the Royal Canadian Air Force Volume 1* (University of Toronto Press, 1981)

Wood, A.C., *Aces and Airmen of World War I* (Brassey's, 2002)

Wragg, D., *A Century of British Naval Aviation, 1909–2009* (Pen & Sword Maritime, 2009)

INDEX